"Probably not since Ruth M. Underhill's *Singing for Power: The Song Magic of the Papago Indians of Southern Arizona* . . . has anyone devoted a study to O'odham pilgrimage traditions. . . . Students of O'odham culture and history now have a worthy companion to Underhill's seminal text."—DAVID MARTÍNEZ, *Kiva: Journal of Southwestern Anthropology and History*

"Twenty years ago Michael D. McNally proposed a compelling framework for decolonizing the study of Native American religions. . . . Nowhere since has that approach found greater resonance than in Seth Schermerhorn's *Walking to Magdalena*, a terrific new book that reformulates McNally's historiographical method as ethnographic practice."—MAXINE ALLISON VANDE VAARST, *Western Historical Quarterly*

"A fine ethnography that contributes to the emerging understanding of embodiment, emplacement, and religious coexistence or layering in contemporary cultures. Schermerhorn demonstrates a mastery of several bodies of academic literature, including anthropology and religious studies."—JACK DAVID ELLER, *Reading Religion*

"This is a holy journey, and the author enriches his account with interviews of various walkers that include discussions about songs, stories, and traditions."—S. J. ZUBER-CHALL, *Choice*

"This is a worthwhile text that demonstrates the deep importance and meaning that O'odham and other Indigenous peoples convey as they complete their yearly walk to Magdalena."—JUAN A. AVILA-HERNANDEZ, *Native American and Indigenous Studies*

"The subject-matter of the book is original: a decade-long partnership with the O'odham, built on trust, offers the reader insights into contemporary, everyday, lived religious experiences of this Indigenous Catholic community. . . . The conscious revelation of self, as it sits alongside the presentation of the O'odham, allows the author to acknowledge his position as the author, without effacing the coproduction of this work with his partners in the O'odham community."—KATHRYN N. GRAY, *Transmotion*

"This book will be of interest to those concerned with Native American Christianities, theories of pilgrimage, and the interaction between selfhood and place. Scholars of Tohono O'odham culture will be particularly drawn to this text, which provides such a careful analysis of material culture and song work."—SUZANNE CRAWFORD O'BRIEN, *Material Religion*

"*Walking to Magdalena* is a book that demonstrates incredible insight and a recognition of a people's ability to adapt to changes in their environment."—KEITH COOK, *Journal of Arizona History*

"This book, while not officially coauthored, is a 'co-labor' of love that focuses on O'odham voices, experiences, and the deep connections they have with their faith. . . . It is evident that the book is a labor of love to the O'odham individuals who are mentioned throughout, as their labor seems invaluable to the study. This book is recommended to anyone interested in Native American religions, Christian theology, linguistic studies, material studies, and the importance and interconnectedness of place and people."—ARTEMIS KING, *Southwestern Lore: A Journal of the Colorado Archaeological Society*

"In the tradition of Keith Basso's *Wisdom Sits in Places*, Seth Schermerhorn's *Walking to Magdalena* grounds the study of Native American religion, and in this case Tohono O'odham Catholicism, in a profoundly sophisticated sense of place and deliberate movement across ancestral landscapes. Theoretically informed and tangibly grounded in respectful relationships with Tohono O'odham elders, *Walking to Magdalena* is as humble a book as it is game-changing. We come to think differently about pilgrimage, the indigenization of Christianity, and what it might mean to become fully human."—MICHAEL D. MCNALLY, John M. and Elizabeth W. Musser Professor of Religion at Carleton College

"*Walking to Magdalena* makes important contributions to the field of Indigenous religious studies. The work will also be of interest to those doing fieldwork with Native communities, regardless of the specific field of research. . . . The writing is some of the clearest academic writing I've read. The author has a unique gift for writing direct, simple sentences, yet within an insightful, engaging narrative."—DAVID DELGADO SHORTER, professor in the Department of World Arts and Cultures/Dance at the University of California, Los Angeles

"Seth Schermerhorn's insightful work *Walking to Magdalena* is a wonderful piece of ethnographic research offering a poignant window on O'odham Catholic beliefs and practices. He was fortunate to become a friend and walking companion to the O'odham."—OFELIA ZEPEDA, author of *Where Clouds Are Formed*

"A sophisticated and engaging ethnography of O'odham expressive culture as it relates to pilgrimages to Magdalena; as an inveterate walker myself, Schermerhorn's discussion of 'being a good walker' reminds us of the fundamental role that walking can have in the constitution of memory and history."—ANTHONY K. WEBSTER, author of *Intimate Grammars: An Ethnography of Navajo Poetry*

"*Walking to Magdalena* makes a vitally important contribution to borderland studies, tracing the making and remaking of place and personhood of the now-transnational Tohono O'odham. It makes contributions to Indigenous and subaltern studies and provides us with a unique set of Tohono O'odham voices."—ANDRAE MARAK, provost and executive vice president of academic affairs, Roosevelt University

WALKING TO MAGDALENA

**New Visions in Native American
and Indigenous Studies**

SERIES EDITORS

Margaret D. Jacobs
Robert J. Miller

Walking to Magdalena

Personhood and Place in Tohono O'odham Songs, Sticks, and Stories

SETH SCHERMERHORN

CO-PUBLISHED BY THE UNIVERSITY OF NEBRASKA PRESS

AND THE AMERICAN PHILOSOPHICAL SOCIETY

The Tohono O'odham pronunciation guide is reproduced from *A Tohono O'odham Grammar* by Ofelia Zepeda. © 1983 the Arizona Board of Regents. Reprinted with permission of the University of Arizona Press.

An earlier version of chapter 2 appeared as "O'odham Songscapes: Journeys to Magdalena Remembered in Song," *Journal of the Southwest* 58, no. 2 (Summer 2016): 237–60.

An earlier version of chapter 3 appeared as "Walkers and Their Staffs: O'odham Walking Sticks by Way of Calendar Sticks and Scraping Sticks," *Material Religion: The Journal of Objects, Art and Belief* 12, no. 4 (December 2016): 476–500.

A small portion of appendix 1 originally appeared in "Global Indigeneity and Local Christianity: Performing O'odham Identity in the Present" in *Handbook of Indigenous Religion(s)*, ed. Greg Johnson and Siv Ellen Kraft, 192–203 (Leiden: Brill, 2017).

First Nebraska paperback printing: 2024
Library of Congress Cataloging-in-Publication Data
Names: Schermerhorn, Seth, author.
Title: Walking to Magdalena: personhood and place in Tohono O'odham songs, sticks, and stories / Seth Schermerhorn.
Other titles: New visions in Native American and indigenous studies.
Description: [Lincoln, Nebraska]: Co-published by the University of Nebraska Press and the American Philosophical Society, [2019] | Series: New visions in Native American and indigenous studies | Includes bibliographical references and index.
Identifiers: LCCN 2018034578
ISBN 9781496206855 (cloth: alk. paper)
ISBN 9781496238764 (paperback)
ISBN 9781496213891 (epub)
ISBN 9781496213907 (mobi)
ISBN 9781496213914 (pdf)
Subjects: LCSH: Tohono O'odham Indians—Religion. | Christianity—Arizona. | Pilgrims and pilgrimages—Arizona. | Pilgrims and pilgrimages—Mexico—Magdalena de Kino.
Classification: LCC E99.P25 S34 2019 | DDC 979.1004/974552—dc23 LC record available at https://lccn.loc.gov/2018034578

Set in Charis by Mikala R. Kolander.
Designed by N. Putens.

FELIX A. ANTONE
AUGUST 16,1933 - JANUARY 31,2012

For Felix

CONTENTS

ILLUSTRATIONS

I use the orthography developed by linguists Albert Alvarez and Kenneth Hale during the 1960s, which was subsequently adopted in 1974 as the official O'odham writing system of the Tohono O'odham Nation. The following list of approximate English equivalent sounds is taken from Ofelia Zepeda's *A Tohono O'odham Grammar*.

a   like the *a* in *father*
b   like the *b* in *big*
c   like the *ch* in *chips*
d   like the *th* in *this*
ḍ   like the *t* with a glottal stop in *but*
e   like the *u* in *hum*
g   like the *g* in *go*
h   like the *h* in *hat*
i   like the *i* in *machine*
j   like the *j* in *job*
k   like the *k* in *kiss*
l   (no similar sound in English—the closest is the *dd* in
    ladder; also similar to the single *r* in Spanish)
m   like the *m* in *miss*
n   like the *n* in *no*

ñ like the *ny* in *canyon*
ŋ like the *ng* in *finger*
o like the *a* in *all*
p like the *p* in *pot*
s like the *s* in *see*
ṣ like the *sh* in *ship*
t like the *t* in *top*
u like the *u* in *brute*
w like the *w* in *win*
y like the *y* in *yes*

Additionally, the symbol ('), which represents an apostrophe in English, represents a glottal stop in O'odham. Long vowels are followed by a colon (:), and short vowels, which usually occur at the end of a word, are represented by a breve (˘) over the letter.

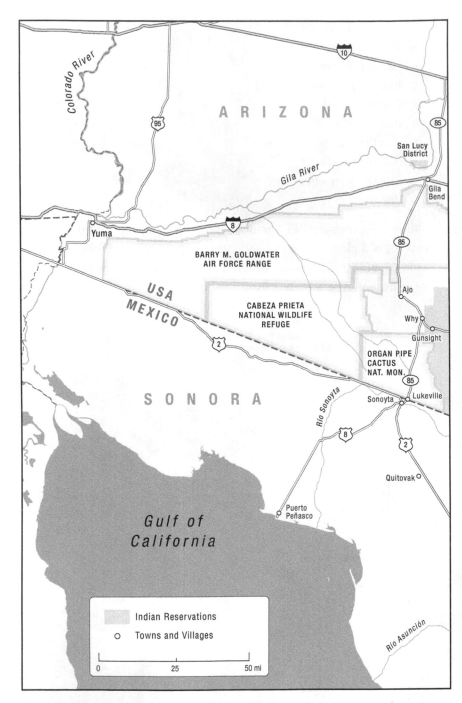

Fig. 1. Traditional O'odham territory. Erin Greb Cartography.

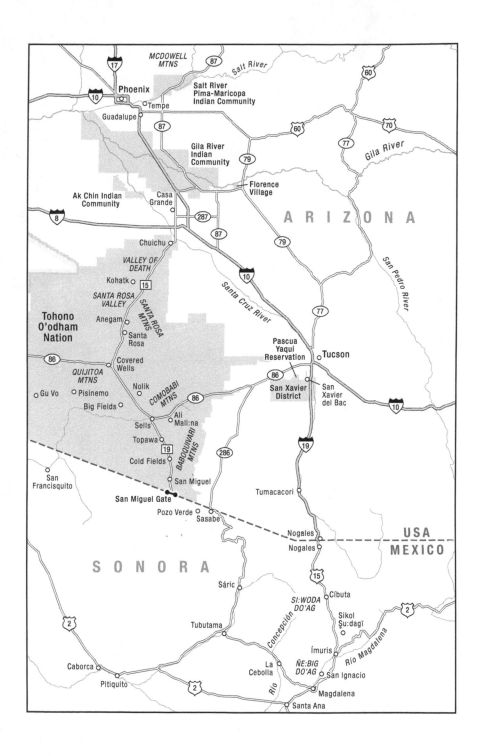

ACKNOWLEDGMENTS

This book is the culmination of almost a decade of learning and working within both O'odham and academic communities. First and foremost, I gratefully thank all of my consultants who shared with me their lives and knowledge about pilgrimages to Magdalena. In particular, I must thank the extended Lopez family of Kaij Mek and beyond for always having an open door for me, especially Simon Lopez and Louis Anthony Lopez. I also thank Ana Antone and Felix Antone, who supported my work on this project before anyone else did, as well as Deacon Alfred Gonzales, Joe Joaquin, Kendall Jose, Verlon Jose, Camillus Lopez, Mary Narcho, Mary Ann Ramirez, Jonas Robles, Bernard Siquieros, and Royetta Thomas. Many other O'odham—far too many to list by name here—also deserve thanks for the hugs, handshakes, and smiles that I receive every time I return to the Tohono O'odham Nation. I have been blessed to have a home away from home and to be part of a large and growing family of walkers. I am deeply grateful for ongoing support from the Tohono O'odham Nation Cultural Center & Museum and Tohono O'odham Community College. This research would not have been possible without the support of the Tohono O'odham Nation's Legislative Council, which passed a resolution approving my research. I have a deep respect for the Nation's mandate to oversee research conducted within its borders. I am particularly grateful to Frances Conde, Billman Lopez, Sandra Ortega,

Frances Stevens, Art Wilson, and the Cultural Preservation and Human Resources Development committees for guiding me through the approval process. To be clear, though, neither the Legislative Council nor any individual tribal member is responsible for my findings, and all errors of omission or interpretation are mine.

I have been very fortunate to benefit from the generosity of many institutions and agencies. I would like to thank the following sources of financial support from Arizona State University: the Lattie and Elva Coor Building Great Communities Graduate Fellowship, the Religious Studies Summer Doctoral Fellowship, the Graduate and Professional Student Association JumpStart Research Grant and Graduate Research Support Program Grant, the Richard E. Wentz Graduate Fellowship in Religious Studies, the Spirit of Service Scholarship, the Graduate College Completion Fellowship, and the Religious Studies Completion Fellowship. My research also benefited from my employment in the American Indian Studies Program, the School of Historical, Philosophical, and Religious Studies, and the Institute for Humanities Research. At Hamilton College I received substantial support from the Office of the Dean of Faculty in the form of Start-Up Funds, Faculty Research Funds, and Sabbatical Research Funds, which gave me time to complete this book. Other valued supporters are the Jacobs Research Fund Individual Grant through the Whatcom Museum, an affiliate of the Smithsonian Institution, the Phillips Fund for Native American Research through the American Philosophical Society, and the Upstate-Global Collective Faculty Fellowship from an award by the Andrew W. Mellon Foundation.

I must also recognize the invaluable mentorship from the faculty at Arizona State University, where this project began to take shape, particularly Eddie Brown, Anne Feldhaus, Tod Swanson, and the late Kenneth Morrison. Religious studies faculty who influenced my research include Miguel Aguilera, Linell Cady, Tracy Fessenden, Joel Gereboff, Leah Sarat, Juliane Schober, and Mark Woodward. I also benefited from the inspiration and guidance of Jolyana Begay, David Martínez, Simon Ortiz, James Riding In, and John Tippeconnic in the American Indian Studies Program, as well as Don Fixico and Peter Iverson in history and Leah Barclay, Sabine Feisst, Dan Gilfillan, and Garth Paine with the Listen(n) Project.

At Hamilton College I am grateful to work in a department and for a college that nurtured my success. In particular, I thank Abhishek Amar, whose friendship and mentorship has been invaluable to me, as well as Steve Humphries-Brooks, Meredith Moss, Quincy Newell, Brent Plate, Heidi Ravven, Richard Seager, and Jay Williams, all in the Department of Religious Studies. Thanks also to supportive colleagues outside of my department, including Nathan Goodale, Chaise LaDousa, and Bonnie Urciolli in anthropology, John Eldevik, Celeste Day Moore, and Tom Wilson in history, and Jace Saplan and the late Sam Pellman in music. I've also benefited from extraordinarily bright and energetic students, including Jade Alvillar, Mike Berrios, Zach Blumenkehl, Shannon Boley, Estella Brenneman, Phoebe Duke-Mosier, Peter Hoogstraten, Suzanne Jacobson, Grant Kiefaber, Lauren King, Tessa Lavan, Jacob Leebron, Eric Lintala, Lindsey Luker, Lillia McEnaney, Marlena Napier-Smith, Frankie Outlaw, Ryan Phelps, Lauren Scutt, David Seavey, Kate Wall, and Cedar Weyker.

Friends and colleagues from around the world have helped me develop my thinking for this book. I benefited immensely from the opportunity to present my research at annual meetings of the American Academy of Religion, the European Association for the Study of Religion, the American Anthropological Association, the Western History Association, the American Indian Workshop, and the quinquennial meeting of the International Association for the History of Religions. For their counsel at these and other forums I especially wish to thank Afe Adogame, Greg Alles, Brandon Bayne, Sarah Dees, Brandi Denison, Fritz Detwiler, Gabriel Estrada, Emily Floyd, Paul Gareau, Sandra Garner, Larry Gross, Rosalind Hackett, Chad Hamill, Graham Harvey, Elana Jefferson-Tatum, Greg Johnson, Sylvester Johnson, Jordan Kerber, Siv Ellen Kraft, Carol Ann Lorenz, Alessandra Lorini, Andrea McComb, John McGraw, Michael McNally, Kristy Nabhan-Warren, Suzanne Owen, Crispin Paine, Peter Pels, Jenna Reinbold, Justin Richland, Lamin Sanneh, David Shorter, Anne Slenczka, Greg Smoak, Bjørn Ola Tafjord, Inés Talamantez, Chris Vecsey, Alaka Wali, Meaghan Weatherdon, Jace Weaver, Anthony Webster, and Tisa Wenger. I would also like to thank the established scholars within O'odham studies for variously inviting me into their homes, discussing the prospects of my work, and sometimes corresponding with me at length: Don and Adelaide Bahr, Husi Cazares, J. Andrew Darling, Coleen Fitzgerald, Bernard Fontana, Ron Geronimo, James Griffith, David Kozak, Barnaby Lewis, Camillus Lopez, Ken Madsen, Andrae Marak, David Martínez, Gary Nabhan, Mary O'Connor, Dean Saxton, David Shaul, and Ofelia Zepeda.

I would also like to thank the many librarians and archivists around the country who supported my research, especially Jeannette Garcia at the Library and Archives of the Tohono O'odham Nation Cultural Center & Museum in Topawa, Arizona. In Tucson thanks are due to Alan Ferg, Mary Graham, and Amy Rule at the Arizona State Museum, Verónica Reyes-Escudero at the University of Arizona Libraries Special Collections, and Kate Reeve at the Arizona Historical Society Library and Archives. In Tempe I must thank Joyce Martin at the Labriola National American Indian Data Center in the Arizona State University Libraries. In Denver thanks to Aly Jabrocki and Sam Schiller at the Denver Museum of Nature and Science. Thanks also to the staff at the Bancroft Library at the University of California, Berkeley. The interlibrary loan staff at Arizona State University and Hamilton College worked hard to fulfill my endless requests.

At the University of Nebraska Press, I am particularly grateful to my sponsoring editor Matt Bokovoy, for his excitement and dedication in taking on this project, as well as Heather Stauffer and the New Visions in Native American and Indigenous Studies series editors, Margaret Jacobs and Robert Miller. Thank you to the anonymous reviewers for their constructive criticism and helpful insights, which have made this a better book. I appreciate the care and precision with which Elizabeth Zaleski as project editor and Jane Curran as copyeditor reviewed the manuscript. Thanks to the *Journal of the Southwest, Material Religion,* and Brill for their permission to adapt my articles for the book. The University of Arizona Press deserves thanks for permission to reprint the pronunciation guide. I'd also like to thank Erin Greb for preparing the map.

None of my work would be possible without my family. My parents, John and Marlene Schermerhorn, raised me to value education and encouraged me to leave behind the comforts of home at an early age.

My brother Quintin and sister-in-law Kelli have long encouraged me and provided welcome diversions. Thomas and Ryna Moss have welcomed me into their family, providing a second home where I have enjoyed needed breaks from my academic life over the past fifteen years. Most importantly, words cannot express my gratitude to my strongest supporter, best friend, colleague, and loving wife, Meredith Moss, and our two inspiring daughters, Zoe and Kirby, whose long naps in a baby carrier on my back gave rise to productive afternoons perusing archives, as well as excited conversations during hikes on desert mountains and walks through wooded glens. Last, but not least, I must thank the extended Lopez family of Kaij Mek and beyond for also welcoming me into their family.

Royalties from the sale of this book will be donated to Himdag Ki:, the Tohono O'odham Nation's Cultural Center & Museum in Topawa, Arizona.

WALKING TO MAGDALENA

Introduction

After an early morning visit to Saint Francis in the San Xavier Mission, I drove past the village's large cemetery, which has multiple signs posted stating "KEEP OUT," "NO TRESPASSING," and "NO PHOTOGRAPHS." When I reached Mary Narcho's home, she welcomed me inside, offering me coffee and doughnuts for our early morning meeting. Mary was eager to begin our conversation, but first I had to set up my video camera, tell her about my project, and secure her informed consent, which she gave verbally. The conversation quickly became very personal as Mary explained to me how grief-stricken she became when her husband, John Narcho, was diagnosed with multiple myeloma. His body "shriveled up," she told me, as he withered away from 209 pounds to 126 pounds and died, only three months later.

MN: You know, for those four years [following his death], I had a candle burning at his, at his grave 24/7. I kept candles [burning]. I was buying candles continually. . . . And I had those there 24/7. And I was going there every single day. *Every single day* [louder] for four years, I was over there. 'Cause *I* couldn't let it go. I couldn't accept his death.[1]

Her anguish was so intense that she became increasingly isolated from others. She had been grieving, excessively, according to some, and for too long. One person who subscribed to this view was an O'odham

1

"medicine lady," as Mary called her, from Sells, the capital of the Tohono O'odham Nation, who knew about her suffering.

MN: She said, *"Let me explain it to you this way* [raised pitch]." She said, "I drove *here* an hour from Sells to, to come to see you." And she said, "When you're, when you, when you're feeling bad and missing John [snapping her fingers], John's here just like that. He doesn't have to drive an hour down here to come see you. [Snapping her fingers, again] John's here like that. And John isn't resting. John's spirit isn't resting. His *body* [added stress] is there, but he's not there. His spirit is, um, gone on, and uh, and his spirit is alive. And uh, and, when you're crying, or feeling bad, you make him feel bad, and he can't rest." That's how she explained it to me [shrugging her shoulders] . . .

So, so, that was when I stopped. *The day before I went* [added stress], started my walk to Magdalena, is the last time that I, that I lit those candles. And I even put a bench over there, a cement bench I have in front of his coffin, in front of his grave, 'cause I was there so much.[2]

Like Mary, many O'odham go to Magdalena for healing from sickness, heartache, and broken lives. Whatever the reason, O'odham and others travel to Saint Francis to directly appeal to him, asking for favors, negotiating deals, and giving thanks. Many O'odham, like Mary, pray not only to God to intercede on their behalf but also to saints, as well as deceased O'odham. "I pray to my husband all the time, you know," Mary added, "so, yes, we pray to our, our deceased also. They're our saints, too." For many O'odham, including Mary, death is not an ending, but rather a transformation. Instead, O'odham dead continue to live, and it is said that they can be accessed by the living at particular places in the landscape and at particular times of the year, like John's grave, for instance, where Mary's tears of anguish, an O'odham medicine woman reportedly told her, brought him back, with the snap of her fingers, "like that."

This book is about the O'odham, their land, their pilgrimages to Magdalena, and their relationships with Christianity. "O'odham"—a pluralization of "odham" through partial reduplication—means "people," or "person" in the plural, in senses both more and less restricted than this English translation might initially suggest. Among those peoples whose indigenous language is mutually intelligible, which linguists have classified as Piman, of the Uto-Aztecan language family, "O'odham" is used perhaps primarily, though certainly not exclusively, in reference to themselves. Within this large linguistic group there has been and continues to be variation between dialects. Socially, culturally, and historically, however, contemporary O'odham primarily distinguish between themselves as Akimel O'odham, Tohono O'odham, Hia Ced O'odham, and O'odham in Mexico.[3]

Those who today call themselves Akimel O'odham, or "river people," more commonly known as Pima, were previously known as "one villagers" because of their permanent settlements along the more-or-less perennial rivers of what is today southern Arizona. Today, they primarily live on the Salt River, Gila River, and Ak Chin reservations and in surrounding urban areas, particularly Phoenix. Those who identify themselves today as Tohono O'odham, or "desert people," or perhaps more commonly as "Papagos," were previously known as "two villagers" because of their seasonal migration between their summer fields and their winter springs or wells. Today they reside on four separate pieces of land that make up the Tohono O'odham Nation: the "main" reservation—the second largest reservation in the United States, the southern boundary of which also shares nearly seventy-five miles of the United States–Mexico international border—Florence Village, San Xavier, and San Lucy. Like the Akimel O'odham, Tohono O'odham also live in nearby urban areas. The Hia Ced O'odham, or "Sand Papagos," who today are struggling for tribal, state, and federal recognition and a separate land base, were previously known as "no villagers" because of their nomadic existence in the considerably more arid regions to the south and west of other O'odham. Today, though, most Hia Ced O'odham live in the western Gu Vo district of the main Tohono O'odham reservation and Puerto Peñasco (Rocky Point, Sonora, Mexico). In addition to the Akimel O'odham, Tohono O'odham, and Hia Ced O'odham, disparate families and communities of O'odham in Mexico, sometimes called "Sonoran Papagos," or "O'odham in Mexico," have for the most part moved to the United States, either living on or in rural communities around what is today the Tohono O'odham Nation or have intermarried and assimilated into other communities in Mexico.

Although this study may include Akimel O'odham, Hia Ced O'odham, and other O'odham in Mexico, it is primarily, though not exclusively, concerned with the Tohono O'odham of southern Arizona and northern Sonora, Mexico. Historically, O'odham occupied a vast area that is considerably larger than many recognize today, extending from the San Pedro River to the east, the Gila River to the north, the Colorado River and the Gulf of California to the west, and the Río Magdalena and Río Asunción to the south. The mere fact that the United States–Mexico international border arbitrarily cuts O'odham land in two should also suggest that the Tohono O'odham Nation—originally known as Papago Tribe of Arizona—is not a political entity with divine sanction from time immemorial, but rather an invention of the United States federal government.[4]

Making Christianity Their Own

Walking to Magdalena builds on the foundational work of religious studies scholar Michael McNally, whose study of Ojibwe Christians privileged insider voices in order to appreciate "what native people *made of* Christianity."[5] McNally argues that in order for an interpretive shift to take place in which indigenous Christianities may be fully appreciated as both indigenous and Christian, academics must redirect their attention "away from what *missionaries intended* [in order] to appreciate what native people *made of* Christianity."[6] Although a broad body of literature has developed addressing what Christianity has done to Native Americans and other indigenous peoples, the literature on what Native Americans and other indigenous peoples have done to Christianity has only begun to emerge.[7] Crucially, this interpretive shift highlights the agency of indigenous peoples in sincerely adopting Christianity—though not necessarily the same Christianity of the missionaries—in ways that have been meaningful to them as indigenous peoples.

While McNally's focus on "what native people *made of* Christianity" is important, it is not original. McNally's position follows from the work of Michel de Certeau, a French Jesuit and profoundly interdisciplinary scholar, who specifically noted in relation to the Spanish colonization of the indigenous inhabitants of the Americas that "consumption"—far from being a passive act—necessarily entails "production," which unavoidably involves agency.

> The Indians nevertheless often *made of* the rituals, representations, and laws imposed on them something quite different from what their conquerors had in mind; they subverted them not by rejecting or altering them, but by using them with respect to ends and references foreign to the system they had no choice but to accept. . . . The strength of their difference lay in procedures of "consumption."[8]

Following this paradigm shift, first signaled by de Certeau and later advanced by McNally, I examine some of the ways in which the Tohono O'odham of southern Arizona and northern Sonora have made Christianity their own by focusing on the annual pilgrimage made by many O'odham to Magdalena, Sonora, Mexico. Using the walk to Magdalena as the point of entry into the larger question of what Tohono O'odham have made of Christianity, I strive to understand Tohono O'odham Christian traditions as they have been understood by their practitioners, in their own words and practices, especially in songs, sticks, and stories. Toward this end, for four consecutive years between 2009 and 2012 and then again for a fifth year in 2016, I accompanied a large group of one to two hundred O'odham walkers on their pilgrimage to Saint Francis in Magdalena in late September and early October. The group was led by the late Felix Antone, an O'odham elder, *ma:kai* (medicine man), resident of Cedagĭ Wahia (Pozo Verde, or Green Well, Sonora), and governor of O'odham in Mexico. In this time it has become clear that, for many O'odham, Christianity is simply the way of their grandmothers and grandfathers. Although scholars agree that the journey to Magdalena is the largest and most significant event in the annual cycle of Tohono O'odham Christianity, it has never before been the subject of sustained scholarly inquiry.[9]

Christianity and Tohono O'odham Landscapes

Tohono O'odham ways of life encompass both "Native" and "Christian" practices, and these "Christian" practices are typically categorized as one of two types, *sasa:nto himdag*, or saints' way, and *jiawul himdag*, or devil way.[10] Judging from phonological evidence alone, George Herzog, a linguist, anthropologist, and ethnomusicologist, concluded that these Spanish-derived religious terms—and perhaps the traditions themselves— "must have come from Spanish indirectly, through the agency of other Indian languages."[11] *Sa:nto himdag*, the singular form of the plural *sasa:nto himdag*, is associated with O'odham relations with various saints who reside in often tiny chapels and in home altars.[12] In contrast, *jiawul himdag* is associated with mountains, mines, horses, cattle, cowboys, and those who work with horse hair. If each O'odham village has a chapel for saints to live in, then it might be said that each village also has a nearby mountain in which *jejawul*, or deceased cowboys, reside.[13] In the O'odham language, saints and devils are classified within a semantic system in which these entities are categorized with other entities including coyote, the ocean, the giant saguaro cactus, and various other plant and animal species as *O'odham* or *hemajkam*, terms that are often translated as referring to "people" or "spirits" with varying degrees of power who are capable of helping and hurting others by causing various types of sickness that are generally said to afflict only O'odham.[14]

In essence, much of the Christian practices incorporated within O'odham traditions are about maintaining proper relations—some intimate, some more distant—between O'odham and these powerful entities that are associated with Christianity: saints and devils. However, as previously noted, these entities associated with Christianity are also classified with various other entities that comprise the desert landscape and should not be understood apart from the larger O'odham context.[15] All of these powerful beings, whether artificially classified by outsiders as "Native" or "Christian," are tied to particular places on O'odham land. All of these entities are decidedly inhabitants of *this* world, embedded in O'odham homelands—whether saints in churches, devils in nearby mountains, or deceased O'odham in village cemeteries or at roadside memorials marking the places of sudden, violent death.[16] In short, O'odham have embedded—or emplaced—Christianity within their ancestral and conceptual landscapes.

Landscapes of Movement

How do O'odham actually live within and move through these landscapes? Since landscape studies sometimes run the risk of being too static, motion and movement have long been at the forefront of landscape studies.[17] As Nancy Louise Frey noted in her ethnography of pilgrims on and off the road on their way to Santiago de Compostela, anthropologists have long used the notion of "landscape" as an ethnographic "framing convention."[18] Moreover, Frey notes that within pilgrimage studies, scholars have tended to conflate "landscape" with "sacred geography," ultimately reducing it to "a backdrop for movement."[19] In response to this trend, Frey counters that "landscape is not only a 'backdrop' but also a central part of pilgrims' experiences."[20] Rather than conceiving of "landscape" as a "backdrop" to movement, I, like Frey, follow archaeologist Christopher Tilley, who argues that it is imperative to understand how landscapes are experienced, how they mark people, as well as how they are socially produced.[21] To rephrase Frey's words for the purposes of this study, landscape is not merely a "backdrop"—as some other scholars in both O'odham studies and pilgrimage studies might have it—but also an agent that actively constructs persons, while persons dialectically produce places, or landscapes, both by thinking of them and by actually moving through them.[22]

Because *Walking to Magdalena* engages the dialogical emergence of personhood and place, the landscapes on which it focuses might more productively be called "landscapes of movement."[23] Walking is the form of movement that I primarily focus on here.[24] The title, *Walking to Magdalena*, highlights this movement as crucial to understanding indigenous landscapes or cosmologies that are not only "imagined," but actually lived in.[25] In so doing, this work perpetuates the trend that religious studies scholar Gustavo Benavides noted: that gerunds dominate the titles of English language scholarly monographs in the field of religious studies.[26] This trend suits my purposes here, insofar as gerunds emphasize process as well as product. Walking, then, is the principal process—though certainly not the only process—through which O'odham become inextricably connected with their landscape.

The category of "landscape," of course, carries multiple layers of meaning. Among other things, "landscape" suggests a way of seeing the world.[27] Hence, the notion of "landscape," like that of "place" (see chapter 1), denotes a social product. In this usage, "landscape" may be understood as a historically and ideologically conditioned aesthetic, or way of seeing, the product of what literary theorist Charles Lock has called "the Protestant optic," in which an optic of distance is privileged over proximity and sensory engagement.[28] *Walking to Magdalena* strives to avoid these pitfalls, with the hope that a focus on movement has the potential to subvert the "landscape" concept's potential to be merely a particular way of seeing.

For ethnographers, such as myself, who are more engaged in participation than observation, landscapes need not be static vistas. Following the lead of historian and critic of anthropology James Clifford, *Walking to Magdalena* "begins with this assumption of movement."[29] Redescribing the problematic figure of the ethnographic "informant" as a "traveler," Clifford declares, the "ethnographer is no longer a (worldly) traveler visiting (local) natives. . . . Everyone's on the move, and has been for centuries: dwelling-in-travel."[30] "The people studied by anthropologists have seldom been homebodies," according to Clifford; "'informants' first appear as natives; they emerge as travelers."[31] In this book, and perhaps unlike most tribal ethnographies, Clifford's chronology is reversed: I first knew most of the O'odham I came to work with as travelers—"walkers" and otherwise—and only later did I come to know them, not as "informants," but as "consultants" who co-labored with me, both in walking and in producing this book.

Method and Theory in the Anthropology of Pilgrimage: Journeys and Destinations

Although there has been an explosion of pilgrimage studies since the 1970s, particularly within the anthropology of religion, many scholars have commented on the general neglect of pilgrimage within earlier studies. For example, anthropologist E. Alan Morinis suggests:

> Anthropologists have tended to neglect pilgrimages because they were, by definition, exceptional practices, irregular journeys outside habitual social realms. Pilgrimage eludes the attention of the traditional

researcher who takes a fixed socio-cultural unit, such as a village, as the subject of study. Pilgrimage also tends not to fit into conventional anthropological categories.[32]

Perhaps even more important than the assumption that pilgrimages are exceptional practices outside of the normal practices of everyday life in the parochial anthropological "village" that dominated most earlier anthropological studies and the inadequacy of anthropological categories that have emerged from "the village" and "the armchair," the constraints of ordinary academic life necessarily impinge on the anthropological study of pilgrimages, limiting the scope of scholarly research. Mary I. O'Connor, an anthropologist who has also studied the Magdalena pilgrimage and fiesta, explains:

> By their very nature as transitory, if regularly occurring, cultural phenomena, pilgrimages are difficult to study extensively in the one- or two-year period that characterizes the bulk of anthropological field research. Because pilgrimages tend to be short in duration, it is not possible to study them intensively over a long stretch of time. The necessity to observe a pilgrimage several times over a period of years makes it almost impossible to study within the ordinary academic frame of reference.[33]

In short, the academic study of pilgrimage does not usually align well with academic years and academic lives.

Furthermore, most pilgrimage studies tend to focus on the destination rather than the journey. This has been noted by many anthropologists of pilgrimage.[34] That is, most pilgrimage studies focus on major shrines rather than the movement to, at, and from these places. A striking departure from the more typical shrine-centered model of pilgrimage is Frey's now-classic road ethnography of contemporary travelers to Santiago de Compostela.[35] Although I had initially hoped to produce a road ethnography somewhat like Frey's, I do not imitate Frey. However, this study is similar to Frey's in that the arrival is anticlimactic, as anthropologists Simon Coleman and John Eade have noted regarding Frey's study; my Magdalena, like Frey's Compostela, "is a largely empty vessel in the text."[36] Given my aims and methods, the city of Magdalena itself is not the focus of this study. In Alan Morinis's classification of pilgrimage studies, this is a "fragmentary" study of pilgrimage, as reflected in the table of contents in which each chapter focuses on a different aspect or topic related to O'odham journeys to Magdalena. In focusing on the journey rather than the destination, like Michael J. Sallnow's study of Andean pilgrims, Ann Grodzins Gold's study of Rajasthani pilgrims, and Hillary Kaell's study of American Holy Land pilgrimages, my examination of O'odham pilgrimages to Magdalena is explicitly aimed at the goal of understanding pilgrimage not as exceptional phenomena, as the Turnerian model of pilgrimage might have it, but as deeply embedded in everyday life.[37]

Since most pilgrimage studies tend to focus on the destination rather than the journey, the trend certainly holds true for previous studies of the Magdalena pilgrimage as well. A major flaw in most academic studies of the Magdalena pilgrimage, then, is that these studies are not actually about the pilgrimage itself—that is, walking to Magdalena—because they are actually about the Magdalena fiesta. As a predictable consequence of this trend, the Magdalena fiesta has been heavily studied, while journeys to Magdalena, whether physical or imagined, have largely passed unnoticed.[38] For example, several studies have been explicitly focused on the Magdalena fiesta.[39] Several more studies have focused on specific aspects of the Magdalena fiesta, such as the behavior of pilgrims in the church, commerce, folk art, milagros, drinking, prostitution, and so forth.[40]

One of the many difficulties of studying destinations rather than journeys is that without some prior relationship or rapport, ethnographers may not be able to learn very much from pilgrims themselves at these destinations. O'Connor noted this limitation in her study of the Magdalena fiesta.

> Because of the temporary nature of pilgrimages, it is almost impossible to create the face-to-face relationships that have traditionally characterized long-term fieldwork. The field researcher is therefore confronted with the necessity of going up to strangers and asking them personal questions. The drawbacks inherent in this are obvious.

Indeed, this lack of rapport seems to have been an important factor constraining O'Connor's ability to study the Magdalena fiesta and pilgrimage. However, as O'Connor notes, folklorist James "Big Jim" Griffith demonstrates one solution to these methodological difficulties: maintaining contact over many years with people who regularly go on pilgrimages to Magdalena, accompanying them on their journeys to Magdalena, and developing rapport through intensive interaction.[41] A somewhat similar approach is employed by Arizona rancher and writer Richard Collins, who journeyed on horseback for several years alongside Mexican riders, retracing the pathways of Eusebio Francisco Kino. Indeed, like both Griffith and Collins, my strategy has been to develop rapport through intensive interaction. However, unlike Griffith and Collins, in focusing on O'odham pilgrimages to Magdalena, I have cultivated relationships with both O'odham walkers and nonwalkers before, during, and after pilgrimages to Magdalena. My method, like religious studies scholar Tod Swanson's model of seeing "though family eyes," has generally been more like what social scientist and criminologist Raymond J. Michalowski and anthropologist Jill Dubisch have called "observant participation" rather than participant observation.[42]

Like O'Connor, I have found the Magdalena fiesta bewildering.[43] This no doubt accounts for my neglect of the Magdalena fiesta as much as the fact that there have been many more studies of the Magdalena fiesta than there have been of journeys to Magdalena. The simple fact remains that I preferred walking out on the road in the rural Sonoran countryside to the sensory overload of the hustle and bustle of the city of Magdalena at its busiest and most chaotic time of year. When I walked into Magdalena for the first time in 2009, my senses were overwhelmed as the combined, yet distinct, smells of urine, feces, vomit, tequila, cerveza, elotes, shrimp, and carne asada filled my nostrils, and my ears ached from the cacophony of carnival rides and a man's voice selling rugs through a blaring loudspeaker in the church plaza. At the same time, I knew that most O'odham did not share my sentiments, dispositions, or pretensions. Most were clearly elated at their climactic arrival, and when I once complained about the blaring loudspeaker, someone said,

"Those are nice rugs." Whereas some aspects of the fiesta may strike me as appalling, the fiesta also has its appeal.

Purposeful Wandering: Movement, Method, and Theory

Religious studies scholar Thomas Tweed turns to Clifford's metaphor of travel in reimagining theories as itineraries, or more precisely, as "embodied travels."[44] In Tweed's conception of theory as travel, he distinguishes between academic theorizing as "purposeful wandering" and "the displacements of voluntary migrants who seek settlement, tourists who chase pleasure on round-trip journeys, or pilgrims who depart only to return home after venerating a sacred site."[45] Neither migrant, nor tourist, nor pilgrim—at least not in any exclusive or simplistic sense—I distinguish between my own "embodied travels" in accompanying pilgrims to Magdalena and back and my own theoretical "purposeful wandering" in other times and places—on breaks alongside the road to Magdalena, in casual conversations at wakes and fiestas, during recorded interviews with my O'odham consultants, reading in libraries and archives, and sitting in front of my computer at my desk. In the former case, my O'odham collaborators might describe my own movements in O'odham as *him*, or "walking," a purposeful movement to a particular place; in the latter case, my O'odham collaborators might describe my own movements as either *oiyopo* or *oimeḍ*, both of which might be translated as "wandering," or, as Donald Bahr—a linguistic anthropologist who spent nearly five decades studying O'odham language, songs, and stories—prefers, "to move about without going anyplace in particular."[46] (See chapters 3 and 4 for more on the distinction between "walking" and "wandering.")

Nonetheless, in extending Clifford's notions of "dwelling-in-travel" and "travel-in-dwelling," I stand with Tweed in declaring that "scholars are dwelling-in-crossing and crossing-in-dwelling."[47] As "the scholar moves back and forth from the desk to the archives, from home to the field, from here to there and now to then," I have experienced, reflected upon, researched, and written *Walking to Magdalena* in crossing and dwelling as I have continually striven toward an articulation of O'odham ways, concepts, and stories of moving through place, challenging "the authorial voice of most scholarly studies [in which] the interpreter is everywhere at once or nowhere in particular."[48] In contrast to the pretentions of such placeless perspectives, my "purposeful wanderings" have taken place primarily in the homes and offices of my O'odham hosts, insightful consultant-theorists, in libraries and archives, and along the road to Magdalena in the company of my fellow walkers. In my scholarly narrative I attempt to illustrate some of these positioned sightings—whether my own, or of my O'odham collaborators—as they have occurred in particular contexts, places, and times. Within pilgrimage studies, the best ethnographers reveal their own field experiences throughout their work and demonstrate how these experiences shape their ethnographies. Indeed, this has long been the mainstay within the anthropology of pilgrimage, with perhaps the best examples being Michael J. Sallnow, Ann Grodzins Gold, Nancy Louise Frey, and Hillary Kaell.[49] In short, I firmly agree with Mary I. O'Connor that "the role of the ethnographer must at the very least be much more prominently displayed in the ethnography itself. The personal experiences of the fieldworker necessarily affect the product and thus must be described in much more detail than is generally found in ethnographic accounts."[50]

Although this study would not have been possible without the support and engagement of my fellow O'odham walkers and conversation partners, *Walking to Magdalena* is not a work of joint authorship. While I am the sole author of this text and as such I am responsible for any errors it may contain—even those errors that might have been avoided through joint authorship—my goal is also to ensure that the voices of my fellow walkers and consultants not only come through in this text but also cut against the interpretive grains toward which I may be inclined. The insider-outsider, ethnographer-informant dichotomies do not, I hope, constitute this work. Indeed, I do not subscribe, in either theory or in practice, to the convention, as Clifford put it, in which "the native speaks" and "the anthropologist writes," thereby ensuring that "the writing/inscribing practices of indigenous collaborators are erased."[51] Rather, like Peruvian anthropologist Marisol de la Cadena, I envision the shared work that has gone into the making of this book to be a form of "co-laboring." "Co-laboring," according to de la Cadena, is distinct from collaborative research, in which the troublesome distinction between "*their* belief and *my* knowledge" is usually maintained, and I endeavor to demonstrate how this book fundamentally depends upon O'odham co-labor.[52]

I wholeheartedly agree with religious studies scholar Robert Orsi that we need "to include the voices of our sources more clearly—and disruptively—in our texts, inviting them to challenge and question our interpretations of them, to propose their own alternative narratives, to question our idioms from the perspective of their own, and, in general to break into the authority of our understandings and interpretations and to reveal their tentative character."[53] This approach also resonates with one of Greg Johnson's methods, particularly in urging religious studies scholars to stop "straining to hear the one 'true voice' of tradition," in order to "be attuned to a cacophony of voices."[54] Similarly, as an alternative to fixating on distinctions between (usually) non-indigenous scholars and indigenous subjects, Swanson urges scholars to see Native American religious life "through family eyes," insofar as "relatives may be loved but they are never mistaken for angels."[55]

In writing *Walking to Magdalena,* I seek to avoid the practices of inscription in the academy that erase indigenous collaborators, sidestepping what de Certeau has called *"writing that conquers,"* inscribing and reinscribing the violence of colonialism through the physical movement of writing itself.[56] Instead, much like Tweed's "purposeful wandering," I aspire, through writing, to achieve a playful—therefore, serious—tentative mode of "messing around," in order "to make a kind of *perruque* of writing itself."[57] *La perruque,* literally "the wig," is a French expression referring to the diversionary tactic of workers disguising their own creative work as work for the employer's profit. De Certeau writes that *la perruque* "may be as simple a matter as a secretary writing a love letter on 'company time,'" and that "the worker who indulges in *la perruque* actually diverts time (not goods, since he [sic] uses only scraps) from the factory [or, college, as the case may be] for work that is free, creative, and precisely not directed toward profit."[58] Rather than conceiving of the broader context in which this book was created as the so-called pressure to "publish or perish" in academia, particularly in competition for tenured and tenure-track positions, my preference has been to conceive of the writing of this book as an extended love letter—replete with endnotes—to the many O'odham who have shared their lives and knowledge with me and the scholars who have trained, challenged, and inspired me over the past decade.

Although *Walking to Magdalena* is about O'odham more than it is about anything else, such as academic theories of religion, or myself, I also use first-person narrative to describe my own experiences of walking to Magdalena with my fellow O'odham walkers. Indeed, several O'odham walkers have assumed that this is *all* that I would write about. In particular, while we were getting jostled around while trying to remain standing in a horse trailer on rough, unpaved dirt roads in Sonora, one O'odham walker in 2009 joked that she didn't want to read about herself in my book, which she spuriously titled *My Time among the Papagos*! I cannot exclude myself from this study, because "lived religion refers not only to religion as lived by others but also to life as lived by those who approach others' everyday experience to learn about culture and history; it refers, in other words, to the conjuncture of two lived worlds in the study of religion."[59] Because ethnographic knowledge is inherently dialogical, such encounters call for profound engagement.[60] As Mikhail Bakhtin, a Russian philosopher and literary theorist, has forcefully argued, "To think about the consciousness of other people means to *talk with them; otherwise they immediately turn to us their objectivized side*: they fall silent, close up, and congeal into finished, objectivized images."[61] To co-opt the titles of two popular oral history manuals, my objective is to establish "a shared authority" while "making many voices heard."[62] This process of co-labor is particularly important because my arguments are necessarily tentative and at times speculative.

Fieldwork Context

Because *Walking to Magdalena* is based primarily on conversations that I have recorded with my O'odham consultants, it is necessary to say something about the context of my fieldwork. I should begin by pointing out that while I spent a total of only five weeks over a period of five years—or one week each year in 2009, 2010, 2011, 2012, and then again in 2016—actually walking to Magdalena alongside other O'odham walkers, I spent approximately another twelve weeks, or three months, living on the Tohono O'odham Nation, spread out over a period of roughly nine years. While living primarily in Tempe, Arizona, near Arizona State University, and later in Clinton, New York, near Hamilton College, I have been studying contemporary and historical Tohono O'odham religious traditions for approximately one decade.

My first trip to the Tohono O'odham Nation was in early May of 2009. At the time I was working as a research associate for the American Indian Studies Program at Arizona State University in Tempe, Arizona. Professor Eddie F. Brown, who was then the director of the program, was eager to put me to work on a significant project that would be of mutual interest to both of us, as well as a service to the Tohono O'odham Nation. At first, the plan was to conduct oral history research on the "Indian Village" right next to the 1.5 mile-wide open pit mine in Ajo, Arizona, a border town on the western-most reaches of the Tohono O'odham Nation. Ajo "Indian Village" was also Dr. Brown's hometown. In addition to preparing for this oral history project, he asked me to accompany him on the walk to Magdalena, which he had been contemplating for some time, particularly at the urging of Mary Narcho, a longtime friend and then peer member of the governing board for Desert Diamond Casinos, the Tohono O'odham Nation's gaming enterprise. This project quickly consumed nearly all of my scholarly attention and much of my personal time and resources. As a religious studies scholar working with indigenous peoples in the Southwest with an interest in indigenous conceptions of religious geography and a growing interest in indigenous Christianities, I quickly realized that this journey would become more than just a passing interest or a side project, and that the walk would be an ideal candidate for a doctoral dissertation—which I needed to write in order to earn a Ph.D. in the School of Historical, Philosophical, and Religious Studies at Arizona State University (ASU)—and a first book—which I needed to publish in order to earn tenure in the Department of Religious Studies at Hamilton College.

I began participating in the journey to Magdalena in 2009, and I had begun bibliographic research on Tohono O'odham in 2008. In the spring of 2011, between my second and third pilgrimages to Magdalena, I started to work on gaining grassroots support among the walk's organizers and other community leaders in the Tohono O'odham Nation for doing an oral history project that would document the history of the walk to Magdalena, particularly for the group of walkers that I had been accompanying. During this period some of my academic advisers were uncertain whether anyone would be willing to talk with me about the walk if I were officially researching the walk, rather than simply participating in it. Indeed, I shared this concern as well, and I grew increasingly worried until one day when I walked into the Department of Human Services' Behavioral Health building in Sells to meet with Louis "Tony" Lopez, one of the organizers for Felix Antone's walk. I told him about the oral history project that I wanted to undertake, and I asked him for his support if he thought that the project would be useful to the Tohono O'odham Nation. Right away he gave me his full support but told me that the person I should really be talking to about the journey to Magdalena and its history was his father, Simon Lopez. From this point on nearly all of the O'odham with whom I spoke in the course of this project were either people whom I met on the walk to Magdalena or people with whom other people told me I should speak.

When I arrived at Simon's ranch in Santa Rosa, he was full of energy and eager to begin working with me. I was scarcely out of my dust-covered 2000 Ford Escort when he began telling me about his earliest memories from his childhood of the journey to Magdalena in covered wagons and how he begged his parents to let him ride to Magdalena on horseback all alone. Of course, I was exuberant: not only was a knowledgeable and respected elder clearly willing and excited to work with me, but it soon became clear that we were building a strong rapport together. Over the time that we spent together between 2011 and 2017, I feel that we grew close. At various points in the gestation of this project I thought that my entire project could easily focus exclusively on his songs, stories, memories, and understandings of the pilgrimage to Magdalena.[63] From summer 2011 through summer 2013, when I was living in Tempe as a graduate student at ASU, I spent many days, weekends, and even a few weeks when I could spare them in the company of the extended Lopez family, talking, certainly, but also attending fiestas and wakes where the family's group of singers and dancers would perform at villages across the Tohono O'odham Nation and working with Simon on tasks that were important to him, such as painting the new Santa Rosa feast house, or working on various other small projects around Simon's ranch, such as hoeing in preparation for a feast day and cleaning up in the feast's wake. When I told Simon at the San Juan feast in June 2013 that I had accepted a position at Hamilton College in central New York, there were tears in both of our eyes. Now, having moved across the country to assume this academic post, I continue to return to the Tohono O'odham Nation at least once or twice per year, usually during breaks in the academic year.

With Simon's support and interest in this project, beginning in summer 2011, everything soon became much easier. Simon and his wife, Florence, welcomed me into their home and frequently fed me their delicious food. They also offered a spare room for me to use whenever I wanted to come and stay with them in a detached house on their ranch or in a room adjacent to theirs. Their hospitality was invaluable and gave me a base from which to work on the Tohono O'odham Nation so that I could spend less time driving back and forth between the Tohono O'odham Nation and my apartment in Tempe or, later, hotels in Tucson or Phoenix. Indeed, their family's hospitality has long been indispensable to generations of non-O'odham scholars interested in Tohono O'odham language, culture, history, and religious traditions, including, most notably, Ruth Underhill, Donald Bahr, and Amadeo Rea.

To call the extended talks that I recorded with the O'odham whom I came to know "interviews" might suggest a degree of formality that was usually, and deliberately, lacking. Most conversations were typically open-ended as I wanted each narrator's interests to guide our sessions. I often merely introduced my research focus and let my O'odham consultants discuss what they considered to be important. Though I did ask direct questions for clarification as a follow-up to each narrator's stories, most of these conversations did not neatly follow a question and answer format. On occasion, though, I felt like I was being interviewed when O'odham wanted to know more about me, why I wanted to pursue this project, and what my intentions were for giving back to the Tohono O'odham Nation, my fellow walkers, and the people who were willing to talk with me. I never felt very uncomfortable during these moments because I agree that these are important questions for any researcher to continually ask one's self, and accountability from stakeholders and community members is a vital part of this process.

I did not pay or offer money to the people who graciously allowed me to record their stories and our conversations. I did, however, try to bring small contributions of food or water to those families—particularly the extended Lopez families of Santa Rosa, Quijotoa, and Anegam—who took me into their homes, took me to the graves of deceased relatives, gave me a place to sleep, and prepared additional food to serve another mouth at the table. I should stress that my contributions were akin to bringing a side dish to a barbecue as basic etiquette, and I rarely gave more food or drink than I received.

Year after year I had hoped to record conversations and stories with O'odham "walkers" on our way to Magdalena. Finally, when I began my fourth year of walking to Magdalena in 2012, I had all of the necessary approvals from the Tohono O'odham Nation and Arizona State University's Institutional Review Board. However, I soon realized, as I surely must have already known from my first three years on the walk, that there never seemed to be an appropriate time to make these recordings. Moreover, though there were frequent breaks during the journey in which I could have pursued my research, I was often exhausted and needed to rest and scramble for what little shade I could find, just like most other walkers. Therefore, no recordings were ever made while en route, in Magdalena, or on the return journey back home. Instead, these conversations took place in a different context, usually in homes and places of work back on the Tohono O'odham Nation.

During the time that I spent on the Tohono O'odham Nation, I recorded the conversations and stories of twelve O'odham narrators, nine men and three women, including both "walkers" and "nonwalkers." This book draws on more than fifty hours of narration, from which I have made a transcript of well over one thousand pages. I have transcribed most of these conversations myself, with only a few exceptions, for which I either hired a transcription service or trained and employed my own students, in both cases carefully supervising and editing the transcripts of the narrations. This transcription process itself took many months and was often quite difficult as well as monotonous since I would frequently rewind and replay the recording to make sure that I got it down right. Like walking, this too was "foot work," with my foot tapping away at the transcription pedal for hours each day and cramping quite regularly. Nonetheless, in spite of these difficulties, this process had many benefits. Not only did the laborious task of transcription boost my confidence in the accuracy of the texts; it also provided me the opportunity to methodically relive the recording process in a deliberate and slow manner, often listening to every word of each speaker at least two or three times.

A note on my orthography for the O'odham language: when citing secondary texts, I have used the orthographic transcriptions as they appear in the sources. In all other cases I have relied on the orthography officially adopted by the Tohono O'odham Nation, so the transcriptions and translations of these narratives follow the orthography developed by Albert Alvarez and Kenneth Hale.[64] I am particularly grateful to Louis Anthony Lopez and Simon Lopez for taking on the difficult and time-consuming task of recording and translating the songs that constitute their "Traditional Rosary," so that this work can contribute not only to the academic literature *on* Tohono O'odham but also the literature *in* Tohono O'odham, and promote reading and writing in the O'odham language.

My O'odham Nickname

The first year that I walked to Magdalena, I was not sufficiently prepared for the journey. Although I had packed everything that I needed, my backpack was often inaccessible during much of the first two days, driving from Sells, Arizona, across the U.S.-Mexico border to Cedagĭ Wahia, where we spent the first night together, and further on south to Tubutama, where we actually began walking the remaining distance of about thirty-six miles to Magdalena. Separated from my supplies—most notably my sunscreen—I was already badly sunburned before we even started walking.

With each passing day, my skin got redder and the layers of dirt, sweat, and sunscreen further browned my exposed skin left unprotected by the T-shirt, shorts, low-cut socks, and shoes I was wearing. Although my sunburn was the source of physical discomfort, it also elicited some sympathy as well as humor from my fellow O'odham walkers.

"You're starting to look like one of us!" Verlon Jose joked. Of course, banter like this can go on for days, even years.

That first year, in the camp on the last night before we walked into Magdalena, I took off my shoes as I did every night before going to bed. Although I somehow avoided getting any blisters, my feet were sore and achy so I delighted in taking off my socks, rubbing my feet, and walking barefoot on the rocky ground.

It was dark, but the moon shined brightly that night illuminating our camp. I remember it was like a super-powered street lamp that shined down so intensely that it was hard for me to fall asleep.

It didn't take long. Walking around camp, I was continually met with soft laughter, murmurs, and smothered giggles. Finally, an O'odham woman explained that my feet were so white that they seemed to glow in the dark. She told me they were calling me "White Feet," or S-tohă Ta:taḍ.

White Feet was a fitting name as well as a good joke. For all the jokes about me becoming an O'odham, my feet betrayed me. My new name memorialized my predicament, I thought.

I had been called other names too:

Smiley. Presumably because of my shit-eating grin.

Sneezy. Presumably because of my notoriously loud sneezing that can be heard from miles away. On numerous occasions, I suffered from involuntary sneezing fits that went on for minutes. "Someone is thinking of you," I was often told. In particular, I tended to go into sneezing hysterics at sunrise each morning when all of the walkers were smudged with the smoke of Ṣegoi, also known as creosote or "greasewood"—the most important traditional medicine to contemporary O'odham.[65] According to O'odham oral traditions, Ṣegoi was the first being created by Jeweḍ Ma:kai, or Earth Doctor, which he made on the "greasy earth" and which he molded from his own skin and sweat.[66] Ṣegoi is a resinous bush with perhaps more than fifty volatile oils, which give the plant its distinctive odor. The plant especially gives off its strong aroma when it is made wet by summer monsoons and when it is burned. Ethnobotanist Gary Paul Nabhan notoriously asked a young O'odham boy what the desert smelled like. The child's immediate response, "the desert smells like rain," provided the title for the now classic book. Nabhan explains that "the question had triggered a scent—creosote bushes after a storm—their aromatic oils released by the rains. His nose remembered being out in the desert, overtaken: *the desert smells like rain.*"[67] However, in my case, if the desert smells like rain, then it makes me sneeze.[68]

According to Alice Joseph, a medical doctor, and anthropologists Rosamond B. Spicer and Jane Chesky, O'odham nicknames given to white people reflect some physical characteristic of the individual named.[69] Anthropologist Ruth Underhill also noted that O'odham names are often descriptive in referring to some peculiarity of the individual named, though she notes that these names are "always slightly derogatory."[70] Returning to my name, White Feet, surely the appellation referred to the relative whiteness of my feet in contrast to the rest of my unprotected and badly sunburned skin. Was my new name also a vaguely disparaging light-hearted insult? As much as my burned skin, my newly exposed white feet were a visible physical sign written on my body signaling that I was out of place in the desert and ill-prepared, lacking the necessary disciplined intentionality required to avoid a sunburn in the first place.

In my third year, during a brief break alongside the road to Magdalena, an O'odham woman walking directly behind me complimented the O'odham man directly in front of me for his steady stride. When she addressed me, she said, "I don't even know what you're doing!" I responded with nervous laughter, worrying that I had been distracting her as I regularly altered my gait to avoid blisters and evenly distribute the weight of my backpack, and myself, on my feet. As time passed, I wondered, could the name White Feet also refer to my characteristic way of walking?

Again, I remembered back to my first year walking to Magdalena. I had assumed that I would be walking around 100 miles over a period of 5 days, averaging about 20 miles per day. This is not uncommon for O'odham who walk to Magdalena from Mission San Xavier del Bac, for example. Imagine my surprise, then, when I learned that we would be walking only 36 miles in 5 days, averaging about 7 miles per day. Even with frequent and sometimes lengthy breaks for resting, walking only 7 miles per day requires an extraordinarily slow pace since we usually began walking each day before sunrise and set up camp typically after the sun had already set. "It's not a race!" I often heard the leaders on the walk say. At the time, I'll admit, particularly during the first year, I found myself daydreaming about sprinting ahead of the group, making my way to Saint Francis before lunch, and rushing back to Phoenix to be home in time for dinner!

Riding north across the border as we returned to the United States, I remember someone asking me how the walk had been. Thinking only of the unhurried, deliberate, and excruciatingly sluggish speed that involuntarily familiarized me with my own hasty, impatient disposition, I exclaimed, "We moved at a crucifyingly slow pace!" Apparently my own impatience caused me so much suffering that I had imagined myself on *la via dolorosa*, bearing my backpack on my achy shoulders and my staff in my arthritic hands as my cross. In that moment I was ashamed of myself. I knew that no one else on the walk would depict their own experiences in such overly dramatic and self-indulgent terms. In retrospect, I might describe the pace and mood of the walk as solemn and prayerful. Clearly my own attempt at suffering alongside O'odham walkers could only take me so far toward a deeper understanding of how O'odham might variously conceptualize and experience the walk to Magdalena; for this I would need to explore how O'odham themselves represent the journey to Magdalena in their own words and practices—in songs, sticks, and stories.

Mapping the Book

Here is the outline of the book. The introduction presents the main argument—that O'odham have made Christianity their own by embedding it within their ancestral landscapes—and briefly describes my own ethnographic research methods. Chapter 1 presents the intertwined notions of personhood and place and further illustrates some of the ways in which people and places become associated with one another. In short, saints are associated with churches, devils are associated with particular mountains, and deceased ancestral O'odham who are tied to particular places in the landscape are said to have grown accustomed to Christianity. Here, place emerges not as a "backdrop" but rather as an agent that actively constructs personhood, while O'odham dialectically produce places, both by thinking of them and actually moving through them.

Chapter 2 explores how O'odham songs map routes through their traditional lands and how these songs construct an ethical landscape. In short, these songs transport the singer and the audience from place to place as they move from song to song, encountering various powerful entities along the way. Cumulatively, each song series documents such a journey. For example, archaeologist J. Andrew Darling and Akimel O'odham traditional singer and cultural preservation officer Barnaby Lewis have demonstrated that fourteen Oriole songs collected by linguistic anthropologist Don Bahr in fact map an Akimel O'odham salt expedition route to the salt flats on the Sonoran Gulf Coast.[71] Much like Darling and Lewis, I have encountered separate song sequences describing journeys to Magdalena via three separate routes from three different dialect groups and three separate points of origin. In short, I explore how O'odham make places and journeys through songs by building upon discussions by Bahr, anthropologist David Kozak and David Lopez, a Tohono O'odham farmer, cowboy, and ritual curer, and Darling and Lewis that treat O'odham song sequences as a form of mapmaking.[72]

Chapter 3 examines the walking sticks that walkers acquire on their first journey to Magdalena. Significantly, although these walking sticks play a prominent role in everyday O'odham Catholic practice, these sticks have not even been mentioned in any academic literature on the O'odham. Here I again build upon the work of Darling and Lewis in their discussion of scraping sticks and calendar sticks, which have been more extensively studied by anthropologists and historians.[73] Darling and Lewis argue that markings notched into scraping sticks—like songs themselves—document song journeys in geographical space, contending that calendar sticks provide a temporal or chronological, rather than geographical, itinerary. This comparison between rasping sticks and calendar sticks is extremely suggestive in terms of O'odham theories and representations of space and time, especially when walking sticks are added into the mix. Indeed, walking sticks not only document chronological and geographical journeys; they are also respectfully treated according to O'odham ethical norms. I argue that as O'odham mature, their sticks become storied and that these stories are told as invitations to the moral imagination.

Chapter 4 situates the journey to Magdalena within O'odham categories of movement in O'odham narratives. Despite the pervasiveness of talk of "pilgrimage" in ethnographic literature about O'odham, most O'odham refer to the trek to Magdalena as either "the walk" in English, or *him* or *himdag* in O'odham. These words bear a heavy semantic load within O'odham language since the verb *him*, "to walk," is the root of *himdag*, which may be translated as "a way of life, a culture, a practice, or a tradition," or "to be a good walker." Significantly, I think that much can be gained by moving away from abstractions of *himdag* as "tradition" or "culture" to focus on what it means "to be a good walker." Following religious studies scholar Tod Swanson, who reunites ethics and aesthetics in order to succinctly argue that "the moral character is a person with style," I hypothesize that whatever it means "to be a good walker" is intimately related to the disciplined, sensuous maturity of O'odham elders.[74] Here I build upon the work of anthropologists Regina Harrison, Elsje Maria Lagrou, and Swanson and as I examine how "walking" is juxtaposed to "wandering."[75] In this ethical and aesthetic sense of the word—rather than its designation of ethnicity—being a "person" or *O'odham* is differentially distributed among those who call themselves "O'odham" since "being a good walker" is an acquired art or skill. Furthermore, focusing on what it means "to be a good walker" is useful for those who are interested in moving toward more sophisticated notions of "culture" as dynamic, processual, living, and in motion.

Chapter 5 returns to the theme of O'odham embedding Christianity into their ancestral and conceptual landscapes by examining divergent O'odham senses of the past in the present in which Christianity is simultaneously both ancient and novel, familiar and strange. I also explore what one consultant called an O'odham need "to be grounded" and O'odham methods for connecting people to places, which include but are not exclusively limited to walking to Magdalena.

The conclusion begins with another pilgrimage, though not to Magdalena. Instead the pilgrimage is to a putatively non-Christian indigenous place that is perhaps regarded as the most sacred place to the O'odham.

Putting a twist on Dakota historian Philip Deloria's *Indians in Unexpected Places*, the book ends with Christianity, and therefore Magdalena, in unexpected indigenous places.[76] The appendixes offer brief outlines of O'odham religious history, particularly relating to the Magdalena pilgrimage, and a narrative map of O'odham genres of speech.

CHAPTER 1

Personhood and Place

Personhood and Producing "Real People"

Western scholars have never had a firm grasp on indigenous worldviews.[1] This is no less true for O'odham than it is for other Native American and indigenous peoples. However, as guideposts, archaeologist, ethnographer, and religious studies scholar Miguel Angel Astor-Aguilera suggests that indigenous "cosmologies are more about a daily social way of life revolving around conceptions of self, personhood, and sense of place relating to what is both visible and invisible."[2] Although Astor-Aguilera made these comments addressing the Mesoamerican context in which he works, he makes the same argument for "Native American relational worldviews" more generally.[3] Indeed, this is why my focus here is on such a mundane activity as walking, in relation to senses of place and the production of "real people."

According to Astor-Aguilera, "Native American personhood concepts should not simply be an aside to our studies. At this point in time they need to take central importance."[4] However, Astor-Aguilera is neither the only nor the first scholar to insist that Native American concepts of personhood should have a far more significant place than they ordinarily do in studies of Native American peoples. In particular Raymond Fogelson shared Astor-Aguilera's sentiments nearly three decades earlier, when he anticipated that there "will be new field investigations in which systematic study of self and person concepts becomes a central rather than a peripheral concern."[5] Therefore, following Astor-Aguilera's lead, as well as Fogelson's before him, the category of personhood, alongside the category of place, is one of the two central categories of this study. In particular, this study further develops Astor-Aguilera's concept of "tethering," a process through which persons, places, and objects become associated with one another.[6]

However, the burgeoning literature on "personhood" has not gone unchallenged. Several scholars have targeted the category of personhood as necessarily and inevitably ethnocentric. For example, religious studies scholar Tod Swanson contends that "in English the word 'person' carries with it a whole Christian and European philosophical history suggesting an individual of a unique class of beings who descend from a single pair, are equal, and of infinite worth because they and only they are made in the image of God."[7] From this perspective, it is impractical to permit the category of personhood to take central importance without carefully working out the similarities and differences between multiple indigenous and European religious and moral histories. Another critic argues that we may study personhood in non-Western societies, but we should first admit that we are really only interested in our own categories, and that we are not truly interested in these other societies.[8]

The focus of *Walking to Magdalena* is almost entirely on anthropocentric models of O'odham personhood, or more specifically maturity and maturation, without going into significant detail regarding O'odham conceptions of personhood that extend to a variety of other species and objects, like anthropologist A. Irving Hallowell's classic conception of "other-than-human-persons."[9] The major exception to this rule is the chapter on staffs (see chapter 3), though the analysis of these and other sticks demonstrates that these staffs also directly relate to anthropocentric models of O'odham maturation. Another minor exception to this rule is a brief discussion of coyote in chapter 5. To use the concepts developed by anthropologists Beth A. Conklin and Lynn M. Morgan, instead of focusing on "structural-relational" models of personhood that might include other species and entities, in this particular study I am more interested in anthropocentric "processual-relational" models of personhood, which anthropologist Sarah Lamb has called "the making and unmaking of persons," and which anthropologist Maureen Trudelle Schwarz has employed in her exemplary studies of Diné (Navajo) personhood.[10]

The most thorough academic model of O'odham life stages comes from David Kozak's unpublished MA thesis. Kozak's model of O'odham life stages directly relates to O'odham models of personhood because distinction between life stages suggests that persons are gradually made, or produced, rather than merely born. His model is reproduced below.

ali pre-toddler infant (from birth to approximately two
   years of age; prior to learning how to walk and talk)
      Literal translation: baby boy (Noun)

ceoj child (from two to approximately nine years of age)
      Literal translation: boy (Noun)

cehia/wiappoi youth (pubescent child, teen
   years; *cehia* = female; *wiappoi* = male)
      Literal translation: *cehia* = young female, virgin;
      wiappoi = a young man, boy (Nouns)

ke:li/oks adult (a person with/without children and/or has
   achieved a special feat; *ke:li* = male, *oks* = female)
      Literal translation: *ke:li* = an adult male; the male of any
      animal; *oks* = an adult female; a lady or a woman (Nouns)

wi:kol an elder or older person (someone with great-grandchildren)
      Literal translation: one's relative of the great
      grand-parent generation (Noun)[11]

In addition to these four life stages outlined by Kozak, anthropologist Ruth Underhill discusses *siakam*, an O'odham notion of maturity pertaining to "ripening" or "ripeness," which might be considered a subset of *ke:li*, *oks*, and *wi:kol*. Underhill translates *siakam* as "ripe man," and missionary-linguists Dean Saxton, Lucille Saxton, and Susie Enos translate the term as "hero," or "one who has endured."[12] Linguistic anthropologist Donald Bahr translates *síakam* as "brave men" or "war hero." Saxton, Saxton, and Enos translate *si* as "real, genuine; ultimate; of good character; precise, very," so if *O'odham* means something like "people," then *siakam* means something like "real people," those ripened individuals who are the physical embodiment of O'odhamness.[13] For example, Maria Chona, the subject of Underhill's *Papago Woman*, is one such portrait of a "ripe" woman, whose life story tells of her maturation and movements within the O'odham desert landscape.[14] Like Chona, Frances Manuel, a well-known Tohono O'odham basket weaver, singer, and elder, was known as "a person who has traveled all over."[15] Alternatively, rather than using the language of "ripening" or "ripeness," Joseph Giff—an O'odham singer from St. John's Village—used the language of "flowering" found in Blue Swallow songs. Giff explains: "Here [in the Blue Swallow song] where it says 'my body flowers' ['ñ-cu:kug hiosim'] what it means is when one really sings with his heart [si e-i:bdagkaj ñei] then his body becomes beautiful similar to flowering all over. If something looks very nice, if it looks very desirable, we say it flowers [s-hiosig]."[16]

Underhill describes four procedures through which males might progress from one stage to another: killing an eagle, going on the salt pilgrimage, encountering a powerful spirit in a dream, thereby acquiring songs and perhaps healing power, as well as the act of killing an enemy.[17] Saxton, Saxton, and Enos suggest a similar model in which four degrees of manhood were attained through "killing a small animal" (often called ban, literally meaning "coyote," though not necessarily referring to an actual coyote), going on the salt pilgrimage (onamed), "meeting an animal or bird with power in a dream or vision," and "killing an enemy tribesman" (o:b).[18] Walking to Magdalena contributes to the literature on O'odham processes of "ripening," "flowering," or maturation, insofar as the very act of walking to Magdalena is a part of the process through which O'odham make mature persons, thereby also contributing to the emerging literature in the academic study of religion on elders, aging, and authority in Native American and indigenous communities.[19]

Making Place

In academic literature "place" is often defined in opposition to "space." Whereas space is abstract and homogeneous, place is concrete and particular. The difference between place and space might be sketched most simplistically in the following constructivist formula:

$$Place = Space + Meaning$$

If place is space transformed by human acts of meaning making—as constructivist dogma would have it—then one can begin to conceive of place as simultaneously encompassing both concrete and particular places, as well as in a variety of more expansive notions of place, such as landscape and cosmos. Building on the elasticity of place, religious studies scholar Anne Feldhaus suggests that a region—such as Maharashtra, the focus of her study on pilgrimage, "connected places," and geographical imagination—may be considered a kind of place. "In such a usage," Feldhaus contends, "a region is simply a large place."[20] Feldhaus acknowledges that other scholars might resist the notion of conceiving of a region as merely a large place, specifically noting that the philosopher Edward Casey prefers to think of a region as a set of places connected to one another rather than a large place. Following Feldhaus's lead in extending the notion of place to include a region as "simply a large place," as well as a set, or series of sets, of smaller, discrete yet "connected places," I maximally expand the notion of place to include cosmology, which is used here more or less synonymously with sense of place. Such an expansion of the category of place is not unprecedented.[21] For example, Feldhaus argues "a sense of place is formative of one's cosmology and basic orientation in the world."[22] Moreover, to speak of the cosmos, a region, or even a landscape as a place is not merely an academic abstraction. Addressing the relation between pilgrimage and the production of regional consciousness in Maharashtra, Feldhaus argues:

> In most pilgrimages in South Asia, the pilgrims enact their conviction that they *can* move through a region by in fact *doing* so. At the same time, they reinforce the same conviction for those who, though they remain at home, are aware of the pilgrims' journeys. Movement through an area with one's own body, or a clear realization of the possibility of such movement, is a condition for being able to imagine the area as a region in *any* coherent sense.[23]

The same thing could very well be said for O'odham who journey to Magdalena: that they enact their conviction that they can move through their indigenous territory by in fact doing so. It is no surprise, then, that on the road to Magdalena, I often heard O'odham walkers declare, "this is our *jeweḍ*"—that is, our "earth," or our "land." O'odham continue to be able to think of Magdalena as existing within O'odham territory, both by actually walking to Magdalena themselves and by praying in their own homes for their loved ones who are making the journey for the people. Although Magdalena now lies outside of any territory recognized as being within the jurisdiction of contemporary O'odham people, the notion that Magdalena continues to exist as O'odham territory in any coherent sense is made possible through the actual physical movement of walking to Magdalena (see chapter 4), imagining journeys to Magdalena through song (see chapter 2), and staffs, ribbons, and saints that evoke the power and presence of Magdalena in the everyday lives of O'odham (see chapter 3).

Most of my O'odham consultants and acquaintances never explicitly invoked or discussed the category of place. However, Verlon "Carlos" Jose, vice-chairman of the Tohono O'odham Nation, takes an explicitly pluralist and relativist stance on place. Even while walking on the road to Magdalena, he often encourages O'odham to make pilgrimages to destinations other than Magdalena. He has also made many of these other journeys as well, and yet, year after year, he finds himself on the road to Magdalena. During one conversation he mentioned that there are multiple groups and individuals who walk to a variety of locations across the Tohono O'odham Nation in honor of Saint Francis. "That's what I've always said: 'We don't necessarily have to go to *Mali:na*. We can go here. We can walk to any church here to make our *manda*, to make our commitment, for our prayers, to humble ourselves, to do that.'"[24] At the moment I was a little perplexed by Verlon's comments, since the pilgrimage to Magdalena is clearly very important to him. When I asked what he thought about "place" and whether particular places are special and distinct from other places, or if all places were more or less interchangeable, his reply was simple: "When it comes to place, place is what you make it and how you make it. . . . You talk about 'place': places are important, but a place is what you make of it."[25] As Verlon's comments about place demonstrate, place and place making is not merely an academic interest.

The municipality of Magdalena in Sonora, Mexico, provides a good example for considering the difference between place as unique and place as interchangeable in some way. Many O'odham travel to Magdalena to visit with their Saint Francis, particularly around the saint's day on October 4. However, there are also several rival destinations for O'odham with their own Saint Francis. Both Mission San Xavier del Bac near Tucson and San Francisquito—meaning "Little Saint Francis," the Spanish name for Cu:wĭ Geṣk, or "Rabbit Falls Down," an O'odham village in Sonora near the international border—have their own rival fiestas for Saint Francis. Moreover, the Tohono O'odham Nation also has a movable feast of Saint Francis that rotates each year across the eleven districts of the nation.[26] This means that each year there are no fewer than three rival destinations for O'odham to travel to in addition to, or in lieu of, traveling to Magdalena. On top of all of this, there is a village named Ali Mali:na, or "Little Magdalena," in the Baboquivari District of the Tohono O'odham Nation. All of these places effectively aspire to be replicas of Magdalena, vying for its prestige, power, authority, and authenticity. As folklorist James Griffith and other scholars have previously shown, some O'odham claim that these rivals of Magdalena are superior to Magdalena because they have the "real" Saint Francis.[27] However, these other journeys and pilgrimage destinations are not the focus of this study. Although each of these might warrant an independent or comparative study at a later date, these other places seem to derive their authority from Magdalena in one way or another. As Feldhaus argues in the Maharashtrian context in India, where the replication of so-called holy places is quite common,

> Even when the ostensible claim is that the nearby place being praised is equal or superior to the distant place in terms of which it is praised, the person making the claim implicitly admits that the distant place is in fact superior. For that place is the one *in terms of which* the praise is formulated. The distant place is the measure against which the nearer place is to be tested, the truly famous place whose fame the other seeks to borrow.[28]

In the O'odham context, these other places invoke Magdalena as the standard against which they should be measured when some O'odham claim that one or more of these other places are equal or superior to Magdalena in some way, though of course some O'odham explicitly disagree with this.

Place and Person

The conjunction of the categories of place and person as the central categories of this study is not without precedent.[29] Keith Basso, the renowned cultural and linguistic anthropologist of the Western Apaches, contends that "what people make of their places is closely connected to what they make of themselves as members of society and inhabitants of the earth, and while the two activities may be separable in principle, they are deeply joined in practice. . . . We *are*, in a sense, the place-worlds we imagine."[30] Or, as put more briefly by ethnomusicologist, anthropologist, and linguist Steven Feld in his coauthored work with Basso, "as people fashion places, so, too, do they fashion themselves."[31] The production, manufacture, or making of personhood and place, then, are coterminous projects pursued in tandem. Moreover, Feld and Basso's quotation above can and should be inverted to state that as people fashion themselves, they also fashion places (for more on this see chapter 4 on walking). Similarly, Feldhaus notes that "awareness of *where* one is (or where one comes from) can become an important element in understanding *who* one is: it can become a vital aspect of a person's identity."[32] Likewise, in the context of the pilgrimage to Magdalena, where one has been (or not), and how one gets there (or not), are significant in the ongoing process of producing O'odham persons.

This chapter has already begun to address how O'odham make persons, but it has not yet begun to discuss how O'odham make places—or, for that matter, how places make mature persons. Living in, moving through, and interacting with places, people are in turn shaped by these places and the people that are sometimes associated with them. On one journey, not to Magdalena but from Cold Fields to Cedagĭ Wahia, not long after the death of Felix Antone, Michael Enis, of San Xavier del Bac, sang songs that were unusual in that the words were sung in ordinary, spoken O'odham, instead of the "song language" that is difficult for even fluent speakers of O'odham to understand.[33] In particular, I remember two lines from one of the songs that he sang:

Mali:na, Mali:na
San Flansi:sko ki:

Mali:na, as I previously mentioned in the introduction, is how the Spanish word Magdalena is usually rendered, through a syllable reduction in O'odham. *San Flansi:sko ki:* might be translated as "Saint Francis's house," or "where Saint Francis lives." The pairing of these lines together in song suggests their equivalence; or, in other words, the person of Saint Francis is associated with the town and church of Magdalena, both of which are, in turn, associated with Saint Francis. Therefore, when O'odham say, "I'm going to Mali:na," everyone knows that the speaker is referring to making a visit to Saint Francis, who—until recently, when a new, separate structure was built next to the main church—was usually lying in a side chapel of the Church of Santa María Magdalena in the Sonoran town of Magdalena de Kino.[34]

By attending to O'odham conceptions and representations of places and how they produce mature persons, the intention is to respond to Bahr's concern that studies of indigenous cosmologies too often neglect the "characters" that inhabit and act within this world—or as Bahr puts it, "what the *persons* . . . are like and how they behave" without assuming, as Bahr does, that O'odham landscapes or cosmos "are just places for characters to act."[35]

In the final pages of his signature work, *Piman Shamanism and Staying Sickness*, Bahr acknowledges that Mircea Eliade's three-part cosmology, or "shamanic geography" (this world and the spiritual worlds above and below), does not fit well with the O'odham cosmology that Bahr elicited from his principal collaborator, Juan Gregorio, whose cosmology, according to Bahr, is decidedly "this-worldly."[36] Despite Bahr's admission of the limitations of working within the Eliadean paradigm, other scholars such as David Kozak and David Lopez have largely adopted this same framework uncritically, without noting Bahr's assertion that the data does not fit the model.[37] This may be why Bahr bemoans:

> I confess to a weariness about studies of the cosmos—the sacred directions, the earth, sky, and underworld, and so on. To me, those are just places for characters to act, and I prefer the characters' actions

over the places. It is a personal preference and I would surely not rule out further attention to the cosmo-visions of Native Americans. I do feel that overattention to that leaves out this other aspect of stories, and orations, namely what the *persons* (godly or mortal, human or human-animal) are like and how they behave.[38]

My goal here, then, is to establish a framework that might satisfy Bahr for attending to place without neglecting persons. Moreover, what O'odham have *made of* Christianity should be understood within these cosmologies, rather than apart from them.[39]

Walking to Magdalena follows what some scholars have called "the spatial turn." Following Michel Foucault's critique of the devaluation of space and hyperinflation of time, in which "space was treated as the dead, the fixed, the undialectical, the immobile" and "time, on the contrary, was richness, fecundity, life, dialectic," critical geographer Edward Soja has forcefully shown how most disciplines in the humanities and social sciences have persistently marginalized space in favor of time.[40] Soja calls this trend "historicism," which he defines as "an overdeveloped historical contextualization of social life and social theory that actively submerges and peripheralizes the geographical or spatial imagination."[41] Instead, Soja urges scholars to recognize that space is agentic—it acts upon individuals (that is, places make people) just as it is shaped by their practices (people make places). Within such a framework, place is agentive and people are emplaced, with each acting upon the other. Places make mature persons, or rather disciplined journeys make persons mature, as people move between meaningful places. Places themselves are capable of calling people to them. Both the production of mature persons and place making, then, are ongoing and unfinished O'odham projects.

"The spatial turn," however, is perhaps less revolutionary for the discipline of religious studies than it is for other disciplines in the humanities and social sciences. No doubt, this is due to Eliade's complex legacy for contemporary scholars of religion. As Manuel Vásquez has recently noted, "by introducing a cyclical notion of time, time as the eternal return to mythical and pristine origins, as a 'continual' or 'atemporal present,' Eliade effectively immunizes religious studies against the bias toward time that has led to the neglect of space in the social sciences."[42] Although Eliade's focus on the spatial dimensions of religious experience corrects the biases and excesses of historicism, this comes at the cost of dehistoricizing and decontextualizing his data. As Vásquez argues, Eliade's inoculation of religious studies against historicism comes at too great a cost:

> Eliade has left unchallenged the untenable dichotomy between space and time, merely switching the duality around, privileging space, particularly the foundational center, against the corrosive power of historicity and change. The result is an essentialist theory of religion that flattens the diversity of religious phenomena across history and cultures. Despite Eliade's remarkable erudition, his history of religions does not seek to provide fully contextualized analyses of changing forms of religious emplacement and materiality. Instead, Eliade summons a myriad of religious practices as surface expressions of underlying transhistorical or supra-historical patterns that are endlessly reenacted. This search for deep, universal 'Platonic forms' flies in the face of his own anti-reductionist efforts.[43]

Instead of following Eliade in defending religion from "the terror of history," my intention is to follow Soja in the goal of articulating "a practical theoretical consciousness that sees the lifeworld of being creatively located not only in the making of history but also the construction of human geographies, the social production of space and the restless formation and reformation of geographical landscapes," so that "social being [is] actively emplaced in space *and* time in an explicitly historical *and* geographical contextualization."[44]

Movement in general, and walking in particular, become that which mediates time and space, making landscapes places that are actually lived in. Again, this is not an original claim. Anthropologist Arjun Appadurai introduced the term "ethnoscape" to draw attention to the "imagined world" of transnational and intercultural human movements across the landscape.[45] Building on Appadurai's theme, religious studies scholar Elizabeth McAlister suggested the term "religio-scapes" to understand "the subjective maps (and attendant theologies) of diasporic communities."[46]

Similarly, religious studies scholar Thomas Tweed describes religions as dynamic "sacroscapes": "Whatever else religions do," Tweed writes, "they move across time and space. They are not static. And they have effects. They leave traces. They leave trails."[47] Following Michel de Certeau, Tweed redescribes religions as "spatial practices" through which people "make homes and cross boundaries."[48]

The Founding of the O'odham Cosmos: Making a Place for "Real People"

Contemporary O'odham sometimes refer to themselves as Wu:ṣkam Hemajkam, or "the people who came out/emerged." This self-identification stands in distinction to Hohokam, or Huhugam O'odham, which means "finished people-like-us."[49] While there is no consensus regarding who the Hohokam are, or were, in relation to contemporary O'odham within either O'odham or academic communities, the crucial distinction seems to be that they are similar to, and yet somehow different from, today's O'odham.[50] The word *huhugam* means "something that is all gone," which Tohono O'odham storyteller Danny Lopez explains can refer to anything that is gone, finished, or disappeared, such as food after a good feast.[51]

During one of our many conversations, Simon Lopez—an observant and knowledgeable Tohono O'odham elder, cowboy, traditional singer, and ritual curer from the village of Kaij Mek (Santa Rosa)—explained to me who contemporary O'odham are as Wu:ṣkam Hemajkam, including how they killed the Hohokam, drove them into the ocean (where they perhaps now reside), and settled in their homelands, an area that is significantly larger than their present land holdings on both sides of the United States-Mexico border. However, according to O'odham oral traditions, this "settling," or "founding," as Eliade might have euphemistically called it, was nothing short of a violent conquest, which Bahr likens to a fraternal or fratricidal civil war. When Simon narrated this history, he explained, "That's why they call us *Wu:ṣkam. Wu:ṣkam Hemajkam.* The I'itoi brought us out there and spread us out to start *war, killing* these *Hohokam*."[52] Simon went on, stating that I'itoi "took them *in the Ocean*," where he killed them in the water.

SL: And that's how they started living here, all over here. And the people started making *their living* here on this *Jeweḍ* [earth or land]. And that's how our understanding *is*. *Now* we're called *Wu:ṣkam*. We got rid of the *Hohokam*.[53]

At the time of the conquest, I'itoi was still with his people, both *Wu:ṣkam* and *Hohokam*. Today, as Simon explained, the situation is very different. I'itoi is absent now, and yet in spite of that absence, he is somehow still present.

SL: Now he's gone, and *where did the I'itoi go?* Disappeared. And we can't see him anymore. If we have any problem, we can't go and call the I'itoi to come and help us the way they helped his people *before*. Yeah, we know where he lives. They'll say, "He's there. He's there, but he's gone like . . . like these others, you know. We can't see him, but he's there. He's around, *like a ghost*, but he can't come back and say this and that to us."[54]

Not unlike the Hohokam, it would seem that I'itoi, too, is *huhugam*. He has retreated to a place known as *I'itoi Ki:*, "I'itoi's home," or "the place where I'itoi lives," in a cave high up on Baboquivari mountain. And yet contemporary O'odham remain vitally engaged with I'itoi and these other *huhugam*, who have gone into the land, connecting O'odham in the present to their past and their relatives that are embedded, or emplaced, within the land. According to Danny Lopez, "These places are what we consider sacred places because they are the evidence that reminds us of the long-ago people, or Huhugam. . . . some of us feel strongly that we are a part of the ancient past."[55]

Personhood and Place in Cosmos and History

In the course of studying pilgrimages to Magdalena, O'odham have discussed three cosmological realms, though these certainly do not exhaust the possible realms within the O'odham cosmos.[56] In addition to *ka:cim jeweḍ*, or the "staying earth," O'odham discuss a place called *da:m ka:cim*, which can be translated as "up above laying," "on top laying," as well as "heaven." O'odham also talk about *si'alig weco*, a place usually spoken of as being in the East where O'odham are said to go when they die. Although the ethnographic literature strongly suggests that O'odham conceive of heaven as a place for God and dead white saints—almost like an exclusive country club—with dead O'odham typically going to the East instead, Simon expressed uncertainty in a conversation about death and heaven.[57]

SS: Do O'odham go to heaven?

SL: I don't know! [Laughing] I really can't say! Like I said, you know, I don't know. Like for instance, that Saint Kateri [Tekakwita] now. She's a saint. And I wouldn't say right now she's with God. She's *seen* God. Maybe when she became a *saint*, maybe she did, maybe she is [in heaven]. Like all these other saints that we have, maybe they are with God, but we don't know. Like I said, I don't know. I don't think anybody would really know.[58]

Like many O'odham, Simon was reluctant to make any definite statements about what happens after death without already having experienced death in order to know from firsthand experience. But what was most striking in this conversation, which took place several months before Kateri was canonized on October 21, 2012, was how Kateri's impending canonization might transform O'odham cosmologies.[59] Because no O'odham, or "Indians," seem to have been admitted to heaven before, or at least not for very long (see chapter 2), Simon stated that the common phrase "he's with God now" seemed a bit strange, at least when spoken *by* one O'odham *about* another O'odham.

When I asked where deceased O'odham want to end up, Simon remembered his grandparents, voicing his grandmother and grandfather, Juan Lopez, which further evoked their memories.[60]

SS: Where do O'odham *want to go* when they die?

SL: They say that O'odham, you know, when you die, you go to where they call it *East*. They say they're gonna go to *si'alig weco*. And they say that there's a place back East where you go when you die. They always say that that's where you go when you die, as O'odham.[61]

According to Simon, O'odham oral traditions state that O'odham go to another realm in the East. However, the boundary between this world of the living and the other world of the dead in the East is said to be porous. Simon went on to describe his grandfather, who he said regularly passed time in the company of his dead relatives.

SL: My grandpa [Juan Lopez] is a real good medicine man. And he talks to the *ghosts*, the people that dies. And when my grandpa is asleep and drunk, he would be talking, talking, and talking in his sleep! And then my grandma would say, "He's dreaming again. That's why he's saying that." And sure enough, sometimes he would say that he's dreaming that he's with *these guys*. And I guess that's why he was talking is because he was talking to those people, and things like that! And he always says that he's dreaming with his *dad*, or his *mom*, or his *brother* that passed away.[62]

As Simon continued to describe O'odham relationships with the dead, it became increasingly clear that "the East" was not some abstract place that existed nowhere in particular. Instead, for Simon, O'odham dead can be found living in particular places in the landscape.

SL: And he was telling me that there's a place back East. There's a mountain, *a big, high, long mountain,* and it's got *seven heads,* that mountain. Maybe you've seen that, by Green Reservoir back here when you go in that side, when they call it Ku'ukcul [Ko'okol, or Chili Mountain]. And he said that there's a place over there, where they call it Wewa'ak Mo'okam Do'ag [Seven Headed Mountain].[63]

Simon knew that I had seen this mountain, known by two names, because it is right next to Felix Antone's home in Green Reservoir—more commonly known in English as Green Well, or Pozo Verde in Spanish, and Cedagĭ Wahia in O'odham—where Felix's walkers assemble to begin their journey to Magdalena together. Although I had walked *on top* of this mountain, Simon stated his grandfather had been *inside* these mountains.

SL: And *beneath* that, *boy*, there's joy there! You can find *all* of these people that's passed away. They're cowboys. They're cowboys. And they would have round up right there. Boy, they'll be *chasing* horses, *roping* horses, cattle, and things like that in that area! And he said,

"That's where they go. You're a cowboy, you die, you go over there. And meet with all those relatives, friends, or whatever, and enjoy yourself over there with all those cowboys." And he says that, "That's where I go sometimes. I dream that I was back there with those guys, doing all this cowboy work, riding broncs and things like that." And he's always saying that when he dreams, he dreams that he's back there. So when somebody is dying, and he would say, "He's gonna go to the Seven Head Mountain to see his friends and relatives when he dies."[64]

Significantly, our conversational topics that day were precipitated by the recent death of Felix Antone, the leader of the largest group of O'odham walkers to Magdalena. Following Felix Antone's death on January 31, 2012, Simon Lopez spoke in O'odham during the funeral services for Felix. Simon's words strongly affected those who were present, bringing most people to tears. Simon later translated, preaching like he did at the funeral:

SL: Now that Felix is *gone* . . . I don't want anybody to say, you know, that you can't make it because Felix is *not there*. *Keep going*. Keep going. Keep doing it even though he's gone; there's others that are helping you, that will be helping you, through the *walk*. And so, you guys, keep going. And I know that in spirit Felix *will* be with you. And Felix will probably help you *a lot*, you know, and give you *strength to walk*, and all that.[65]

Essentially, Simon exhorted Felix's walkers not to say or think that Felix is not present with them when they walk to Magdalena. Instead, Simon claimed that Felix would be with his walkers, helping them along the way. Simon went on to explain that not only Felix but also many O'odham dead make their way to Magdalena, even in death, as they once did in life.

SL: And as we understand in our *culture* that we're there, they're there, even though they're gone. I know *myself* that I've *always* said that when I get to Magdalena, I always get things that my dad likes, or my grandpa, or my mom, and put it somewhere, where I know that they're there and do their shares, you know, the time when we're at

Magdalena. Because I know that my grandpa tells me and my dad and everybody that, "They're there. The ones that we *lost* that always go over there. They're, they're over there with us. You *can't see them*, but *they'll see you*." And so, you know, that's how we say, you know, that "they're there *in spirit*." So that's what I was telling *them*, you know, that Felix will be with you guys on your walk. And so you just think about that, and just keep going.[66]

For many O'odham, Christianity is simply the way of their grand-mothers and grandfathers. When contemporary O'odham journey to Magdalena, they are retracing the paths of their relatives and walking in the footsteps of their ancestors. Moving across the land, whether by foot or in song, O'odham follow those who have gone before. Moreover, these movements connect O'odham in the present with loved ones whom they have lost, with powerful entities embedded in the landscape, and with histories embedded within the land that have not been written. These movements across the landscape, or landscapes of movement, constitute what anthropologist Jack Waddell has called "an emotional space" through which "something important about man's environment feeds back into Papago awareness through ritual participation," such as walking to Magdalena.[67] As anthropologist Michael J. Sallnow has argued, "Landscapes exist in time as well as in space."[68] In conceiving of landscape as a medium for materializing time in space, or making the past present in place, Sallnow borrows from Russian philosopher and literary theorist Mikhail Bakhtin's concept of chronotopes, in which "time, as it were, thickens, takes on flesh, becomes artistically visible; likewise, space becomes charged and responsive to the movements of time, plot and history."[69] In this sense *Walking to Magdalena* strongly supports Bernard Fontana's view that "to be on the road to Magdalena in early October is to take part in the richest kind of living history, to participate in the weaving together of past, present, and future."[70]

A journey through space toward Magdalena may also become a jour-ney backward through time as each step evokes the memories of those who have passed that way before. Past, present, and future seem simul-taneously tangible, as O'odham become a part of a living history and a larger community united by a shared journey. And many O'odham feel the presence of their ancestors and the dead as they walk along the road to Magdalena.[71] Remember the words of Simon Lopez's grandfather: "They're there . . . . they're over there with us. You *can't see them*, but *they'll see you*."

Summary

This chapter shows some of the ways in which O'odham have made Christianity their own by embedding—or emplacing—Christianity within their ancestral landscapes. Crucially, *Walking to Magdalena* is situated within what I have previously referred to as "landscapes of movement." Following Tweed, as well as the theme of movement, these theoretical and methodological inclinations are named "theoretical wandering." The chapter has introduced the intertwined notions of personhood—or better yet, "real people"—and place, illustrating some of the ways in which both O'odham places and persons become associated with one another. Each of these themes is further developed in the following chapters.

CHAPTER 2

O'odham Songscapes

March 18, 2014. On a Tuesday night during the second week of Lent, I attended a wake for Francisco "Harry" Encinas in the Tohono O'odham village of Kohatk. This is the first time that I've been in the village. Were it not for the fact that I was accompanying the Lopezes, who came to sing their "traditional rosary" at the wake, I might have felt out of place. Inside the small village church, like so many others on the Tohono O'odham Nation, there is one prominent Saint Francis and several other San Franciscos. All are reclining. Outside of the church, there are field crosses in multiple directions, including one facing south toward Magdalena. Photos of Harry, horses, cowboys, saguaros, mountains, and either sunrises or sunsets appear together on the makeshift altar constructed for the wake outside of the little church, which is far too small to contain all of those who have come to pay their respects. As I listen to the rosary, singing along to some of the words that I have learned, my thoughts begin to stray. In particular, alongside the photos is a sign that reads, "Rest in Paradise." Usually, at least in a non-O'odham context, I assume the letter *p* in RIP stands for "Peace." Spelled out clearly in front of me, that assumption is not safe here. But then I think again, even wondering what "rest" might mean in this context, considering O'odham propensities for movement, in both life and in death. Then again, given the visual cues of the photos, and the fact that Harry was a cowboy, I think that the "Paradise" referred to is probably terrestrial, and not celestial or heavenly. I imagine *jejewul* moving about for all eternity inside mountains in the "East." Finally, my thoughts are interrupted when an O'odham woman brings me back to the "traditional rosary" that the extended Lopez family is singing. She asks me, "Do these songs remind you of being in Mali:na?" Without any hesitation, I answer with a smile, "Always." Wordlessly, she smiles back, seemingly in approval.

This chapter poses two questions. First, how do O'odham evoke movement across their land through songs? Second, how do these same songs evoke the O'odham past embedded in these places? "Evoke" is used here with the meaning of causing to recall unspoken memories embedded in the land. Moreover, not only words but also sounds, smells, and movements evoke O'odham pasts embedded in these places. Present-day O'odham "walkers" on their pilgrimage to Saint Francis in Mali:na, or Magdalena, Sonora, Mexico, in late September and early October also participate in past movements, particularly when these past movements across their land are evoked through songs that contain the memories of previous journeys.[1] Moving across their ancestral lands, contemporary O'odham walkers often think about their parents, grandparents, and great-grandparents who have made the journey before them. Indeed, the land itself holds the past of these people, including past movements, which are evoked through retracing the steps of those who have gone before both through walking (see chapter 4) and through song, which Ofelia Zepeda—an O'odham linguist and poet—describes as "pulling memory from the depths of the earth."[2]

Although the tremendously influential Dakota theologian, historian, and activist Vine Deloria Jr. established the primacy of place in the study of the indigenous religious traditions of the Americas, and this emphasis has been upheld by other scholars, such as Mvskoke theologian James Treat and religious studies scholar Greg Johnson, the intention in posing these two questions together is to follow the Russian philosopher and literary theorist Mikhail Bakhtin in privileging neither time nor space.[3] Bakhtin's concept of "chronotope," or "time space," which was already introduced in the previous chapter, expresses "the intrinsic connectedness of temporal and spatial relationships that are artistically expressed in literature."[4] Following Bakhtin's synthesis of time and space, O'odham senses of time and space are interdependent and should be studied as such.[5] In this chapter my analysis follows a line of inquiry established by linguistic anthropologist Keith Basso, who invoked Bakhtin's notion of "chronotope" in his study of Western Apache senses of place.[6]

Archaeologist J. Andrew Darling and Akimel O'odham traditional singer and cultural preservation officer Barnaby V. Lewis have shown that O'odham song series encode geographical knowledge.[7] On the other hand, linguistic anthropologist Donald Bahr as well as anthropologist David L. Kozak and Tohono O'odham farmer, cowboy, and ritual curer David I. Lopez have demonstrated that O'odham songs encode historical knowledge.[8] For many O'odham, no journey is too far, and the past is never so far away that it cannot be viscerally felt through song. Those who listen closely to O'odham songs are transported not only through space, but also through time. Indeed, the "ancientness" of the past is palpably present (never too distant) for many O'odham in the present, and faraway places are never inaccessible, so long as the audience may be transported to the place, and the place made palpably present, through song. O'odham songs, then, evoke movement across the landscape, which I have previously called "landscapes of movement." As Kozak explains, "The contents of O'odham song lyrics feature two related signature characteristics: nouns that describe the landscape and verbs that tell of the song subject's actions."[9]

O'odham songs evoke movement across their land through what Bahr has called "filmicness"—or the "filmic" quality of O'odham songs—in which each sentence (usually three or four in each song) produces a different "word picture."[10] When heard or read together in sequence, these songs evoke movement. Bahr explains, "Since the songs are so short, the shifts of focus across the sentences give an illusion of motion."[11] Moreover, O'odham songs evoke movement through more means than the "illusion" of apparent motion caused by the succession of images or "word pictures," as Bahr also notes that the verbs in O'odham songs usually describe things in motion, particularly noting the occurrence of "run" in almost every song.[12] In turn, as O'odham songs evoke movement, these movements (as well as the songs themselves) evoke memories of past journeys. Movement across the landscape is common in O'odham songs, and as Kozak has noted, "the movement (often frenzied) of the song's 'I' or 'it' is a signature feature of Tohono O'odham song-poetry."[13] Like the Apache cowboy Basso overheard talking quietly to himself and "talked names" all the time, enjoying the pleasure of reciting a long list of Apache place-names, O'odham songs transport their audiences to the places through song. The Apache cowboy told Basso, "I ride that way in my mind."[14] No doubt, many O'odham feel the same way about these songs that evoke a sense of journey as well as memories of past journeys. On one occasion, for example, after I turned off my video recorder following a long conversation with Louis Lopez—who is introduced later in this chapter—he told me, "Yeah, I do that sometimes, when I am singing. I close my eyes, and it's just like watching a movie." After saying our goodbyes, I scrambled to write down as quickly as possible the words that he spoke, before I forgot them. I remembered that Louis mentioned other song sets too, like ocean songs that involve certain birds flying upside down, dipping just the tip of one of their wings in the water as they fly across the surface, and Huhugam at Superstition Mountain singing "We're gonna drown!" as they watch the water rising higher and higher in yet another song.

The narratives below aid in answering the two questions posed at the beginning of this chapter through the analysis of six O'odham songs, while at the same time considering how O'odham songs map journeys and constitute an O'odham form of historical knowledge.[15] Rather than treating O'odham statements as mere data, this method draws upon and elaborates upon O'odham exegesis of their own songs.

Kendall Jose's Mixed Magdalena Songs

One day, long before Kendall Jose was born, his great-grandfather needed a ride from the village of Nolik to Tucson. And fortunately for Kendall, he was inclined to sing. While he was singing, Kendall's grandmother turned on the tape recorder and began recording. As Kendall tells the story, he voices his grandmother who was there with his great-grandfather on the day in question.

KJ: She said, "We were going to Tucson, and my Dad showed up, and . . .
he wanted a ride." She said, "But we were going to Tucson, and he
wanted to *sing*." So she said, "So, I got my recorder out, *and he sang
those six songs*, real short, he sang 'em real quick." And there's just
the vocals. No rattle or anything. He sang those songs for her. . . . And
those were the first six songs I started singing.[16]

Decades later, the tape itself is probably unplayable, the reel long
ago stretched out and damaged from overuse. Kendall may not even
have a copy any longer. Instead of preserving the recording itself and
archiving his great-grandfather's songs, Kendall prefers a more active
and engaged method of cultural preservation: *singing* the songs himself.
By all accounts, he picked up the songs quickly, after hearing them only
a few times.

KJ: Thank God for cassettes and VHSs, because that's how I learned.
Nowadays a lot of people don't like recording things, especially culture
and history and stuff like that. They don't like doing it for whatever
reason. But, like I said, thank God there was such a thing for me,
because that's how I learned. I never met him. I never knew him. I
just, all I knew was a tape my Grandma had.[17]

After memorizing the songs, Kendall taught them to his father, Verlon Jose, and his son, Jojo Jose. Now the Joses are usually busy most
evenings and weekends, singing these six songs and doing rosaries for
elders who are near death and at wakes, death anniversaries, fiestas, and
other events throughout the year including the pilgrimage to Magdalena.
Significantly, the six songs that Kendall and his family sing map a journey
to Magdalena. Although the songs are usually sung in the transportable
rosary format, in which the same six songs may be sung anywhere with
one song inserted at each decade, the songs are also sung along the actual
road to Magdalena taken by contemporary pilgrims.

When I first encountered the Jose family and their songs on the road
to Magdalena in 2009, the songs were presented in a particular sequence,
or what ethnomusicologist George Herzog referred to as "mythic dreamt
song series."[18] This was the stress of the literature.[19] For example, in their

discussion of a much longer sequence of thirty-five devil songs, Kozak and Lopez explain, "A set's sequence is fixed in memory to recall it — in sequence — when needed. It seems to us that intentionally scrambling the sequence would prove tremendously difficult and a frankly improbable maneuver."[20] Moreover, within this literature, songs are said to be associated with particular powerful beings or entities, usually called "spirits" or "mythic persons" by Bahr and by Kozak and Lopez, who give these songs to particular O'odham dreamers.[21] For example, according to Bahr, around 1900 an Akimel O'odham named Hummingbird was "the first Pima of record to go to and return from Heaven," where he learned 16 songs from Jesus and Mary.[22] In the same way, in his study of three Tohono O'odham Airplane songs, Bahr states, "The Airplane songs are said to have been dreamed from (overheard from) an airplane in the 1940s."[23] Likewise, for Kozak and Lopez, devil songs are said to have been given to living O'odham by devils, or deceased O'odham cowboys.[24] If these entities have songs associated with them — illustrating an O'odham strategy of local consumption of the global — then surely, these Magdalena pilgrimage songs must have been given to living O'odham by Saint Francis, their patron saint!

This analysis, however, is certainly incorrect. In this research, no one has ever suggested that these six songs constitute a "mythic dreamt song series." No one has ever suggested that these six songs associated with pilgrimages to Magdalena, or other songs like them, were given to O'odham by Saint Francis. In fact, Kendall states that these six songs did not even belong to the same series, or song set, and he was uncertain of exactly what sets these six songs originally came from.

ss: Do you know if any of those songs are associated with any particular bird or birds? I know you told me that they're kind of mixed.

kj: Yeah. And again, this is the way I've understood it was that *the birds* that are referred to a lot in the songs that we sing are the Ṣu:g, the Mockingbird, and the Gigitwul, the Swallow. And again, I don't really remember. I think it is the Swallow, the Gigitwul. I know in Gila River, they have different series: the Mockingbird, the Oriole. I know I've been asked that question before. To me, I don't know.

All I know is that they're social songs. But what I can tell you is that as far as I know, the birds that are referred to in these songs are the Mockingbird and the Swallow.[25]

Simon Lopez's Mixed Magdalena Songs

The conversation took place on a cold February morning in 2012 with Simon Lopez in his house in Santa Rosa, also known as Kaij Mek, or Burnt Seeds. Much like the Joses, the Lopezes also have a set of six songs that map a route to Magdalena, which they also are often requested to sing for elders who are near death, at wakes, death anniversaries, fiestas, and other events throughout the year including the pilgrimage to Magdalena. On several of these occasions, such as at the wake in Kohatk with which I open this chapter, the Lopez rosary has been billed as a "traditional rosary." When I asked Simon about these songs, Simon, like Kendall, explained that the songs were "mixed."

SL: There's a lot of places, you know, *journey songs*, songs here and there. All these mountains, the villages, and places like that where we go. A lot of times they told me, you know, my ancestors, you know, they said, "Even if you just *sit* and just *sing, maybe mixed*, mixed songs and sing, it's okay. I mean, you know, as long as you're singing. But if you want to you can do like that, journey around with the songs and come back home." So *that's what I've been doing all the time*.[26]

Because this was the first time that I had encountered the suggestion that songs might be "mixed" to achieve a particular geographical purpose, or to evoke a sense of journey, I asked Simon to elaborate:

SS: You talked about singing different *mixed* songs. For those songs that you sing going to Magdalena and back, are those mixed songs? Or are they a single kind of song, like Swallow songs, or something like that? How would you classify or label those songs?

SL: Yeah, they're mixed. I mean, they're not the same songs. They're all different songs, but different places. What I meant when I say *mixed* songs is that when we sing for a journey song, we sing where we're gonna go. But if you don't have to, you can just mix it. You can pick

one South, North, West, East, or middle, or things like that, you know. Pick a song like that and just mix 'em and you don't have to go like, you know, line 'em up like a journey type. And just like that, the songs for Magdalena is a mix. I mean, you know, it's a different song that goes along the road.[27]

Generally speaking, it may be said that O'odham song series map routes through their traditional landscape. According to Bahr, song sequences are something like "postcards sent from someone on an impassioned journey."[28] Bahr contends that for O'odham audiences of song, "on receiving the card one speculates about the mood of the sender, about all that was happening at the moment of the message (the card can't say much), about what could have changed since the last message, and what the next step in the journey might be."[29] In their brevity, these songs are similar to the minimalist aesthetic of condensed moral truths in the Apache discursive genre that Basso calls "speaking with names," in which "depictions provided by Apache speakers are treated by Apache hearers as bases on which to build, as projects to complete, as invitations to exercise the imagination."[30] In short, these songs transport the singer and their audience from place to place as they move from song to song.

Cumulatively, each song series documents at least one such journey. For example, Darling and Lewis identified fourteen Oriole songs related by Akimel O'odham singer Vincent Joseph to Bahr as mapping an Akimel O'odham salt expedition route to the salt flats near the Sonoran Gulf Coast.[31] Similarly, the song sequences used in the Lopez and Jose family rosaries sing of particular mountains along the way to Magdalena, mapping routes to Magdalena from the areas of Santa Rosa and Quijotoa, and Nolik and Big Fields, respectively, via two separate points of origin and two different dialect groups. In short, O'odham evoke movement and make journeys through songs such that O'odham song sequences constitute a form of mapmaking. This is an indigenous cartographic method. In addition to mapping journeys, song sequences present an unfolding narrative, which also has an overall narrative moral that the audience

Fig. 2. Simon Lopez. Courtesy Louis "Tony" Lopez.

is invited to contemplate. Thus, not only are O'odham inhabitants *of* their landscape, covering it with songs, but they are also inhabited *by* an ethical songscape.[32]

And yet, song series not only map journeys, constituting ethical land-scapes in song; they also encode historical knowledge. These same songs evoke the past embedded in these places, recalling unspoken memories embedded in the land through the haiku-like brevity of O'odham songs that Bahr has called "a subjective, action oriented, pictoral and shamanic poetry."[33] To be more precise, the words of songs are considered by many O'odham to be historical speech. As Bahr has shown, O'odham songs are historical documents insofar as O'odham take them to be the actual words of powerful beings with whom O'odham have maintained relationships from time immemorial.[34] Therefore, those who listen closely to O'odham songs are transported not only through space, but also through time.

In their otherwise spatial interpretation of the place-making capabilities of O'odham song, Darling and Lewis ask a historical question: "How old are O'odham songscapes?"[35] Although they concede that archaeological evidence suggests that the places mentioned in these songs have been used since the time of the Hohokam, they foreclose the possibility that O'odham songs and songscapes encode historical knowledge, asserting that "songscapes refer to the spatial and spiritual order of places and things, not to historical events."[36] However, this interpretive move is hardly novel. In their study of O'odham devil lore, Kozak and Lopez acknowledge that "O'odham think of song-poetry as a kind of ancient talk," but much like Darling and Lewis, they immediately undercut the possibility of interpreting songs as historical documents when they assert that this "ancient speech" originates in the "mythical world of spirits."[37] Significantly, Kozak and Lopez reached an impasse regarding the historicity of devil lore and the "ancient speech" in devil songs: "Our individual opinions on origins appear to be irreconcilable, because one hypothesizes a historical and secular origin, and the other a mythical and sacred origin. . . . Kozak argues for a materialist under-standing, whereas Lopez argues for a spiritual one."[38] This analytical move, made by Darling and Lewis and by Kozak and Lopez, is premised on the incommensurability of indigenous and Western ways of knowing, further reinscribing an "us/them" dichotomy that is characteristic of most anthropological studies. Interpretive moves such as these may be misguided for at least two reasons. First, they depend on a questionable, Eurocentric distinction between "myth" and "history" to which I cannot subscribe (see chapter 5 and appendix 2).[39] Second, it spiritualizes O'odham conceptions of these entities, which are regarded by some O'odham to be very real, material, physical beings.[40] These two moves work in tandem, marginalizing indigenous knowledge and worldviews by relegating them to an unreal world outside of history.

Bahr has done the most to emphasize how O'odham songs encode historical knowledge and illustrate O'odham historicity, or senses of history. According to Bahr, O'odham songs "are taken to be the actual words of ancient characters, quite like Western historians' quotations from primary sources. Therefore, the O'odham have what they consider to be historical documents."[41]

In the course of one of our many long conversations that covered many topics, without elicitation or prompting, Simon Lopez began to elaborate on how O'odham songs are historical documents.

SL: Some of the songs that we sing is way back there, but we didn't know [through direct experience]. But we just learned the songs, and that's why they're sung. Yeah, it's true, I guess, all these other songs that I've heard, you know, that it's from way, way back, like the birds songs, you know, what they said. And we heard about it, but we didn't see it. And that's the same way with me, I always tell these guys that I didn't see it. I guess it's happened way back. There's very little things that I say that I've seen.[42]

And yet, while it is productive to think about songs as historical documents containing ancestral speech, it is also imperative to remember that although O'odham songs may be more or less fixed, they are in a special song language that is not directly accessible, even to fluent contemporary O'odham speakers. Because the meanings of the texts within these songs are somewhat elusive and encoded in a song language that is distinct from contemporary spoken O'odham, they may be differently translated and understood by contemporary O'odham. While O'odham song texts may remain fixed, O'odham engagements with these texts—bridging the past and the present, as it were—are much more fluid.

On another occasion, again without elicitation, Simon shared that he often wonders about the somewhat inaccessible ancient speech in O'odham songs and oral traditions.

SL: *I wonder sometimes*, you know, "*How is it like* way, way back in the years back, how the O'odham were, especially in *speaking*, the language, and things like that, you know? How, what words are?" And I *heard* a lot of these, you know, from my great-great-grandmother and father, when they would talk, and sometimes I would say, you know, "*What does that mean*?" And then he would tell me, you know, what that means, what they used to say in O'odham *before*, you know, the word. . . . They used to talk something like that *before*, even the songs, when he would sing the song a long time ago. And sometimes I wouldn't understand what it *means*. But from what he was telling me, it's the same thing, you know, it's like that, which it's different now. So a lot of these things that I've heard from way back, I don't really understand, you know, *how it used to be*.[43]

At the same time, even though Simon did not claim to know directly "*how it used to be*," the ambiguity of O'odham songs is an invitation for the historical and moral imagination.

If one accepts that song series constitute an O'odham cartography (they map journeys) and historiography (they contain the historical speech of powerful nonhuman or proto-human entities), what could this possibly mean for the song sequences that constitute journeys to Magdalena if they are "mixed," as both Kendall Jose and Simon Lopez insist for their own separate song sequences? How might O'odham song journeys to Magdalena be understood, knowing that the songs themselves were removed from their original song series contexts? What kinds of maps are these? What becomes of these song texts as encrypted historical documents?

Before I attempt to answer these questions, the songs should be presented and analyzed. Following Bahr, these songs are examined as a set.[44] As previously mentioned, the Lopez family's song series featured in this chapter consists of six songs. Songs 1–3 constitute a journey from home to Magdalena. Songs 4–6 constitute a return journey from Magdalena to home. What follows is a three-step translation process of the Lopez family "traditional rosary" songs. At my request, Simon Lopez's son Louis Anthony Lopez translated these songs in collaboration with Simon, by transcribing the O'odham song language, translating the song language into ordinary O'odham, and then translating the ordinary O'odham into a freely translated English text. This method somewhat follows Bahr's method of translating songs, but skips the step of an awkward literally translated English text between steps two and three.[45] My grasp of O'odham is weaker than Bahr's, so any attempt at a directly translated English text will have to wait until a later date. Although Bahr has strongly criticized scholars such as anthropologist Ruth Underhill for skipping this same step of a literal English translation, this method is justifiable for four reasons: (1) this is the method that Louis Lopez preferred, (2) the free translation is written by an O'odham rather than a non-O'odham, (3) some of the missing steps of the literal translation are discussed in the interpretations of the translated texts that follow, and (4) it is an artifact of contemporary O'odham engagement and interpretation with O'odham texts from an O'odham past that is not directly accessible to O'odham in the present. When my transcription or translation departs from Louis's, it appears in brackets. Following the three-step translation process, Simon Lopez and Louis Lopez offer interpretations of the texts that were recorded separately on various occasions in the course of ongoing conversations with each of them.

Songs

(1) Kuñs am o himeta
*Kuñs am o himeta
Kam ñena cu gamhui ñetam a cemai tonoda
Taṣ a tonlig a wehm tonoda

Kuñs am him
Kuñs am him
K c am ñedacug gamhu ñ-tam cem tonod
Taṣ tonlig wem tonod

As I'm walking
As I'm walking
I'm watching the light in the distance over me
As it shines with the light of the sun

The first song, lacking any direct reference to an O'odham place-name, begins "here," which is either in Santa Rosa or in Covered Wells, just north of Quijotoa—mentioned in the next song—which was also the site of the conversation with Louis and where the Lopez family lived before migrating to Santa Rosa. As Simon put it, "It starts from here . . . here in our home. . . . The *sun* shined at us towards Magdalena and headed us down that way. And that's where we started going down that way."[46] In other words, the light of the sun in the South beckons O'odham toward Magdalena. Louis also commented that "the sunlight is giving us strength as we're running towards this [Magdalena]. . . . That's all the first song is saying, running towards the South with the guidance and the strength of the sun, I guess."[47]

Another striking feature about Simon and Louis Lopez's interpretations of this text is that the first person singular "I" in the free English translation automatically became a first-person plural "we" and "us" in both of their interpretations (see especially song 6 for more). Also, while the O'odham word "him" is literally translated as "walking" in English, both Simon and Louis broaden the meaning to include "running" (*meḍ*) and the more generic "going" (also, see chapter 4).

(2) Kuñs am a himeta
*Kuñs am a himeta
Iowag tamai cenhai tonoda
Ma:lina cenhe ka wesai koiwe donlida

Kuñs am him
Kuñs am him
Iowag tam cem tonod
Ma:lina [Mali:na] ce k-wesko donod

As I'm walking
As I'm walking

On top of Iowag [Giho Do'ag, "Burden Basket Mountain"] is a dim light
Then I notice the lights of Ma:lina [Mali:na] shine all over

Presumably, "Iowag" is "Giho Do'ag," or Quijotoa, as the O'odham place-name and mountain range usually appears on maps. Like the first song (or, to be more precise, songs 1–4), the second song portrays a brightly colored and beautiful landscape, which Claude Lévi-Strauss has called "chromaticism."[48] Both Simon and Louis called attention to the light in this song. Simon explained that the sunshine "shines *the road*" to Magdalena. "And from *there, we see the shining,* the road to Magdalena is where it's [the light] gonna be taking us . . . clearing it [the way] to us from there [Magdalena, the source of the light] to there [Quijotoa]."[49] Louis added, "as they're getting closer they see the *lights* . . . the shine of Mali:na. . . . And so that's what you *saw* as you're going. You saw this certain mountain [Quijotoa] and there was the gleaming of the light. That's what you're running towards . . . knowing that these are the lights of Mali:na. *And I see them very dimly.*"[50]

(3) Siwok anonowaga
*Siwok anonowaga
Hugitanai hemeda, Nupi nonowano sisiwone tonoda
Ma:lina cenhewa kowesekoiwe tonoda

Siwol duag [Si:woda Do'ag]
Siwol duag [Si:woda Do'ag]
N-an hugitam him, Nupig duag [Ñe:big Do'ag] si'iskol tonod
Ma:lina [Mali:na] ce k-wesko tonod

Siwol Mountain [Si:woda Do'ag]
Siwol Mountain [Si:woda Do'ag]
As I'm walking by it I notice lights around Nupig Mountain
    [Ñe:big Do'ag]
From ther [there] I see the lights of Ma:lina [Mali:na] shine all over

This is the first song of this sequence that mentions more than one place-name. Indeed, it mentions three: Siwol Do'ag (Onion Mountain), Ñe:big Do'ag (Sucking Monster Mountain), and Mali:na (Magdalena).

With this relatively dense clustering of place-names in a single song, both the song itself and the interpretations by Louis and Simon suggest excited and frantic movement from the first named place, Si:woda Do'ag, to the second named place, Ñe:big Do'ag—a mountain said to hold songs within it, where O'odham may go to learn songs from within the earth itself—and on toward the third named place, Mali:na. Moreover, as David Kozak has previously argued in his analysis of O'odham Swallow songs, "Locations and movements create a poetic, or semantic, sense of dizziness [*nodagig*]."[51] This frantic, or manic, movement is common to O'odham Swallow songs, even when dizziness, or *nodagig*, is not explicitly mentioned in the songs.[52]

Because the giddy movements between these three locations are so sparsely indicated in the song text, Louis and Simon are quoted at greater length:

LL: The third song is actually kind of two different places connected together if you listen to the song. And the first mountain is the Siwol Do'ag, where we camp at on the third night in that little community, Cebolla. And that Siwol Do'ag that runs this way, and then Ñe:big Do'ag runs this way. And as they're running below Siwol Do'ag, they see this other mountain [Ñe:big Do'ag] standing on this other side. And from the other mountain [Ñe:big Do'ag], the lights of Mali:na are a little bit brighter, where they shine a little bit more, and that's what they're running to. Actually, that this song is kind of running along Siwol Do'ag and then getting to that mountain where Mali:na is, right on the other side of the Mali:na, which is those mountains that we go through when we get to Mali:na. And so the third song is actually the song that gets us there to Mali:na.[53]

Simon's comments build upon Louis's, commenting on the theme of chromaticism that unites the first four songs of the song set, explicitly juxtaposing the dimness of the light far in the distance in song 2 with the brightness of the light in the presence of Mali:na in song 3.

SL: When we're getting *close, close* to there, and from a *distance* away, we can see the Ñe:big, the mountain there. And we can see on top it's shiny. *And that means* that we're there. We're there. And when we *got* to the top of there, we can *see* the shining of the holy city, Magdalena, all over, from our imaginations, you know, that we see *all that* is *shining* for us [Simon pounds on the table for emphasis] to know that we're there in Magdalena. And that's what it really means when we sung those songs. And when we got there, from the start [Santa Rosa] to where we got [Mali:na], there is still the same thing, you know, that shine. That song that we sung about the mountain is that that's when we're getting right close to it. And *we can see the shine* on top of the sacred mountain. *And when we got there*, we see all that *shining*, you know, on the grounds. That's all it really means.[54]

Significantly, while song 3 marks the final song in a journey *toward* Magdalena, before beginning a return journey *from* Magdalena in song 4, the climax—or, the *arrival at* Magdalena—is elided, falling, though only implicitly, between song 3 and song 4. This spare, or minimalist, aesthetic is common to a variety of O'odham speech genres in which the climax is deliberately obfuscated or mystified. For example, in Bahr's analysis of Tohono O'odham war (*gidahim*) speeches, which similarly mystify the necessary violence of hand-to-hand combat in O'odham warfare prior to the twentieth century,

> Such brevity concerning the climax of a ceremonial journey is common in Papago oratory as well as in prose. Whatever its cause, its effect is of extreme modesty. One can easily miss the part of a text which by Anglo-American standards should be its main point, as for example the mention of wine in a wine feast speech, the killing of deer in a *ma'm'aga* speech, or the battle in a text on war.[55]

Such brevity, I would add, is also common in song. At the very least, it is a prominent feature of *these* six songs. Indeed, if the word "Mali:na" had not been used in the final line of song 3 (as well as earlier in song 2), or if Simon and Louis Lopez had neglected to explicitly mention Magdalena in their commentaries, we might not have known, at least not from the song texts, that the songs describe a journey both *to* and *from* Magdalena.

Finally, a somewhat lengthy note on the difficulty of translating from O'odham song language is in order. Louis translates "siwok" in song language as "siwol" in ordinary spoken O'odham. "Cebolla" is the Spanish word for onion, which entered O'odham vocabulary and phonology as "siwol." La Cebolla, which O'odham more frequently call Siwol, is a small town in Sonora about half way between Tubutama and Magdalena. The small town, where O'odham walkers usually spend one night each year, is also nestled near a mountain—a mountain that could very well be called "Onion Mountain," but to my knowledge is not. While walking to Magdalena near this mountain, I've even seen truckloads of onions either come from, or at least pass through, the area on their way to the fiesta in Magdalena. However, given the fact that Siwol Do'ag appears nowhere in any inventory of O'odham place-names, it may more accurately be translated as Si:woda Do'ag, meaning something like "Topknot Mountain," or perhaps even "Headdress Mountain." Initially, I privileged Louis's "Siwol Do'ag" translation, which he made in consultation with Simon.[56] However, on April 30, 2017, Simon mentioned that this translation was incorrect, and that "Siwok" should have been translated as "Si:woda" instead. Notably, unlike Louis, who discussed Siwol Do'ag, or "Onion Mountain," in some detail, Simon never mentioned the place-name.

I now consider the evidence in support of translating "siwok" not as "siwol" but rather as "si:woda" to be rather compelling. According to Harry J. Winters Jr.—a geological engineer and prospector who is fluent in the O'odham language and an amateur O'odham place-name enthusiast—"si:woda," or as he writes the word in a slightly different orthography as both "siivoda" and "siivodag," "can refer to feathers sticking up from a bird's head such as the quail's topknot."[57] Si:woda was the name of an O'odham village positioned between Nogales to the north and both Ñe:big Do'ag and Mali:na to the south. Perhaps first mentioned by Spanish chroniclers in relation to the 1695 revolt (see appendix 1), by 1700 Kino established a ranch at Si:woda, giving it the name San Simón y San Judas Tadeo del Síboda. By 1706 a small church was constructed in the village. Because Si:woda lay along an important O'odham trail going south to Magdalena, and eventually to Caborca, Kino visited Si:woda several times in his multiple journeys crisscrossing

O'odham territory. Today, Si:woda appears on maps as Cibuta. Winters speculates why the village was given its O'odham name:

> I do not know the reason this village was called Siivoda, but as a place name it is probably because there was a mountain nearby that had a projection fitting the meaning of the word. In 1977, describing the routes used on pilgrimages to Magdalena, Dora Lopez of San Pedro . . . in the Schuk Toak District, told me that there was a mountain called Siivoda Do'ag, "Siivoda Mountain," on one route. She may well have been referring to a mountain near Siivoda, today's Cibuta. The mountain range to the west of Cibuta is called the Sierra Cibuta.[58]

I suspect that Winters's speculation is correct. Furthermore, Ron Geronimo—an O'odham linguist and the director of Tohono O'odham studies at Tohono O'odham Community College—argues that unlike many O'odham-derived place-names in the United States, for most O'odham living north of the international border,

> place names in Mexico . . . are unfamiliar to most O'odham, and are considered to be non-O'odham communities with non-O'odham names. Although these places were originally O'odham communities, there is no sense of belonging or connectedness because O'odham are not aware that these communities were formerly theirs. There is a lack of awareness about traditional O'odham communities in Mexico because the history of these communities is seldom seen or heard.[59]

In light of the inherent ambiguity of "Siwok" in O'odham song language as well as Louis's greater familiarity with La Cebolla, and perhaps his relative lack of familiarity with Si:woda, I suspect that Louis assimilated the (less-known) geography of the song into the (better-known) geography of the pilgrimage route that he took with Felix Antone's walkers between Tubutama and Magdalena. In short, the ambiguity of the particular place-name within the song language permitted Louis to offer, and even embrace, a new translation for an altogether different place, Siwol, along one particular pilgrimage route to Magdalena, from what I suspect was once a significant traditional O'odham village along a different pilgrimage route.[60]

Additional evidence of Si:woda Do'ag as a significant O'odham mountain, likely referred to in song 3, comes from a somewhat unexpected place (see also the conclusion): a church. In Pitiquito, Sonora, just east of Caborca, stands an old mission church built with O'odham labor in the eighteenth century called San Diego del Pitic. According to folklorist James Griffith, the Pitiquito church is the sole colonial mission church in traditional O'odham territory on either side of the international border, "whose decorations seem to show clear evidence of an Indian 'hand' and Indian ideas." The walls of the church were once covered by a quarter inch of multiple coats of plaster, which left the church interior immaculately white. But when some women cleaned the walls of the church in 1966, their corrosive detergent began to dissolve the thick layers of plaster. Images crafted centuries earlier by O'odham hands began to emerge from behind the whitewashed walls. "The oldest group of these paintings," according to Griffith, constitute fourteen Stations of the Cross. While not all of these Stations of the Cross have been uncovered, the twelfth station—the most complex station yet to be uncovered—appears on the west wall of the south transept. If you look closely at the image, you can see five triangles on the upper and lower edges, with the central and outside triangles red and the other two white. As Griffith describes the image, "Four of the triangles on the top appear to have heads. Red dots seem to indicate eyes and mouth on the left-hand 'head,' which also has rays of red and white emanating from its top and sides. The central triangle has no 'head' but rather a series of curving red lines issuing from its top."[61] As with other indigenous iconography from the greater Southwest, the triangles are presumably mountains, or perhaps clouds. I prefer to see them as mountains, though I cannot prove that they are. What can be said with greater certainty is that the central triangle, which could very well be a mountain, has a headdress-like topknot. So we have a stylized image of a "si:woda" on top of a stereotypical depiction of a mountain: Si:woda Do'ag.

The next song begins the return journey home from Magdalena.

(4) Kuñs am a himeta
*Kuñs am a himeta

Sikola ṣunai gamhu cenhewe
Gamhuñ tamhai cemai tonoda

Kuñs am him
Kuñs am him
Sikol ṣudag [Ṣu:dagĭ] gamhu cen
Gamhu tam cem tonod

As I'm walking
As I'm walking
Way over there is Sikol ṣudag [Ṣu:dagĭ]
On top of it is a dim light

The transition between songs 3 and 4 implies movement away from Magdalena, the final destination in song 3, toward Sikol Ṣu:dagĭ in song 4. Sikol literally means "round" or "circular," and Ṣudag literally means "water," usually referring to a pool of water. A creek originating from the place, which may have had a round pond, giving the place its name, flows south to Imuris, where it flows into the Magdalena River. The O'odham village of Sikol Ṣu:dagĭ is scarcely mentioned by Spanish chroniclers and was likely abandoned by 1764.[62] Alternatively, as both Simon and Louis Lopez insist in their commentaries on song 5, Sikol Ṣu:dagĭ may also be an O'odham name for a different place that is also north, but more west of Magdalena. This could either be yet another example of contemporary O'odham assimilating the (less-known) geography of the song into the (better-known) geography of the pilgrimage route, or it could simply be an identically named, but different, place. In either case, song 4 signals a directional shift away from Magdalena and back north toward Quijotoa and Santa Rosa. Louis notes this change in direction, commenting, "We're going straight North where there's a mountain where one of the main trails used to go through . . . They say they see this other mountain further up ahead where the *fifth* [emphasis added] song comes in."[63] Simon further explained the significance of Sikol Ṣu:dagĭ, mentioned first in song 4 and then again in song 5, where in both songs it is "way over there," far off in the distance. "There's this place where we call Sikol Ṣu:dagĭ. . . . They stop there and give away things to the

Sa:nto that's there before they come home for good lucks, and things like that. And that's why we had to sung *that* before we come back home."[64]

(5) Gahu Sikola ṣunai kac
*Gahu Sikola ṣunai kac
Dam heg ñeahanai gikgowa ṣuliga
Kuñ heg a tamai kukam a himeda

Gahu Sikol ṣudag [Ṣu:dagĭ] kac
Gahu Sikol ṣudag [Ṣu:dagĭ] kac
Dam ant g ñ-a'an am ṣul
Kuñ heg tam am him

Way over there is Sikol ṣudag [Ṣu:dagĭ]
Way over there is Sikol ṣudag [Ṣu:dagĭ]
On there I offer my eagle feathers
As I'm walking on it

Louis translates Sikol Ṣu:dagĭ as "Where the Water Goes Around in Circles," which he locates on top of a mountain that he says might be "strong" or "powerful."[65] Notably, the image of swirling water, as in an eddy, is a pervasive symbol across the O'odham landscape, found on many Hohokam and O'odham historical artifacts as well as in contemporary O'odham art. Simon further explained:

SL: I think you guys spend the last night there [near Sikol Ṣu:dagĭ] before you get to Magdalena on your pilgrimage. There's a little place there, and *at that place* there's a *shrine*. There's a statue. It's about this big [gesturing with his hands]. It's called Teresita. Teresa. And it stands there. And according to Felix and my son, Louis, he said that it's there. When they come back from Magdalena, they'll stop by there, last at that place called Sikol Ṣu:dagĭ and they'll . . . give something to that statue. We call it Mat o 'iagc ha'icu, offering to the saint. It can be *money*. It can be grocery, it can be anything, your belonging, you know, like your necklace, or ring, or whatever, you know. Your belonging that you can give to them, and then go home.[66]

If Simon is correct that the group of walkers spend the last night near the place called Sikol Ṣu:dagĭ, where there is a shrine for Saint Teresa, then this place is less than ten kilometers northwest of Magdalena on the road to Tubutama. It is interesting that this song is placed after Magdalena in this sequence because most walkers give no more than a quick sign of the cross with their staffs at this site, sometimes without even stopping on the long, slow march to Magdalena. The song's placement within the sequence here is also consistent with the ideology and practice of purposeful, disciplined walking (see chapter 4), insofar as it is often said that O'odham "walkers" should go first to Saint Francis without interruption before commencing other activities in and around Magdalena.

(6) Inha wa t-weco kacim cenhewen
Inha wa t-weco kacim cenhewen
*Am hegwuwai wañiok kom ñena him
Tam haig gihawal ñeñe mamato

Ina t-weco kacim [jeweḍ]
Ina t-weco kacim [jeweḍ]
Am hegwui ñeñoikim
Tam g gigitwul ñeñei amto ka

Under us (from the top of the mountain [literally, "earth," or "land"])
Under us
I am walking toward the sounds
On top of it you will here [hear] the songs of the swallows

According to Louis Lopez, song 6 is about descending and moving frantically toward the songs of the Swallows, which is the familiar sound of social songs, and therefore celebrations, in Santa Rosa. The scene is essentially that of a homecoming celebration (see also chapter 4).

LL: So when we're coming back, that's what we hear down here are the songs of the Swallows. And that's what we're going towards. We're going towards the songs, which basically means *our area*, because the songs of the Swallows come from our area. So we've returned home, back to where the songs of the Swallows began, or are from. And that's what I think it [song 6] represents is that our home is where the songs of the Swallows are. And that's what we hear as we're coming home. That's what we're running towards: the songs of the Swallows.[67]

Louis elaborates by stating, "Depending on what area you come from, there's certain birds that the different areas use as their [long pause] messengers. We use the Swallows, so *in most of our songs that we sing*, we sing about the Swallows."[68] The songs or sounds of the Swallows seem to entice and excite the ambiguous traveling "I" returning to the village of Santa Rosa in the valley below. Like the oft-heard O'odham phrase "Smells like village," the sounds of Swallows, or Swallow songs, signal a return home for residents of Santa Rosa.

Sensual and affective connections between various birds and O'odham run deep.[69] For example, ethnobiologist Gary Paul Nabhan, who has noted the symbiotic mutualism between bird populations and O'odham villages, recorded an O'odham farmer stating that birds "come where the people are. When the people live and work in a place, and plant their seeds and water their trees, the birds go live with them. They like those places, there's plenty to eat and that's when we are friends to them."[70]

Indeed, the relationships between Santa Rosa O'odham and Swallows are so close that at times Simon collapses the distinction between Swallows and O'odham, at least for those O'odham who sing Swallow songs.

SS: Are they mostly the birds [Swallows] that are *speaking* in those songs?

SL: Yeah, part of it; but part of it is just us.

SS: Oh.

SL: You know, that we're going to there. And the others songs that we made, that they made, you know, *is* about us, you know.

SS: Oh.

SL: Where we went to those different places. So it's really about *us*, you know, going to Magdalena and back.[71]

While Simon's interpretation echoes, at least in part, Louis's explanation, Simon's analysis is more complex. First, as previously noted, Simon collapses the distinction between Swallows and O'odham. Second, according to Simon, the speech in these songs is primarily that of living O'odham in a sort of poetic ethnographic present. For Simon, it seems that the speech is, at most, only secondarily Swallow speech. Third, and perhaps most interestingly, the ahistorical speakers in the unspecified transportable present are drawn toward their imminently future social selves—or to put it slightly differently, moving toward the sounds of themselves celebrating, singing, and dancing in the tangibly near present.

SS: So is it more like they're hearing the Swallows, or are they singing those Swallow songs, or is that kind of like the same thing?

SL: *Yeah.* Yeah, it's about the same thing. It's about the same thing . . . . We're hearing all of the Swallow's songs that we'll be singing. And most of it is the Swallow songs that we sung when we do the celebration, or singing, you know. And that's when we'll be singing all these songs about the Swallows.[72]

Simon consistently maintains that what has been translated as the first-person singular "I" of this and other songs is really always a first-person plural "we," a traveling entourage of O'odham and Swallows.

SL: When they say that "*I* am walking here," or "*I* am going here," and things like that, it's just *put* in there *so people understand.* Now, we could be talking about a *group* of people that's going there, or even the birds. So if they *knew* that it's the Swallow's song, we'll know that it means that it's the birds going here and there. *And it could mean the people,* for the people that go around there. It's the same thing with the other songs, like you said, you know, about the Swallows, the birds, whatever we're singing is the group that's going around, and things like that, *not only one* person, you know. A lot of times it'll state on there [in O'odham song translations], you know, "*I* am here. *I* am going. *I* will be going here," but it could mean the whole group. You know, *not only just one,* or things like that, or when we get home to celebrate the songs and things like that, it's for *everybody,* you know, the whole group that'll be doing that. So that's what really is on that thing, "I." Yeah, I've seen a lot of this, you know. . . . "*I'm* here. *I'm* there. *I* go here. *I* go there." But, usually it's the group. But *the song sounds like* it's just the one person or something like that. But most of the time it's the group that does everything like that.[73]

In his study of O'odham Swallow songs, Bahr suggests that "the interesting question is who are the 'I's'?"[74] Noting the ambiguity of "I's," Bahr offers three answers: (1) I the Swallow; (2) I the dreamer being taken on a journey by the Swallow; and (3) the O'odham "I's" singing and dancing the Swallow songs in the present—whenever that may be. Crucially, Bahr states that the third meaning is only circumstantially or implicitly present. Bahr claims, "The standard native interpretation is, 'Swallows do this, they act just like humans.' What I have not heard is the additional statement, 'and so the "I's" of social dancing songs also refer to the people dancing.'"[75] As shown above, my conversations with Simon have yielded a statement very close to this, unlike Bahr. Consequently, Simon's interpretation of these songs (again, described mostly as Swallow songs) as being "really about *us*, you know, going to Magdalena and back" is the clearest O'odham statement in support of Bahr's third meaning of the deliberately ambiguous "I's" in O'odham social songs.[76] Therefore, Simon's analysis of these songs (especially song 6) is significant in and of itself for those who are interested in the interpretation of O'odham social songs.

Summary

Two questions were posed at the beginning of this chapter. First, how do O'odham evoke movement across their land through songs? Second, how do these same songs evoke the O'odham past embedded in these places? These questions gave rise to still more questions. In light of the preceding discussion on the "mixed" arrangement of these six songs, as both Simon Lopez and Kendall Jose label each of their separate song sequences, how might O'odham song journeys to Magdalena be understood, knowing that the songs themselves were removed from their original song series contexts? What kinds of maps, or postcards, are these? What becomes of these song texts as encrypted historical documents?

The evidence presented above suggests that the songs themselves, as well as the O'odham interpretations of these songs that have been included in this chapter, are somewhat more geographist than historicist, to adopt and play with cultural geographer Edward Soja's critique of historicism as that which "actively submerges and peripheralizes the geographical or spatial imagination."[77] At the same time, it is not entirely fair to conclusively state that the songs or their interpretations are more geographist than historicist. There is no submergence or marginalization of the historical imagination here, as Simon Lopez in particular has shown. While the cartographic characteristic of these songs is more or less stable (though I have also noted that they certainly are not fixed), the historiographic quality of these songs is clearly much more flexible, complex, and nuanced between these songs (as more or less stable texts) and contemporary O'odham audiences of these songs.

While the places mentioned in these songs may seem to be somewhat stable, it is important to note that these songs can be, and frequently are, sung in various places. Therefore, in the sense of *performance*, and perhaps to a lesser extent *reference* (to named places), these songs are eminently transportable. However, in terms of audience—that is, who the songs (1) are sung for, (2) are sung to, and (3) are about—the evidence suggests a transferability, flexibility, and reflexivity of audience and subject. After all, while these songs are "mixed," they are also mostly Swallow songs (for the Lopezes) or Mockingbird songs (for the Joses), and yet at the same time the songs are said to be *about* and *for* "us," the present-day O'odham walkers to Magdalena.

This chapter confirms that in the O'odham context, Vine Deloria Jr. was correct in arguing that "American Indians hold their lands—places—as having the highest possible meaning, and all their statements are made with this reference point in mind."[78] Indeed, O'odham pasts are embedded within these places (concealed behind as little as a quarter inch of plaster, in some cases), evoked through movements across the land in both songs and actual walking (see chapter 4).

The evidence from O'odham song texts and interpretations of these texts included in this chapter also demonstrates, at least in the cases of Simon and Louis Lopez, *how* O'odham have embedded Christianity within their ancestral landscapes through song.

LL: So even going back to those [six] songs that we sing now in between the decades, those songs are not any songs having to do with church, or any songs having to do with the religion [Catholicism]. They're traditional O'odham songs, but the songs of the path of going to Mali:na, prior to the Catholicism, prior to [laughter] . . . you know, Father Kino. This path O'odham had originally followed to go to that little village of Mali:na, and that's where these songs come from. They come from way back before the whole Spanish thing. That's how they journeyed to Mali:na. . . . That path has been *there*, for centuries prior to, you know, the whole Saint Francis movement thing.[79]

CHAPTER 3

Walkers and Their Staffs

There's a lot of use for those. Those are important belongings to people that get them. I don't know if you were *taught*, I mean if you were *told*, when you were first given that walking stick, that *it can help you* in many other ways, you know, *not only the walk to Magdalena*. And anywhere else that you have to go—an important walk, or a *place*, you know, that you go—that you have to have it. *Take it, and it'll help you*. And so it's not only there [to Magdalena] that that'll go. Just like I've told my kids, you know, when they first got it, "*It's yours. You can take it*, even to other people's *celebrations*," especially the Feast of Saint Francis or some things like that. "*You can take yours too*, you know, *and use it*. And *this way*, you know, *it'll help you a lot*, you know, *not only* when you go *down there* [to Magdalena]." . . . So, there's a lot of ways that it can be handled: those walking sticks.
—Simon Lopez, Tohono O'odham elder, cowboy, traditional singer, and ritual curer

For Felix Antone's group of O'odham walkers, those who made the walk for the first time were each given a staff, or walking stick, at the beginning of their journey.[1] Felix and others instructed them to keep their staffs close to them at all times, make sure that the staffs are always upright, and otherwise treat the staffs with respect.[2] In some ways, these sticks are treated as though they were sentient beings. Having

73

Fig. 3. Partial staff. Courtesy Bernard Siquieros.

seen how veteran walkers have beautified their sticks after many years of working on and walking with them, most new walkers are eager to attain and begin decorating their own. Nevertheless, walkers are told not to alter their sticks in any way until they have completed their first walk and ribbons have been tied on their staffs. Regardless of how O'odham decorate their staffs and otherwise make them their own, they almost always seem to record history, or at least the number of times that the stick and its owner have made the journey to Magdalena.

At camp each night, these staffs are collectively made into a moveable altar by standing them up in a line and partially burying them in the desert sand.[3] In front of these sticks, O'odham place their saints and candles, do their rosaries, and sing. Outside of the context of the journey to Magdalena, these staffs perform a similar function as they are integrated into home altars and travel with their owners from village to village for various fiestas, wakes, and other events throughout the year. Indeed, one of the primary objectives of O'odham who travel to Magdalena is to acquire the trappings of Christian material culture to bring back to, and distribute within, O'odham villages.

Significantly, although these staffs play a prominent role in everyday O'odham Catholic practice, they have not even been mentioned in any academic literature on the O'odham. This chapter aims to fill this gap within the academic literature on the O'odham by focusing on these staffs. Scraping sticks and calendar sticks are two other types of sticks that have been historically used by O'odham, and those have been extensively studied by anthropologists. Archaeologist J. Andrew Darling and Akimel O'odham traditional singer and cultural preservation officer Barnaby Lewis argue that markings notched into scraping sticks, or rasps—like songs themselves (see chapter 2)—document song journeys in geographical space, and that calendar sticks provide a temporal or chronological, rather than geographical, itinerary.[4] Indeed, songs are not the only way in which O'odham map journeys and record history (see chapter 2). This comparison between rasping sticks and calendar sticks is suggestive in terms of O'odham theories and representations of space and time, especially when examined alongside O'odham walking sticks. I aim to contribute to this larger discussion as it offers a deeper understanding of O'odham theories of personhood and place—as well as materiality more generally—given that these staffs not only document chronological and geographical journeys, but they are also treated with respect, as though they were sentient beings. In order to avoid speculation on the matter, I have spoken extensively with several O'odham consultants about these walking sticks, the relationships that walkers have with their staffs, and any relation that these staffs may have with these other sticks that have previously been the subject of scholarly inquiry.

In this chapter I argue that the past as well as personhood and place accumulate and become embedded in these staffs, evoking memories of past journeys in the present, and the ubiquitous presence of Magdalena in everyday O'odham life. In making this case, I begin with an exploration of an O'odham model of how history accumulates in objects through the examination of an O'odham oral tradition about the flute; then I briefly survey the literature on O'odham calendar sticks and scraping sticks before finally turning to an analysis of O'odham staffs, or walking sticks.[5]

History in Objects: How the O'odham Lost the Flute

Today, O'odham do not use flutes in their songs.[6] And yet their Yoeme (Yaqui) neighbors do. According to some, O'odham once used flutes in the distant past. In the version of the story recorded by Tohono O'odham linguist Juan Dolores, titled "The Yaquis Won the Flute from Us," the story begins by establishing the context: "It is said this happened to a man when the puberty ceremony first appeared. He lost his wife through these ceremonies, because she ran around following the ceremonies, and was told about everywhere."[7] The man's wife was one of the women who enjoyed the first puberty ceremony (see also chapters 4 and 5) so much that they could not stop dancing until they had destroyed their homes, becoming displaced, homeless women whom nobody wanted and who could only bring their placeless condition to an end by becoming the Pleiades.[8] At the loss of his wife the man became filled with shame and sorrow, and so "he wandered around feeling like crying" until he came to Reed Mountain, or Vapk Do'ag, more commonly known as the McDowell Mountains northeast of Phoenix, where he drank from a well.[9] Thinking of what was ahead for him, "the thought suddenly occurred that he would make a flute and cry in it, imitating the whip-poor-will. That way no one would know he was crying, and he would overcome the sorrow in his heart."[10] So he took a reed from the place, made a flute, and played it there in a cave. Women were drawn to the beautiful music, and when he saw them, "he forgot his wife right away and no longer cried. He just played and sang his songs over and over."[11] After playing his songs for an unspecified length of time, he eventually attracted four Yoeme women from the south. He was attracted to the youngest woman, so he married her. She took him home with her, which according to the narrator is how "the Yaquis learned about the flute from us, and we don't have the flute."[12]

This version of this story recorded by Dolores suggests that the O'odham man's flute playing drove the plot toward a resolution in which his overwhelming sorrow was overcome, and his placeless condition of wandering came to an end when his crying into the flute attracted another mate. Like his former wife, who became one of the Pleiades, the O'odham man had to move to the Yoeme woman's home and bring his flute with him in order to restore a dynamic sociable balance thrown off by the undisciplined movement of O'odham women who could not stop dancing.[13] Yet a single line suggests that "crying" into the flute was itself disruptive, perhaps contributing more to the ongoing problem of undisciplined movement than its resolution: "He just played and sang his songs over and over." The O'odham man's unending repetition of "crying" into the flute bears a striking resemblance to the unconstrained and ceaseless movement of women like his wife who became the Pleiades.

Another version of the same story, recorded by anthropologist Ruth Underhill, supports this interpretation of undisciplined movement (ceaseless dancing) provoking further undisciplined movement (ceaseless "crying" into the flute). In Underhill's version the chronology is reversed: "the playful women were called out long ago by a youth who played the flute and drove them mad."[14] In this case, the man's flute playing is responsible for the undisciplined and amoral movement of O'odham women, and yet again—though this time with the cause and effect switched—undisciplined movement ("crying" into the flute) provokes further undisciplined movement (ceaseless dancing). Either way, in both versions of the story a history of shame, sorrow, crying, ceaseless dancing, alienation, love lost and regained are embedded into a particular object: the flute.

VERSION OF THE STORY	CAUSE	EFFECT
Dolores	Dance	Cry
Underhill	Cry	Dance

Like the notion of the past becoming embedded into the landscape (see the introduction, chapter 1, and chapter 2), "The Yaquis Won the Flute from Us" poignantly demonstrates how the past can become embedded into objects. Anthropologist Peter Nabokov has called this "memories in things."[15] For the purposes of the present study, this story suggests an O'odham theory of materiality in which history accumulates in objects, including the flute, as well as sticks and ribbons.

Within this indigenous context, O'odham theories of materiality are necessarily imbricated with O'odham theories of personhood, and consequently as anthropologist Fernando Santos-Granero put it, there are "multiple ways of being a thing."[16] Much like flutes are a reminder of the unintended consequences of the first puberty ceremony, certain objects such as staffs and ribbons—as well as saints, rosaries, holy water, and so forth—that have been imbued with Saint Francis's borrowed power in Magdalena are, as anthropologist Bernard Fontana noted in his brief discussion of the pilgrimage to Magdalena, "reminders of the journey to Magdalena."[17]

Calendar Sticks

O'odham staffs and flutes are not the only objects into which history accumulates and becomes embedded. *Hikanaba,* or "calendar sticks," are made from the ribs of the *haṣañ,* the giant saguaro cactus that is iconic within the Sonoran Desert.[18] According to anthropologist Donald Bahr, O'odham stopped making or adding to calendar sticks in the 1930s or 1940s, marking printed calendars instead.[19] Writing about O'odham calendar sticks, historian of religion Tod Swanson maintains that with each passing year, "as the seasons pass, the stick becomes historied."[20] Throughout the period of its use, the stick is gradually covered with cuts, aiding the historical memory of the stick's keeper, who experiences and narrates the stories held within the stick. For Swanson, at least ideally, the stick's keeper "becomes, like the stick, a seasoned character."[21] Crucially the sticks themselves mature and become storied along with their keepers. Darling and Lewis provide further support for the notion of history accumulated in calendar sticks when they assert, "The historical narrative and the symbols for each event become part of the stick itself. . . . Even after the keeper has died, the stick remains a repository of personal historical knowledge."[22]

Ethnomusicologist J. Richard Haefer notes that O'odham histories are found primarily in calendar sticks and narratives.[23] However, most historians and anthropologists have been suspicious of these sources as reliable histories. For example, in 1871 United States Army Captain F. E. Grossmann complained that the Akimel O'odham "have but vague ideas of the doings of their forefathers, and whatever accounts may have been handed down to them have been so changed in the transmission that they cannot be deemed reliable now."[24] Ethnologist Frank Russell similarly called the calendar sticks "annals" rather than "history," because, as he put it, "chronologic sequence is subordinated to narrative."[25] Moreover, Russell adds: "As usual with Amerindian records these contain much that is trivial and omit much that is important."[26] Likewise, when José Santos of San Xavier del Bac related his calendar stick covering the length of one six-foot stick and a portion of another to Ruth Underhill over a period of two weeks, Underhill called the calendar stick "gossip rather than history," due to its failure to mention policy history, such as the Gadsden Purchase in 1854, the Civil War extending into Arizona in 1863, and Arizona becoming a territory and then a state in 1912, as well as the establishment of reservations, churches, and land allotments.[27]

Nevertheless, not all scholars have been as skeptical of calendar sticks and their accompanying narrative histories as reliable sources of history. A. T. Kilcrease, for example, significantly noted that O'odham calendar sticks are important because they tell us what particular O'odham regarded as noteworthy and important in their own histories, as well as "by implication, what was not regarded as important."[28] Noting that the marks on these sticks are "not writing," but rather memory aids, Kilcrease suggested that "calendar sticks" might better be called "memory" sticks.[29]

Scraping Sticks

As Simon Lopez explained to me, an O'odham *hivkuḍ* (scraping stick or rasp) "makes a good sound."[30] When he spoke these words, he felt compelled to demonstrate the sound, so he retrieved a scraping stick made of greasewood, playing it by quickly and rhythmically rubbing a smaller stick perpendicularly across the larger, notched stick as he continued.[31] "And if there's about six people using it, and with different sizes, you can hear *real nice sound*, you know, and you can hear it. And they start going and you can hear it *real* good. *Real* nice sound." According to Frances Manuel, a Tohono O'odham traditional singer and basket weaver, and ethnomusicologist J. Richard Haefer, the sound is associated with rain and wind.[32] Haefer classifies these sticks as a "song maker," like the flute. According to Russell, these sticks were historically used in Akimel O'odham rain ceremonies and therefore are usually spoken of as "rain sticks."[33]

Like flutes and calendar sticks, the past and past journeys can also become embedded into these scraping sticks as they are transformed through use. Not only history but also journeys to faraway places accumulate in these sticks. "After repeated performances," according to Darling and Lewis, "the spiritual essence of the songs becomes part of the scraping sticks used to perform them. Even when the sticks are no longer used, they retain this spirituality and should be handled respectfully."[34] Like calendar sticks, scraping sticks also have markings etched into the wood. Although Bahr calls these markings o'ohon, or "writing," Darling and Lewis call these markings o'ohadag, or "song flowers." For Darling and Lewis, these "song flowers"

> are representations of the spiritual presence of the songs in these instruments, obtained through their use in performances. The designs are not strictly decorations but are emblematic of the singers' spiritual accomplishment, particularly the song journey . . . song marks appear on the rasping sticks only when the performance is completed. The designs on rasps document spiritual song journeys in geographic space, whereas calendar sticks provide a temporal or chronological itinerary—a time line—relating the present to the past. This is an important distinction between O'odham systems of geographical and historical reckoning.[35]

Crucially, not only do the songs themselves become embedded in these sticks, but the places mentioned in these songs that evoke a sense of movement and journey across the landscape in these songs also accumulate, becoming embedded in these sticks. These "song flowers" document song journeys, evoking journeys—whether in body or the imagination—that the singer has made previously. Like the keeper of these sticks, these sticks themselves become well traveled, storied, emplaced, and marked by the landscape.

Moreover, as Swanson said of calendar sticks and their keepers, they mutually become "seasoned" or "well-weathered."[36] Simon Lopez agreed that these designs could document previous journeys through geographical space, and as such they held the enduring past within them:

SL: These are Greasewood. These are *hard*. Very hard. It's not gonna break, like Ocotillo, or Mesquite tree, and things like that. This is just like uh *Iron*wood, but *Ironwood is heavy*. Greasewood is not heavy. And it's *hard*. It's not gonna break. It's gonna last for *years*. I have some that belongs to my late Grandpa. And he's using it for a *long* time.[37]

Like his *ma:kai* (medicine man) grandfather, Juan D. Lopez, his grandfather's scraping sticks are strong and durable, evoking his presence and power through the continued endurance of his hardened greasewood rasps (see also chapter 1). Therefore, much like flutes and calendar sticks, these scraping sticks hold an accumulated past within them, a past that evokes memories of previous journeys and movements.

Walking Sticks: *'U:s* and *'lagta*

As the preceding discussion of flutes, calendar sticks, and scraping sticks illustrates, songs (see chapter 2) are not the only O'odham means of evoking memories of the past and memories of previous journeys across the landscape. Staffs are much like songs, just as songs are much like staffs, as one Akimel O'odham old man once told ethnomusicologist George Herzog: "songs are a good bracing-stick to go through life with."[38] O'odham staffs are usually made from the branches of *kui* (mesquite).[39] However, in a few noteworthy exceptions, staffs may also be made from the ribs of the *haṣañ* (saguaro cactus), just like calendar sticks. As previously mentioned, these staffs or walking sticks have somehow eluded the ethnographic gaze. For example, Frank Russell's otherwise extensive inventory of O'odham artifacts makes no mention of O'odham walking sticks.[40] In the conversation featured below, Simon Lopez stated that anthropologists are not alone in neglecting and misunderstanding these staffs:

SL: Right now, a lot of these *young* people, you know, they *think* that *only the old people* uses [staffs] for the cane, for their *cane*! You know, because they're old and they have to have that cane, but it's not [a cane]! There's a lot of ways that people use those walking sticks.[41]

Simon's concern here is that younger O'odham think these staffs are merely canes. But staffs are not only used by elderly O'odham who need them in order to avoid falling while walking. Simon explained that previous generations used walking sticks far more widely than they generally do today. When I asked if he noticed any changes between how walking sticks were used in previous generations and how those who walk to Magdalena use them today, he responded:

SL: *They don't really understand what it is.* . . . And so that's why they don't consider the walking sticks as important as it is. Now days, *the young people* . . . most of them *think* that the only people that uses [them] is the *old people,* and so they don't use it. But there *is* ways, you know, that they could *use.* So, I guess that's the only thing, that the difference is that they don't use it *anymore* until they start the *walk* to Magdalena.[42]

To borrow Simon's words, then, the challenge for both ethnographer and many contemporary O'odham is to understand what this stick is, what it is for, how it can be used, and why it is important. In short, how are these sticks not merely canes?

In the O'odham language, staffs or walking sticks are typically spoken of in two ways, either as *'u:s* or *'iagta*. According to ethnobiologist Amadeo Rea, *'u:s* may be used to refer to an entire tree.[43] In their dictionary entry for the word, missionary-linguists Dean Saxton, Lucille Saxton, and Susie Enos also translate *'u:s* (rendered in their orthography as *'uhs*) as "a tree; a bush; a stick; a crutch; wood."[44] Bahr, who translates *'u:s* as "stick," notes that *'u:s* may refer to a tree's trunk, its branches, or even twigs.[45] But if Bahr is correct in stating that *'u:s* refers to "a length of wood in its natural state," then O'odham staffs or walking sticks—especially when referred to as *'iagta* rather than *'u:s*—are lengths of wood in a cultural state, transformed by O'odham use. Crucially, the O'odham whom I consulted almost always referred to these peripatetic lengths of wood in the O'odham language not as *'u:s* but as *'iagta*, and in English not as sticks but rather as staffs.

'Iagta is derived from the transitive verb *'iagcud*, which means something like "to make an offering, gift, or sacrifice of something to someone."

Saxton, Saxton, and Enos translate *'iagta* as "a propitiating gift" and "an article for the harvest ceremony [*Wi:gita*]."[46] In the context of translating devil songs with anthropologist David Kozak, Tohono O'odham cowboy and ritual curer David Lopez explained that *'iagta* "means something like devil's things, medicine man things, the devil's tools. You know, like a feather or rock, a crystal, the things that a shaman uses."[47] Without elicitation, Simon's son, Louis "Tony" Lopez, explained to me in the course of telling me about his staff, "Your *'iagta* are your effigies, those things, those items that you use that becomes a part of you that you use for healing, like your feathers, your rattles, you know. Those are your *'iagta*. . . . You take care of it, it will take care of you. It will become a part of you."[48]

These various translations of *'iagta* focus on an object's use in the context of traditional O'odham religious practice. But these translations do not definitively explain why many O'odham would refer to a staff as *'iagta*. The key to understanding how the category of *'iagta* might include staffs could hinge on their use in a ceremonial context as well as the notion of *'iagta* as a gift or sacrifice. As O'odham walker and vice chairman of the Tohono O'odham Nation, Verlon "Carlos" Jose explained to me: "I was given this staff by the late Felix Antone. . . . It was just a stick [*'u:s*]. It was a piece of wood. But like I always say, 'This is your *'iagta*.'"[49] Having just introduced an O'odham term, he went on to define it and explain how the term might apply to a staff.

VCJ: *'Iagta* is like, uh, to make an offering, to give something, you use it to pray with. As I mentioned, [your] staff would become very handy when you go out for days, helps to keep you balance, helps to keep you walk, but more so, it becomes a sacred item. It becomes, uh, a religious artifact of yours. It becomes whatever you want it to become.[50]

Verlon seems to suggest that the description of his staff as "just a stick" or "a piece of wood" is somehow inappropriate or potentially disrespectful. Instead, he insists that he must always exhort young people, preaching, "This is your *'iagta*,"—which he pointedly calls a "staff," and not a "stick," or *'u:s*—which "becomes a sacred item" or "religious artifact." Although Verlon's staff was given to him as a gift from Felix Antone, Verlon also stressed that the stick that became his staff was once a living thing that sacrificed its life for his benefit. "To other people," distancing his own position from that of hypothetical others, "Ah, it's just a piece of wood." In contrast to this perspective, Verlon insists that his staff "gave its life for me and I have to protect it. I have to treat it like that, because it gave its life for me."

In the attempt to "really understand what it is," in Simon Lopez's words, Peter Pels's conception of "materiality" as "a quality of relationship rather than a thing in itself" is a useful analytic framework for understanding the relationship between O'odham walkers and their staffs, or walking sticks.[51] Moreover, following Pels, once materiality is conceived of relationally, or as particular modes of relation, it becomes possible to begin to see how these relations may vary. Or, as Verlon "Carlos" Jose has said of the indeterminate relation between walkers and their staffs, "It becomes whatever you want it to become."

On Receiving Staffs: Processes of Identification and Dis-identification

Much like O'odham walkers themselves, sticks are not all the same. Sticks vary by shape, size, color, weight, and strength, among other attributes. In his discussion of the "Age of Sticks" in O'odham architecture, Bahr suggests that sticks may be "long," "short," "thick," or "thin."[52] Most O'odham walkers whom I consulted are keen on identifying these and other differences, evaluating their attributes, and seeking an adequate fit between walkers and their staffs. As Verlon "Carlos" Jose explains, "The staffs come in many different shapes, sizes. Some are big, some are small, some are skinny, some are fat."[53] These distinctions are important, especially when walkers don't perceive a good match between themselves and their staffs.

Verlon's son, Kendall—a robust, full-bodied O'odham man and vice chair of the Chukut Kuk District, who was introduced in chapter 2—described the first staff that he received when he was about fourteen or fifteen years old as "a little skinny."[54] Having arrived late that year at Felix Antone's residence in Cedagĭ Wahia, where his group of walkers assemble before moving on to Tubutama and Magdalena, there were only about two sticks to choose between. Kendall explained, "So, I went to pick my staff up. . . . And they were the *real little, skinny, skinny, skinny*

Fig. 4. Felix Antone tying ribbons on Mary Narcho's staff in Magdalena. Courtesy Mary Narcho.

ones. And this one I thought was gonna break! My first year [my staff] was *real thin*. It was like a *twig*! It was about, see, about the size of a quarter. It was *real skinny*." Indeed, the relative size of Kendall's staff was not only a matter of concern to Kendall, but also to others, including Felix, who, according to Kendall, asked him, "'Are you sure it's gonna *handle* you?' . . . To be honest, that one couldn't hold my weight if I tried. So, you know, he made a comment. . . . '*You should have got something bigger,*' you know, '*more your size.*'" So the next year Kendall arrived at Felix's earlier and got another staff that he described as "a lot *thicker* and *stronger.*"

When I asked Mary Narcho, who served for many years on the Saint Francis feast committee at San Xavier and on the management board of the Tohono O'odham Gaming Enterprise (see also the introduction), what she most remembered from her five years of walking to Magdalena, she said, "My main memory of my walk is this staff."[55] Like Kendall, she acquired her staff at Felix's place in Cedagĭ Wahia during her first year as a walker.

MN: They had this big pile of staffs laying there. I remember that I went over and I kind of put one aside because that was the one that I wanted. So we were in this long line getting ready to get our staffs . . . *and somebody went and got that staff and I was so disappointed.* And then somebody said to me, *"You're not supposed to pick out your own staff. You take what they give you* [laughing]."[56]

According to the intervening "somebody" who reprimanded her, Mary's staff had to be given to her by Felix or one of his assistants, rather than chosen by her. Initial disappointment inevitably resulted when she was given an unsavory staff that seemed inadequate for its purpose. Mary continued:

MN: Well, when it got to be my turn, they gave me this *little, tiny, skinny staff* [laughing] *and they gave it to me and it had little tiny—I guess that was termite holes?—all over it,* and I thought, *"Well, I can't lean on this thing, it would break!"* But I swear that was the *strongest staff.* I mean I leaned on that thing *all those years* and it's just as *strong* today. *And it's just a little skinny, ugly, ugly little staff.*[57]

Mary was disappointed with her staff at first, particularly noting how scrawny it looked. Mary went on to explain, "A lot of the staffs were white and they were *fatter.* Some were *real fat* [laughing]. Mine was real skinny and uh, *it looked like it was going to break any day.*" Mary hastened to add, though, *"It never did."* Strong, yet riddled with small holes and covered with cracks, Mary eventually came to identify with her staff. Mary focused intently on her staff, slowly twirling it in her hand as she spoke:

MN: I was really looking at my staff one day when we were on our rest break and I was thinking uh, that this kind of symbolizes my *life.* I had a very hard life. I went through a lot of hard hard times, a lot of um. . . . I don't really want to say suffering, but just hard times; *and it looks like the staff went through a lot of hard times too* [laughing]! And maybe that was why it was given to me. This kind of symbolizes my *life.* All the ups and downs that I had. And maybe that's why I was supposed to and that's another reason that it's special to me.[58]

Through the gradual process of walking, thinking, and maturing with her staff, Mary clearly came to identify very closely with her staff and its ability to endure "all the ups and downs" of life, just like she had. She eventually came to see her staff—once a termite-ridden stick that she described as "*a little skinny, ugly, ugly little staff*"—as something like an extension of herself, both metaphorically and metonymically.

Holy Ribbons: "Every Ribbon Is a Journey"

O'odham often refer to the ribbons tied onto their staffs as "holy ribbons." In O'odham, these "holy ribbons" are sometimes called *ku:lañ li:ste*, which is derived from the Spanish *curan listón*, meaning "curing ribbon" or "healing ribbon." Many O'odham who have been to Magdalena, particularly children, will wear these ribbons, often tied around their necks, until they fall off. Historically, ribbons may also be tied to the tail of one's horse. And while this practice continues today, more frequently ribbons are tied to the rearview mirrors of O'odham trucks. For the group of O'odham walkers that I accompanied, Felix tied the ribbons to the staffs of walkers at the end of their journey after visiting Saint Francis in Magdalena.

What is the difference between an ordinary ribbon and a "holy ribbon"? Verlon "Carlos" Jose explained the difference as follows:

VCJ: This ribbon is no different than a ribbon you'll go buy in the store. If you scientifically look into it, they're probably both made up of the same thing. What sets it aside, is this holy ribbon has come from Mali:na [Magdalena]. This has come from Mali:na; this has been taken to the church; this has been taken to Saint Francis; and asked Saint Francis to offer prayer; and to offer guidance; and to help us on our journeys; been blessed by the Holy Water; when the one in the store has not.[59]

Essentially, there is no discernible difference between an ordinary ribbon and a "holy ribbon," other than the fact that the latter is from Magdalena, where it has been blessed by Saint Francis and possibly a priest. Verlon also went on to explain how "holy ribbons," unlike ordinary ribbons, are not only highly respected but also sought after by O'odham.

VCJ: I could get a bunch of ribbon and sell them to people and they won't buy them here. But if you know, when people go to Mali:na, now they're buying these ribbons at, you know, five for a dollar. I could set up a shop here in Sells [the capital of the Tohono O'odham Nation and the location of the interview] and they probably won't sell because we're not in Mali:na, because we're not at the church. [But,] we could set up a shop and say, "Oh, these holy ribbons have been blessed and taken down to Saint Francis," and so forth, and probably they would now sell. It's the idea of going somewhere to retrieve them. For us, every ribbon is a journey we've made.[60]

But there are multiple ways of being a ribbon. In contrast to Verlon's understanding in which "every ribbon is a journey," he recounted another use in which a single journey resulted in countless ribbons. Even in the spur of the moment of our conversation, Verlon anonymized the identity and even the gender of this individual, whom Verlon most frequently referred to in the third-person plural, "they":

VCJ: I've seen one person walking around Mali:na and they have a bunch of ribbons on their staff, but I think that was that person's first time walking. They just come down and just got a bunch of ribbons, tied them on there. I don't know. And that's okay. I guess that's okay. If that's what they want to do, to beautify their sacred item, then that's, you know, that's okay. Um, but to each is their own.[61]

Although Verlon clearly wanted to adopt a tolerant stance toward this different mode of relating to the ribbons on one's staff, the practice he describes—of buying rather than earning ribbons in order to have more ribbons and a more beautiful staff—demonstrates how highly many O'odham regard ribbons and particularly the labor through which they are normally acquired: walking to Magdalena. Instead of going to Magdalena to get "a bunch of ribbons," Verlon stated that at least for Felix's walkers, they had to earn the ribbons by walking:

VCJ: They usually tell you, "Don't put anything on there. Don't put anything on there until you get [to Magdalena] and make your first journey." The first things that we put on that staff was the holy ribbons.

We're given the first year you walked four holy ribbons. And then every year thereafter you get one.[62]

To summarize, "holy ribbons" are those that have come back from Magdalena. As Verlon so succinctly put it, "every ribbon is a journey." However, if this is the rule, then there are at least three noteworthy exceptions. First, new walkers are often given four ribbons in the first year: red, blue, green, and the fourth in a color of one's choosing. Second, ribbons are easily and inexpensively acquired in Magdalena. And third, O'odham regularly "honor" one another by giving ribbons to people who have done something significant for the people.

History and Memory in Staffs

Regardless of how O'odham decorate their staffs, they almost always seem to record history, or at least the number of times that the staff and its walker have made the journey to Magdalena together. Because each ribbon is a journey, these ribbons evoke memories of previous journeys and invoke the power and presence of Mali:na wherever they may be. Speaking about his staff, Verlon stated: "It reminds me of the journey to Mali:na. It reminds of the journeys I've taken."[63] Speaking about the ribbons on his staff, Louis "Tony" Lopez declared, "Truly, the ribbons itself automatically kind of reminds you of Mali:na. That's about the only place that we get the ribbons, from Mali:na. So, when you see other people wearing it, it's kind of like, 'You know, they must go to Mali:na.'"[64]

Mary Narcho also explained how the ribbons on her staff evoke memories of both walking to Magdalena in different years and Felix Antone. Eager to show her staff to me as we talked in her living room, Mary ran to her home altar in her bedroom to retrieve it. When she returned, her hands gently caressed the staff, and she tenderly ran her fingers through the ribbons and her "finger rosaries" with which she always said the rosary while she was walking to Magdalena. Mary explained the two different ways that her ribbons record history and evoke her memories of previous journeys to Magdalena:

MN: I think I have eight or nine ribbons on here, but these first four, they were all put on by Felix. And on this yellow one, every year I would put another knot to show how many years I made it. And um, I made it five years and so I have five knots on here. My fourth year, I thought it would be my last so I went and I bought four ribbons and I added four ribbons on it. But the first four are the ones that Felix put on and now they're very special to me since he's . . . since he's gone.[65]

Essentially, Mary has recorded history with three different methods. In the first method, each ribbon reminds her of a particular journey. In the second method, each equally spaced knot on a yellow ribbon marks the number of journeys she has made to Magdalena.[66] In the third method, thinking her fourth year would be her final year, as it is customary to walk to Magdalena for four consecutive years if possible, she memorialized the completion of her four years by adding four more ribbons. Although the last two methods of recording history seem to have been her own idiosyncratic way of remembering her accomplishment, the first and more common method, in which each ribbon represents a journey, is particularly meaningful in retrospect since these were the only ribbons that were personally tied onto her staff by Felix, who originally gave her the staff. These four ribbons evoke memories of Felix, who passed away at the age of seventy-eighty on January 31, 2012, and his absence. But tied as they were on her staff by Felix, they also invoke his enduring presence.

Mary Ann Ramirez, of Tucson, similarly handled her staff with care. As she looked at the well-worn ribbons on her staff and tactilely experienced their sheer physicality, they also gradually evoked memories of the walk for her. Her speech below illustrates how her ribbons eventually brought back memories of Felix as well as thoughts of the imminent future when his absence would be most salient in the coming year's journey to Magdalena after his death.

SS: Is there anything on your staff that brings back memories?
MAR: Um, no. Maybe. I don't know. I guess when I look at them [the ribbons], they're kinda getting ratty, like these here. The tips are getting old and then some of them are kinda [pause] . . . I have to tie knots in them. That way they won't start coming apart, so I have to tie knots in them. But I guess, um, I would say probably just the

ones with the knots because they've been with me all this time and the ones without the knots are, I guess they're doing okay, but no, not really. I guess maybe now, now when I think about it, you know, I guess maybe Felix tied all of them on here and now, this year, he's not going to see them. He's not here anymore and, um, that will be different, you know, 'cause all of these, he's tied them. I guess that would be something to remind me of this, knowing that Felix tied all of these ribbons.[67]

Mary Ann Ramirez's knots are distinctly not the same as Mary Narcho's knots. Whereas Mary's equally spaced knots marked five consecutive years of journeys to Magdalena, Mary Ann's knots are intended to keep her fraying ribbons from completely unraveling. "Kinda getting ratty" and "getting old," Mary Ann's ribbons have clearly seen many journeys, not only to Magdalena, but to wherever else she takes her staff. But amid all of her well-worn ribbons, one of them in particular stood out among the rest: a lone black ribbon. This black ribbon evokes the presence and memory of the dead.

MAR: I have one black ribbon on here, and the black ribbon represents, um, my Mom who passed away, my friend who died from cancer, and, um, and I guess probably now, all the other people who have passed away since I've been walking. So that's one that I believe I put on. All the other ribbons are, you know, are the ones that Felix tied on there.[68]

The black ribbon evokes the presence and memory of the dead. And yet, at the same time, at least for Felix's walkers, all of the other ribbons, and therefore the staff as a whole as well, evoke loving memories of the recently deceased Felix Antone. During his wake, as well as in Mali:na in the year after his passing, Felix's walkers were each given one black ribbon.

Walkers and Their Staffs

Staffs, and particularly ribbons, can evoke memories both of previous journeys to Magdalena and of Felix, as well as deceased family and friends. But how might these staffs themselves be regarded as sentient beings that should be treated with respect? "That's why you have to take care of them the way that you do," Mary Narcho began her explanation.

MN: Every year, you know, I dust the staffs and it's always standing next to my little altar. Because it's so sacred to me and so special to me. You take care of it like you would yourself or your child because it got me through five years of leaning on it and walking with it. And everything that I went through in those five years, this staff was right there beside me and it was helping me to make it.[69]

After a brief pause, Mary pensively added, "I leaned on it [pause] . . . and maybe it leaned on me." Mary cares for her staffs like members of her own family and stands them upright next to her saints. She leaned on her staff for five years, and they mutually depended on one another as they experienced the struggles and joys of walking to Magdalena together. Like Mary, most O'odham walkers practice a relational materiality, or material rationality, in which they seem to relate to their staffs through practices that are categorized by O'odham as either respectful or disrespectful.

Kendall Jose explained that a staff should be treated like a person.

KJ: *You take care of it as if it is a person, you know.* You know, *we don't leave it behind.* Don't just *leave it laying around on the ground.* I know we always tell the kids along the road [preaching], *"Don't be playing with them like swords,"* you know. . . . If you don't use it right, *it can hurt you,* meaning, *if you're disrespectful to the item,* you know, *it'll hurt you.*[70]

When I asked him to elaborate on what he meant by taking care of a staff as though it were a person, Kendall described how and why he takes care of his family's staffs in their home altar throughout the year:

KJ: *It being a person:* you take care of it; it takes care of you. The way I take care of my staff [pause] . . . keep it inside the house with our altar, the saints, and everything. *Stand* 'em right there and time to time take 'em, set 'em outside, and *get* that air, *get* some sun. And occasionally, you know, [with raised pitch] *sprinkle some water.* You know, [with raised pitch] *just little things like that.* They say to *offer it some food.*[71]

Kendall stands his family's staffs next to standing and reclining saints in the altar inside of his home, like additional members of the family. Moreover, like the saints—who, much like O'odham, putatively don't like being cooped up all of the time and like to have feasting, singing, and dancing from time to time—staffs need to go outside from time to time to take in the air, the sun, as well as food and drink.

Like Kendall, without any leading questions, Royetta Thomas of San Miguel described her staff as being "like a person." Having brought up the subject of staffs in her own narrative, I asked her to elaborate.

SS: Can you tell me more about the staffs?

RT: They're like your backbone, your backbone, that will carry you on, like a helper. You respect it. It's like a person. You don't just leave it laying around anywhere. It's given to you for a reason [coughs]. That's what I was told. I keep mine by my saints, so it's there.[72]

After Royetta stated that a staff is "like a person" and that it is to be respected as such, I asked her how she shows respect to her staff. She explained that she occasionally brushes hers off, burns cedar for it, and takes her staff with her to different events. Since I did not completely understand what she meant by stating that her staff was "like a person," again, I asked her to elaborate.

SS: You said that the staff is "like a person."

RT: Mmhmm [affirmative].

SS: Can you, um, expand on that at all?

RT: If you start throwing your staff around and everything, you're hurting it too. All the elements that are taken from different plants and all that, they're all beings. You don't just take it and disrespect it. It helps you. It heals you. You meditate with them. It takes care of you. That's why you respect it and treat it like a person. . . . If I didn't take care of it, you know, it's gonna come back on me. Only time will tell.[73]

Much like walkers themselves, staffs can get hurt. Royetta stressed that staffs can either help you and heal you or make you sick. As with other forms of sickness outlined by Donald Bahr, Juan Gregorio, David I. Lopez, and Albert Alvarez in their study of O'odham theories of sickness "playing," or "playing around" is a disrespectful offense that is usually paired with the consequence of "sickness."[74] When children play with their staffs, spinning them around, pounding with them, throwing them, or "sword fighting" with them, they are quickly reprimanded. On rare occasions in which adults—or even ethnographers—are perceived as "playing" with their staffs, they too might be reprimanded.

Although most O'odham in the study stated that staffs may be treated in a variety of ways, they also consistently stated that staffs should not be played with. For example, Simon Lopez explained:

SL: The only thing that is no good, is when you *play with it*, start playing with your walking stick, instead of using it *like you're supposed to*. And I think that's the only thing that is no good, is when you play with it, and don't take care of it like you're supposed to. A lot of times there's uh people that *don't care*, you know, they just leave it somewhere, so somebody—kids, or things like that—will get it and, you know, misuse it. And that's no good.[75]

If caring for one's staff shows respect, then "playing with" one's staff shows disrespect, as though "playing with" were synonymous with "not taking care of" and "misusing" in this usage. I also asked Simon about the potential consequences of these actions.

SS: And what are some of the things that might happen if you're playing with that stick, or you just leave it somewhere unattended? What are some of the risks of doing that?

SL: There is a lot of things, you know, that they do. If the kids get it, and take, lose it somewhere, or throw it away somewhere, and things like that. And a lot of times they say *there is sickness that you can get because you're not taking care of this*, you know.[76]

Staffs, like other volitional beings discussed in Bahr's study of O'odham theories of sickness, can cause sickness to O'odham with whom they have a relationship. Consequently, this chapter makes an important contribution not only to the ethnographic literature on O'odham "objects" but also to the ethnographic literature on O'odham theories of sickness as well as O'odham theories of materiality, personhood, and place.

Summary

To conclude, I return to the question with which we began: what is the relationship between walkers and their sticks? Following Tod Swanson's analysis of O'odham calendar sticks, this chapter has suggested that as seasons pass, O'odham become seasoned and staffs get historied.[77] Storied staffs and seasoned characters, then, are the results of the productive labor of walking to Magdalena. Ideally, walkers become attached to their sticks and identify with them because they have endured much together and helped one another. However, it is also clear that relationships between walkers and their sticks can be less than ideal, as demonstrated by undisciplined actions—such as thoughtlessly "playing with" a staff, or forgetting where one's staff is and leaving it unattended and uncared for—that might result in sickness.

Verlon "Carlos" Jose explained: "You don't walk around, and drink beer, and do whatever with these staffs. It's not what they're meant to be. Yet, some young people would do that."[78] In short, from Verlon's understanding, these staffs are meant for journeys, not aimless wandering and distraction seeking (see also chapter 4); they get thirsty and need water, not beer. Without elicitation, Verlon narrated two ways of relating with one's staff that came to his mind as being particularly disrespectful.

VCJ: I was told that there was one person who was running around, breaking all their windows in their home with their staff. It's very disrespectful. I was told there was a young girl who didn't want to have her staff anymore and she was gonna break it. And I was asked to go talk to her, and she said that staff does nothing for her. I talked to her and told her, "It's not gonna [do] anything for you. It's not gonna cure you. It doesn't have magical powers. It could, but that depends on you. That depends on you and what you put into it that it gets its power from."[79]

Whether they are used respectfully or not, these staffs accumulate years of thoughts and actions in relation to their walkers. History is embedded in these objects, but these objects hold different histories within them: the histories-in-the-making of walkers who are themselves persons-in-the-making, journeying to and through places-in-the-making. These staffs—whether or not they are spoken of and interacted with as persons in and of themselves—make persons who are placed and places that are personed. Staffs *can* aid in the gradual production of mature O'odham personhood, but of course there are other—less productive and counterproductive—modes of relating to one's staff as well. Since history—tragic, comic, and otherwise—accumulates, becoming embedded in O'odham "objects," there are "multiple ways of being a thing" and consequently multiple "memories in [multiple] things."[80]

As Darling and Lewis have shown, scraping sticks encode geographical knowledge (though this too is historical), while calendar sticks encode historical knowledge (this too is also geographical, since calendar sticks tend to be village-based).[81] So long as their ribbons and staffs are ever present, for O'odham walkers, Magdalena, Saint Francis, and all of the blessings associated with them are never too far away. And the memories of these journeys that they have taken with their staffs and the stories that they together tell inextricably link walkers and their sticks, sticks and stories, persons and places, the past and the present, as well as the living and the dead. Thus, Magdalena is palpably present in the everyday lives of the walkers who cannot help but be transported by their sticks to stories—whether told or untold—and memories made along the road to Magdalena as well as dreams of future journeys.

CHAPTER 4

Walking to Magdalena

> When he [Christ] walked among his people, he walked everywhere. He
> walked from community to community. [Christ] never, you know, rode
> anything. He was always *on foot*. He did everything on foot. And you know,
> he didn't really have a house. He did everything on foot, and he prayed, you
> know. He healed. That's what this journey, you know, kind of, represents.
> That we can be that if we want to be. We can be in that kind of realm, I
> guess, as Christ walked in. And that's what this journey, especially with
> the prayer, is really about.
> —Louis Anthony Lopez, remembering Felix Antone's teachings about the
> pilgrimage to Magdalena

Pilgrimage has long been the focus of much attention in both academic
and popular literature about Tohono O'odham.[1] However, most O'odham
refer to the trek to Magdalena as either "the walk" in English, or *him* or
himdag in O'odham.[2] In lieu of perpetuating the "pilgrimage" as a valid
anthropological category for cross-cultural comparison, focusing on the
physicality of "walking" and the conceptual notions of what it means "to
be a good walker" as expressed in O'odham narrative discourse is useful
for scholars interested in moving away from static notions of "culture"
toward more sophisticated notions of "culture" as dynamic, processual,
dialectical, living, and in motion. Indeed, the category of "movement"

has long been at the forefront of pilgrimage studies, at least since Alan Morinis's declaration that movement is the essence of pilgrimage.[3]

O'odham understandings of walking to Magdalena are grounded within wider O'odham conceptions of movement. Much about "walking" and "being a good walker" or a "good" O'odham person is about maintaining proper kinship relations with one's kin as well as with other entities in O'odham landscapes. As such, these relations seem to follow the same principles whether one is encountering one's grandmother, a "saint" in one's home altar, village church, or even in Magdalena, or a deceased cowboy "devil." Indeed, these "saints" are not necessarily "saintly" and these devils are not particularly "diabolical," but both entities are regarded as capable of causing harm and "sickness" to those who mistreat them and their property.[4] Walking—or, to be more precise, a particular O'odham way of walking—is instrumental in the incremental production of *siakam*, an O'odham notion of maturity pertaining to "ripening" or "ripeness." As previously mentioned in chapter 1, *siakam* means something like "real people," those ripened, matured, and modest individuals who exude O'odhamness. As pinnacles of O'odhamness, *siakam* are inextricably linked to what it means "to be a good walker."

In the opening epigraph to this chapter, Louis Lopez explained how one of Felix Antone's teachings was that those O'odham who walk to Magdalena are walking in Christ's footsteps. However, in purposefully moving through the landscape on foot toward Magdalena, O'odham may also find themselves on a path toward becoming a "real person" as they become more familiar with, and are in turn shaped by, the places through which they move. One example is the productive juxtaposition of Louis Lopez's homeless Christ, who according to Felix Antone is temporarily and productively imitated by O'odham walkers on their way to Magdalena, and the story of the Homeless Women who were transformed into the Pleiades as recorded by Juan Dolores.

> At that time there was no puberty celebration. . . . The first time they had the celebration the people liked it. But some women did only that all the time. It wrecked their homes and no one wanted them. People called them "homeless women," because they ran around and

had no home. They wandered everywhere in the country and finally went to a powerful medicine woman. When they arrived, they told her to do something to them so they would soon find rest from their homeless condition.[5]

The story of how the Pleiades appeared (see also chapter 3)—which are referred to in O'odham as Cecpa'awi U'uwi and are variously translated into English as either Homeless Women, Prostitute Women, Promiscuous Women, or simply the Travelers—tells the origins of O'odham puberty rites. At that time, I'itoi sang beautiful songs, giving them to the people, who in turn sang the songs and danced. The people enjoyed the first puberty celebration, but some enjoyed the celebration too much, seemingly unable to stop singing and dancing. Such undisciplined and frenzied merriment had grave consequences. According to the story, "some women did only that all the time. It wrecked their homes and no one wanted them. People called them 'homeless women,' because they ran around and had no home." After wandering everywhere, they finally happened upon a powerful medicine woman whom they begged to put an end to their homeless, kinless, and displaced condition. The medicine woman acquiesced, saying, "Alright, I'll do it. I'm going to put you out in plain sight of all. Every evening your relatives will see you and tell their daughters why you were called Homeless Women (the Pleiades). In this way women will know what a good home is. Even though a puberty celebration is enjoyable, no one should go around just doing that." Having spoken thus, she transformed the women into stone and threw them into the sky where they are now.

Being a good walker is intimately related to the disciplined, sensuous maturity of O'odham elders, with a life full of experience and a body full of knowledge and skill.[6] In turn, such disciplined maturity (or the lack thereof) is manifest in the everyday movements of O'odham men and women. These movements include not only walking but also dancing, as well as cooking and eating. Movements are bound by certain informal rules, which become most salient when the rules of proper form are broken. In particular, the embodied practices of walking and dancing are linked in the analysis that follows. As two skillful, foot-wise, embodied knowledges of how to move through the world, dancing and walking are mutually related arts of carrying oneself that provide exquisite vantage points for viewing, participating in, and analyzing O'odham "kinesthetics" (ways of moving) and "kinesthetic ideologies" (evaluations of movements) that relate aesthetics of particular ways of moving and ethical judgments of value and taste.[7] Focusing on walking and dancing together is not unprecedented within pilgrimage studies. Most notably, in his analysis of a Quechua pilgrimage to Qoyllur Rit'i, anthropologist Michael J. Sallnow observed that the journey was so pervaded by melody and rhythm that "the pilgrimage, in a sense, is not so much walked as danced."[8] Insofar as the songs analyzed in chapter 2 accompany O'odham walkers on their way to Magdalena, it is not unreasonable to suggest that this journey too, is "not so much walked as danced."

Before examining O'odham practices of walking, categories of movement, and narrative discourse that illustrate O'odham kinesthetic ideologies of what is at stake in "being a good walker," this chapter includes a discussion of practice theory as developed by French social theorists Marcel Mauss, Pierre Bourdieu, and Michel de Certeau, religious studies theorists Thomas Tweed and Manuel Vásquez, and others in order to highlight the significance of walking as an "epistemologically actualizing" embodied practice.[9] Moving away from the discussion of practice theory and toward a discussion of O'odham movements or kinesthetics and O'odham kinesthetic ideologies, the analysis draws upon intimate ethnographic observations of O'odham ways of walking as expressed by Ofelia Zepeda, an accomplished Tohono O'odham linguist and poet, and Byrd Baylor, a well-known nonnative author of fiction with a keen ethnographic eye. Because O'odham ideologies of walking are somewhat underarticulated, this chapter on "walking" takes a brief detour to consider O'odham kinesthetics and kinesthetic ideologies of "dancing" in contemporary *waila* performances, which have been far more extensively studied by anthropologists than O'odham ways of walking. Finally, I examine several O'odham narratives about going to Magdalena and O'odham categories of movement.

This chapter explores the physicality of movement in general with an emphasis on walking in particular. In addition to attending to these actual movements, or kinesthetics, my analysis also includes a discussion of O'odham discourses on these movements, or kinesthetic ideologies. Here, I employ my own observations and experiences from five years of participating in the walk to Magdalena, as well as stories that O'odham told me about "good" (*s-ape*) and "no good" (*pi o ape*) (i.e., "bad") walkers.

Practice Theory: From "Body Techniques" to "Embodied Cosmologies"

French sociologist and ethnologist Marcel Mauss's concept of "body techniques," which he uses to describe "the ways in which from society to society men [*sic*] know how to use their bodies," foreshadows both French social theorist Michel Foucault's "technologies of the self" and French sociologist and anthropologist Pierre Bourdieu's notion of "habitus."[10] In addition to noting how habits of swimming had changed in his lifetime and how French and English troops had different techniques of digging that could only be learned painfully and slowly by the other, Mauss also noted, significantly, how French and English walking techniques differed considerably by frequency and stride so that one "could recognize the gait of an Englishman and a Frenchman from a long distance."[11] Mauss was particularly struck by a revelation that came to him when he was ill in a New York hospital:

> I wondered where previously I had seen girls walking as my nurses walked. I had the time to think about it. At last I realized that it was at the cinema. Returning to France, I noticed how common this gait was, especially in Paris; the girls were French and they too were walking in this way. In fact, American walking fashions had begun to arrive over here, thanks to the cinema.[12]

Walking figures prominently in Mauss's exploration of body techniques. He discusses more examples of walking as the quintessential body technique, necessarily acquired, and never natural.[13]

> I think I can also recognize a girl who has been raised in a convent. In general, she will walk with her fists closed. And I can still remember my third-form teacher shouting at me: "Idiot! why do you walk around the whole time with your hands flapping wide open?" *Thus there exists an education in walking, too.*[14]

Mauss's analysis of "the techniques of the body" provides a foundation for practice theory upon which Bourdieu later builds, which in turn—at least for the purposes of the present study—provides a vantage point from which practice can be seen as integral to the production of disciplined, mature, "ripe," or "real people."[15] Already in Mauss there is a dialectic: tradition is embodied as bodies comport to tradition; tradition forms bodies as bodies make tradition. Moreover, Mauss's classification of body techniques according to efficiency opens the possibility for further consideration of the connections between the capacity for embodied knowledge (disciplined skills, or practice), since Mauss signals that he is primarily interested in "those people with a sense of the adaptation of all their well-co-ordinated movements to a goal, who are practiced, who 'know what they are up to.'"[16]

Significantly, as Mauss suggests, and on which Bourdieu elaborates, the embodied knowledges of practice do not necessarily, or easily, rise to the level of discourse.[17] Taking this dichotomy between discourse and practice to its logical extreme (though it should be noted that Derrida deconstructs the dichotomization of discourse and practice, arguing that discourse *is* a practice), Bourdieu promotes *"learned ignorance"* as a mode of practical knowledge that "can only give rise to a misleading discourse of a speaker himself [*sic*] misled."[18] For Bourdieu, this "learned ignorance" belongs to "the field of doxa, of that which is taken for granted," when "the established cosmological and political order is perceived not as arbitrary, i.e., as one possible order among others, but as a self-evident and natural order which goes without saying and therefore goes unquestioned."[19]

As Manuel Vásquez notes, Bourdieu's notion of habitus is useful in the study of embodied religious practices.[20] Bourdieu defines habitus as "a system of dispositions" that "designates a *way of being*, a *habitual state* (especially of the body), and, in particular, a *predisposition, tendency, propensity*, or *inclination*."[21] In the context of O'odham pilgrimages to Magdalena, the embodied knowledge of religious practices such as walking to Magdalena is a "practical mastery . . . transmitted in practice, its practical state, without attaining the level of discourse. The child imitates not 'models' but other people's actions. . . . In all societies, children are particularly attentive to the gestures and postures which, in their eyes, express everything that goes to make an accomplished adult," including mundane everyday acts, such as a way of walking, that are grounded in routine bodily dispositions, or what Bourdieu calls "*hexis*."[22]

Although O'odham discourses on "walking" are not necessarily "misleading discourse of a speaker himself misled," as Bourdieu would have it, walking does seem to be one of those things that usually "goes without saying."[23] In my conversations with O'odham elders and walkers, for the most part, I repeatedly found that O'odham kinesthetics and kinesthetic ideologies of "walking" were often articulated in hesitant, halting, and otherwise unconvincing ways when elicited through leading questions. A way of walking, then, is precisely that which for Bourdieu "*goes without saying because it comes without saying*," which the French Jesuit social theorist Michel de Certeau glosses as "a cleverness that does not recognize itself as such."[24] De Certeau extends Bourdieu's radical distinction between discourse and practice in his memorable and illustrative example of the spatial practices of jaywalking "Walkers in the City"; largely unaware of their subversive spatial tactics, positioned as they are on the ground, they cut across the grid system of city streets, illegibly writing texts with their feet that they themselves cannot read, and that can only be read from high above.[25]

Because ways of walking tend to be nondiscursive, my own observations are vital to understanding unmarked normative O'odham ways of walking. In the following attempt to represent an O'odham theory of walking that imbricates the ripening of "real people" and senses of place, it is productive to follow religious studies theorist Thomas Tweed, who conceptualizes theories as "*sightings* from sites."[26] Like Tweed, "my position . . . obscures some things as it illumines others."[27] This is necessarily the case since my own perspective in walking to Magdalena was often and necessarily confined, walking in a single file line with eyes mostly focused on the feet or the backpack of the person directly in front of me in order to avoid collision when the line slowed suddenly or abruptly came to a halt. My analysis also draws upon the close ethnographic observations of Ofelia Zepeda and Byrd Baylor in order to articulate a particular O'odham way of walking that usually "goes without saying" as the normative unmarked mode of walking.

Walking to Magdalena meets Bourdieu's challenge to study "*religious labor* carried out by specialized producers and spokespeople invested with power, institutional or not, to respond to a particular category of needs belonging to certain social groups with a definite type of practice or discourse."[28] Indeed, O'odham "walkers" are specialized producers, producing religious labor—walking—for their kin and homeland.[29] At the same time, the physicality of walking to Magdalena itself manufactures persons and place, further suggesting the interpenetration of O'odham anthropologies (concepts of personhood) and cosmologies (concepts of place).[30] Hence, this chapter investigates the inculcation of embodied *himdag*—that is, ways of being a person—through *him*, or walking.

Religious studies scholar Vasudha Narayanan proposed the notion of "embodied cosmologies" to address embodied and emplaced practices such as walking to Magdalena.[31] Significantly, religious studies theorist Manuel Vásquez argues that Narayanan's "embodied cosmologies" are not mere texts to be reenacted or performed, as anthropologist Clifford Geertz would have it in his now infamous textualization of practice.[32] Instead, for Vásquez, "embodied cosmologies" are at the heart of "religion-in-the-making," as practices and cosmologies are transformed and contested as they are embodied and emplaced.[33]

A Brief Literature Review of O'odham "Walking" (and "Dancing")

For O'odham linguist and poet Ofelia Zepeda the physicality of certain iconic O'odham movement is embedded in the soundscape of her memory as an O'odham child. In her poem "Landscape," Zepeda reminisces about an old O'odham woman, perhaps her grandmother, articulating the sounds, kinesthetics, and metaphysics of walking.[34]

> The early morning sounds are so clear.
> Familiar in my memory.

> The sound of shuffling feet, a step, a shuffle.
> She didn't lift her feet when she walked.
> She shuffled to her own rhythm.

She didn't lift her feet.
She was in constant contact with the earth.
With each shuffle she pushed the earth along,
with each step she dragged time along.[35]

The sounds of shuffling feet that remain "in constant contact with the earth" are ingrained in her memory and elegantly articulated in her poem, which brings O'odham practices of walking to the level of an O'odham discourse on walking.[36]

Zepeda's auto-ethnographic memories, observations, and ontological musings may also be placed in relief against novelist and amateur ethnographer Byrd Baylor's observations in her novel about Tohono O'odham living in Tucson in the 1970s.[37] Baylor describes the characteristic movement of one of the fictional characters in her book, Maria Vasquez, as she walks from her home, passing the shrine of St. Jude with a simple glance and "half a nod" on her way to the B-29 bar. According to Baylor, Maria's manner of walking is distinctly O'odham, which Baylor juxtaposes with the characteristic manner in which she perceives (or imagines O'odham to perceive) how Mexican and Anglo women move.[38]

> Maria walks down the dusty sidewalk slowly, slowly, evenly as Indian women walk. Though she is still young, her hips don't swing; she doesn't dance along the way Mexican girls do. Instead, she moves her feet on the city sidewalk as though she were moving barefoot across the desert. As though that journey might take all night, all week, a lifetime. The foot falls solidly to meet the earth, feels the pull of the earth. A heavy walk, but easy and animal-like. No man who watches women walk here mistakes the black-eyed, black-haired Indian girls for Mexicans. You can tell that walk from a block away.[39]

Although Baylor's portrait of O'odham walking is romantic ("moving barefoot across the desert . . . animal-like") and ahistorical (Maria's journey to the B-29 bar could last "a lifetime") compared to Zepeda's historical portrayal of O'odham walking, both depict a physical and metaphysical closeness between the earth and the soles of O'odham feet. Unlike Zepeda, who juxtaposes an old O'odham woman's shuffling with her own step-wise maneuvering of an uneven urban Tucson landscape—Zepeda tells us, "I consciously lift my foot with every step"—Baylor goes on to draw distinctions between O'odham, Mexican, and Anglo movements.[40]

O'ODHAM WOMEN	MEXICAN WOMEN	ANGLO WOMEN
"slowly" [2x]	[implicitly faster]	"almost runs"
"evenly"	"dance along"	"bouncing"
"a heavy walk, but easy, and animal-like"	swinging hips	"a little-girl motion no Papago woman uses"

According to Baylor, O'odham valuations (kinesthetic ideologies) of these various movements (kinesthetics) are clear. The characteristic movements of Maria Vasquez, and presumably of other O'odham women, are markers of disciplined, sensuous maturity lacking in Mexican and Anglo women—that is, non-O'odham women—who are referred to as "girls," who move in ways that "women" do not. Therefore, Baylor's description of these movements reveals what she understands to be an O'odham prescription for movement, revealing O'odham kinesthetic ideologies.

	O'ODHAM WOMEN	MEXICAN WOMEN	ANGLO WOMEN
IMMODEST/ IMMATURE	-	+	+
MODEST/MATURE	+	-	-

Moving from ethnographically informed poetry and novels toward my own experiences and observations of O'odham on the walk to Magdalena, my analysis in this chapter follows ethnomusicologist Janet Sturman, whose study of O'odham *waila* traditions asserts the necessity of studying what she refers to as "kinesthetics," or movement itself, and "kinesthetic ideologies," or discourse on movement.[41] Sturman forcefully argues that in O'odham *waila*,

> patterns of movement (and conceptions behind them) link modern *waila* performance to much older ceremonial music and dance traditions as well as to long-standing cultural values. *Waila*, then, is not

just O'odham music because O'odham play it; it embodies O'odham identity because of how O'odham play and respond to it—or more precisely, how they move at *waila* events.[42]

Although Sturman is interested in identity while this study's focus is on personhood and processes of maturation, or ripening, Sturman's embodied conceptualization of O'odham identity dovetails with the conceptualization of O'odham "ripeness" as an embodied condition.

Sturman recorded Angelo Joaquin Jr., the Tohono O'odham director of the annual *waila* festival in Tucson, stating that "O'odham don't *bounce* when they dance. . . . Keep your feet close to the ground, *glide*."[43] Prompted by Joaquin's comments to attend to how musicians and dancers moved in *waila* performances, Sturman found that "Angelo [Joaquin] was right; O'odham barely move their bodies as they dance."

Angelo Joaquin Jr.

+ (Minimalist)	- (Maximalist)
"glide"	"bounce"

Janet Sturman

+ (Minimalist)	- (Maximalist)
"sliding"	"galloping"
	"hopping"
"gliding"	"bouncing"
	"head bobbing"

The differences between Sturman's analysis of O'odham and non-O'odham "kinesthetic ideologies" might be glossed as minimalist and maximalist aesthetics of movement, insofar as the minimalist aesthetic is equated with modesty and maturity while the maximalist aesthetic is equated with immodesty and immaturity. Sturman questions whether non-O'odham critics of O'odham *waila* who "have described *waila* versions of familiar melodies as 'too steady,' 'too repetitive,' or 'deadly still,'" might be "more influenced by the actions of the performers than by the sound itself . . . [because] plenty of non-O'odham dancers respond with abandon and high-energy movement to *waila* music."[44]

Musicologist and ethnomusicologist Joan Titus also continues Sturman's focus on "kinetic ideologies" in O'odham *waila* performances. Following a particular song at a *waila* event, Angelo Joaquin Jr. translated an O'odham master of ceremonies' public commentary in the O'odham language for Titus. Although the comments were made publicly by a public figure at the event, in effect, Angelo disclosed to Titus part of a "hidden transcript" revealing an O'odham kinesthetic ideology.[45] Angelo translated the MC's response as "That was a very painful cumbia!"[46] Cumbia is the most popular *waila* song and dance style among non-O'odham audiences, for whom such songs frequently elicit animated movements that some older O'odham consider to be not only less "traditional" than other *waila* dances such as the mazurka and the *cho:di* (or, schottische), but also potentially disrespectful. This led Titus to observe "that dance style, indeed movement in general, seemed to be an important part of the O'odham aesthetic."[47] In contrast to these ostentatious and potentially disrespectful movements, Angelo explained to Titus that O'odham highly regard *still*ness, or what folklorist James Griffith has called a "visual aesthetic . . . of smoothness, with little or no vertical movement."[48] Through Angelo's explanation, Titus came to understand that "to be 'still' and smoothly glide across the dance floor was a sign of proficiency and grace, and a way of behaving modestly that is closely related to the *himdag*, or Tohono O'odham way of life."[49] In contrast to the "bouncy" movements of younger dancers, Titus observed that some older O'odham dancers, whom she estimated had been dancing for many years, appeared to be "floating across the ground."[50] Her attempts to emulate such stillness were met with much difficulty and even pain the following morning in her hips and lower back. Learning the hard way, Titus found that "stillness was an acquired skill that may appear simple, but was in fact a significant challenge."[51]

Because Titus uses the language of identity and performance, she concluded that "movement is an identity marker linked to Tohono O'odham philosophy about conducting oneself in daily life."[52] However, if this claim were rearticulated in the language of "ripeness," embodiment, and indexicality, then it is possible to say that movement is an index of "ripeness," modesty, and maturity of O'odham-ness. Moreover, movement is not only the product of persons, but movement—including journeys, such as walking to Magdalena—makes persons or manufactures ripe O'odham maturity. Stated another way, particular types of movement produce (and are the products of, as indexes of) particular kinds of people.[53] For example, Titus's analysis of O'odham movements in *waila* is particularly suggestive when she claims that "attracting attention to oneself [such as through ostentatious or immodest movement, for example] . . . is not just inappropriate, but is considered a form of bad luck, which could attract 'devils' and create 'devil sickness.'" In *Devil Sickness and Devil Songs*, anthropologist David Kozak and Tohono O'odham farmer, cowboy, and ritual curer David Lopez similarly attend to ostentation and immodesty, contending that "the conspicuous display of wealth is the prerogative of devils."[54] Describing O'odham "devils," linguistic anthropologist Donald Bahr likewise asserts, "They dress as supercowboys, they ride the wildest horses, use the gaudiest saddles, [and] carry the shiniest ropes."[55] In addition to overt displays of wealth, ostentation more generally (even "showy" dancing or walking) is expected of devils, and therefore also of cowboys, who—as an occupational hazard—are at the greatest risk of contracting devil sickness.[56]

Anthropologist Ruth Underhill identified what she considered to be three distinctively O'odham characteristics of human behavior. According to Underhill, O'odham "never raise their voices. . . . And they are always laughing." In addition to these two traits, Underhill adds, "their movements are deliberate; our swift jerkiness can hardly comprehend the rhythm slowed down by desert heat . . . and these same slow movements have been going on in the same desert since prehistoric time."[57] Although Underhill naturalizes and romanticizes the timelessness of O'odham "kinesthetics" and "kinesthetic ideologies" as a natural human response to the heat of the desert, Sturman cautions against such ecological determinism in maintaining that "cultural values shape movement as much as physical practicalities."[58] Hence, in agreement with Sturman, it is necessary to attend to what she refers to as "kinesthetic ideologies," or otions of which movements are "good" (*s-ape*) and which are "bad" (*p'o ape*) by listening closely to what people say about movements in addition to attending to *how* people actually move through careful observation and participatory engagement. For example, recall the story of how I got an O'odham nickname (see the introduction) and how an O'odham woman complimented the steady stride of the O'odham man in front of me while adding in her next breath, in reference to my own stride, "I don't even know what you're doing!" These statements, I contend, were firmly grounded in O'odham aesthetics and ethics of movement—or "kinesthetic ideologies"—which entail normative judgments no less than ethnographic description.

Walking to Magdalena: O'odham Categories of Movement in O'odham Narratives

As previously mentioned, most O'odham refer to the trek to Magdalena as either "the walk" in English, or *him* or *himdag* in O'odham.[59] Movement across the desert ideally—though not necessarily in practice—involves a particularly disciplined and stylized type of movement that involves a sensuous exchange with nature. This movement bears a heavy semantic load within the O'odham language since the verb *him*, "to walk," which can refer to spatial and temporal movement as well as reflect O'odham conceptions of the maturity and agency of persons, is the root of *himdag*, which may be translated either as a noun, "a way of life, a culture, a custom, or practice, or traditions," or as a stative verb, as "to be a good walker."[60]

I suggest that much can be gained by moving away from abstractions of *himdag* as "tradition" or "culture" in order to focus on what it means "to be a good walker." In this regard my analysis again follows religious studies scholar Tod Swanson, who reunites ethics and aesthetics— notoriously divided by German philosopher Immanuel Kant—in order to succinctly argue that "the moral character is a person with style."[61] For O'odham, whatever it means "to be a good walker" is intimately related to the disciplined, sensuous maturity of O'odham elders, with a life full of experience and a body full of knowledge and skill. Narayanan's notion of "embodied cosmologies" in her discussion of diasporic Indian performances from the *Ramayana* or the *Mahabharata*, in which "the movements of the actors are as important as the lines they utter," is also useful here.[62] O'odham ways of walking constitute such an embodied cosmology, or as Vásquez puts it, "a particular way of carrying oneself, an embodied aesthetic or poetics of life."[63]

In O'odham narrative discourse *him*, or "walking," is juxtaposed with *oimeḍ*, or "wandering," which is characteristic of undisciplined, immature characters who lack disciplined intentionality, are easily distracted, lazy, sexually loose, and neglect their kinship obligations in seeking their own self-interests and pleasures.[64] This point has already been illustrated in the story of how the Homeless Women became the Pleiades. These women have "the wandering heart."[65] In this ethical and aesthetic—rather than its ethnic—sense of the word, being a "person" or *O'odham* is differentially distributed among those who call themselves "O'odham," since "being a good walker" is an acquired art or skill. *In short, it is not people who make journeys: rather, journeys make people.* The "pilgrimage" to Magdalena should be understood within this context in which—as anthropologist Jean Sybil La Fontaine put it—"not all individuals are persons," and "personhood is the fulfillment of a socially significant career."[66] Indeed, several O'odham narratives about journeys to Magdalena that I collected suggest this interpretation insofar as these stories are preoccupied with the consequences of one's own thoughts and actions.[67]

For example, Simon Lopez related two stories: one of a "good walker" and the other about falling short of this ideal. The first story Simon shared is about his daughter, Rozy, who walked to Magdalena in order to ask Saint Francis to spare the life of her nephew, Robert, who was on life support and expected to die after suffering severe brain damage in an automobile accident that had claimed the life of his two parents. Simon told me the first story when I asked what walkers should be thinking about when they are walking to Magdalena.

ss: You had said earlier that if you are thinking the right thoughts, that it [the journey to Magdalena] is supposed to be easier. What are those good thoughts that you're supposed to be thinking when you are going down there?

SL: Even these people, like my kids, when we go on the walk, we always do the prayers, rosary, for them. The next day [pause] . . . they leave. And I always try to tell them, you know, "When we go down there, there's a lot of things *that you're going there for*. You're not just going there for the walk. But there's a lot of times that you might have something in your family that's not working right, or your jobs, or things like that that you ask for. And that's the only thing that you have to think about when you go: why you are going to Saint Francis. And all this that you can think, you know, the kind of help that you need."[68]

As Simon preaches to his own family, walkers should have a singular purpose in mind when they are walking, and "that's the only thing that you have to think about when you go." Simon went on, adding, "Or there's a sick[ness] in the family."

SL: Like my daughter, my oldest daughter [Rozy], when Robert got injured with his head injury. And the doctors in Phoenix said that, "He can't live. He can't live. Because too much blood got into his *brains*, and he can't live, so might as well take the machine off of him and just wait."[69]

Rather than passively accepting a medical diagnosis of certain impending death, Simon's daughter Rozy took the initiative to do everything that was within her power to save Robert.

SL: So right away, my daughter thought about her *faith*, so she told those doctors that "We're gonna ask for the help from our faith. If you can just *leave those machines* for at least a week. And we'll see what he can do. Maybe he'll come back." So they said, "Okay." So they *did*.[70]

Buying time from the medical establishment to seek another way of healing for Robert, Simon stated:

SL: And *right away, I* thought of that medicine woman that was here that do[es] a lot of curing and things like that. So I told her. So, right away she got ready and she went to Phoenix. And she told us, "He's not going to die, he's not going to die. *He's gonna live, he's gonna live.* You guys, just pray, and do what you can, and *he's gonna live*, he'll be okay." So that's what that medicine woman said.[71]

So, Simon and his family did just that, they prayed and sang together in the Phoenix hospital room while Rozy made her way to Magdalena.

SL: She took her patron saint over there and we took the others [saints] when we prayed over there in his room and the chapel for three days. And sure enough, he opened his eyes.[72]

Even as Robert began his slow recovery, Western biomedicine continually offered a grim diagnosis.

SL: And the doctors said, "He's not going to see. He's probably not going to see. He'll be blind. Or maybe he's not going to talk, or walk." *But he did. He's talking* right now, and *walking,* you can hear him *singing* as loud as he can and walking. And he can see better. Well, he has a little problem with his sight, but they said it's from that head injury that he had. And sure enough he did![73]

Though his doctors said he would be blind, he regained his sight. Though they said he would be mute, he regained his speech. Though they said that he would never walk again, today, Robert walks to Magdalena. Not only can Robert talk and walk, but he can dance and sing, including the Lopez family's songs for journeying to Magdalena (chapter 2), and many other traditional O'odham social songs, thanks to Rozy's walk to Magdalena as a labor of love. Simon continued, "So at *that time*, it was time for the walkers to go, so my daughter said, that she's going to *walk*." Simon's voice trembled on the word "walk," saying, "Walk to Magdalena for Robert and ask Saint Francis that he's gonna get help from him, for Robert."

Returning to my original question about thinking "good thoughts," Simon resumed his narrative, preaching to his daughter Rozy:

SL: So I said, "Okay, if that's what's on your mind, then you can do that. It's the only thing that you can do, think about Robert." *And so she did.*

And when she came back, she really felt good. "I'm really, really, really good. I think that something's telling me to go." . . . And *that's* what most people *do* if they walk or go to Magdalena. And that's what they think [about], you know, is their family, their health, or whatever that they go down there to pray to Saint Francis to get all of these back.[74]

When I explicitly asked Simon what it might mean to translate *himdag* as "to be a good walker," and how *himdag* might be used to describe or refer to an actual person, he replied as follows, illustrating not only that his daughter Rozy is a "good walker," but also that such disciplined, modest, mature, or "ripe" persons are acted upon by an agentive *himdag*. This is what moved Rozy to action, telling her to go.

SL: Yeah . . . I guess it's just the same way, like they say in the *himdag*. It's something, like I've already mentioned: *Why, why* do you do the walk? And *why*—like for instance, like my daughter, my daughter—*why* she did that walk for Robert. And that's a good walker. If somebody *feels* or thinks of something like that, we consider *himdag*. "It's *himdag*, that's making him [*sic*] do that." That would be, you know, [how] I'd describe him [*sic*], like that.[75]

Although Simon's first story stresses the positive consequences of positive thoughts and actions for mature O'odham as "real people," the second story that Simon shared follows different characters with different motives, and therefore a different character arc as the plot unfolds. In short, the story is about a couple that tries to go to Magdalena but ultimately fails to do so successfully because of their failure to overcome their own immature, undisciplined lifestyle. Significantly, Simon claimed no one in his family had ever experienced any problems such as these, which is why the following story was about nonrelatives.

SL: And this guy and his wife, he never goes to Magdalena. So, they wanted to *go* to *Magdalena*. And so they got ready. They left, and they went around Sonoyta, and along down that way. There's a *long* stretch of the road, you know, a *long* stretch of the road, and *way* past, you can see that *mountain*! And *there's* a place there, which is kind of like uh . . . a rest area over there, somewhere there. So they went. *And so I don't know*, I guess . . . his *cegidag* [or "state of mind"] is way far off. And when they got there, they stopped. And they were sittin' there, looking at the road. "Oh, it's too *far*." 'Cuz he can see the road.[76]

Since Simon knew that I had never gone to Magdalena through Sonoyta, and therefore that I was unfamiliar with the area that he refers to in this story, he compared this dauntingly long stretch of road that seems to go on forever to the "Valley of Death" that I encounter every time I drive between Phoenix, where I was living as a graduate student at the time, and Simon's home in Santa Rosa. The road that runs through this particular valley is comparatively densely populated with crosses alongside the road, marking the places of sudden, violent vehicular death.

SL: It's just like when you're coming out from Casa Grande. . . . That area. And then you see where those crosses are, where the road goes. And you can see the road [pause] . . . *way* over there.[77]

Simon stressed that "this one is *further*" than the "Valley of Death," which I knew. He went on:

SL: So they sat there. They were *lookin'* at the road [pause] . . . stretched. And *no cars!* So *anyway*, that's what happened to *this guy*. When they get there, he was sittin' there, wondering, "*gosh*, we're gonna go . . . [trailing off]," and look *way*. So as he *thinks* of things like that, the road gets stretcher and stretcher. And he'll think, "Oh, it's too far. It's too far out. I think we can't." *So they just turn around right there.* Turn around and came back *home*, and they never made it to Magdalena.[78]

As previously mentioned, Simon insisted that no one in his family has ever experienced any problems such as these. And at the end of this story, Simon shifted from a narrative mode to a speech genre that Don Bahr calls "preaching," in order to drive home the pedagogical and moralizing value of the story for his own family.[79]

SL: That's *why*, we tell you, "*Don't* think back. And think of where you're going. And the trip's going to be shorter. The road's going to be shorter." Instead of, what you're doing is you're saying, "No, it's too far. I don't think we can make it. We might as well head on back." And *that's* what made you turn around and come *back!* And *that's what happens*, you know, a lot of times, with a lot of people. And *that's why* I tell my kids, "*Never think back; always think ahead of where you're going.* And nothing will, you know, be hard for you."[80]

Here, the connections between place and ripeness become more explicit: Those who know the land—and therefore *how* to move across the land—are more fully developed persons than those who do not know the land, and who are therefore less capable of achieving a socially significant career. If walking to Magdalena is more difficult and time-consuming than driving, it is also more prestigious. The first story describes a disciplined character who is familiar with the areas through which she will travel, successfully undertaking a journey for a clearly defined and socially privileged purpose. The second story concerns a couple of undisciplined characters who are unfamiliar with the areas through which they are driving, unsuccessfully undertaking a journey for vaguely defined and perhaps even for socially and ethically dubious purposes. In other words the juxtaposition of these two stories is essentially a juxtaposition of *him* ("walking") with *oimeḍ* ("wandering"), which as previously stated is characteristic of unruly, immature characters lacking disciplined intentionality, who are easily distracted, lazy, sexually loose, and neglect their kinship obligations in pursuing their own self-interests.

Many of these stories about journeys to Magdalena are passed down through generations. As Felix Antone, the recently deceased leader of the walk to Magdalena, began to fall ill, Simon's son and Rozy's brother, Louis Anthony Lopez, inherited and embraced an increased leadership role in planning and executing the walk. Louis explained how his experience of walking to Magdalena under Felix's tutelage had the effect of epistemologically actualizing his father's traditional oral knowledge of the areas around his family's traditional routes to Magdalena. He had grown up hearing about these places, but he never himself experienced being in and moving through them. Louis described how when he began walking to Magdalena, he would approach Felix to learn from him in the evenings and during times of rest.

LL: If we had like [an] opportunity where we weren't so tired [pause] . . . I'd go sit with him. He'd tell me about the area and the surrounding areas. And I'm sure that, you know, you've probably gotten stories from my dad [Simon Lopez], where they used to go there [to Magdalena] on *horseback* and on the *wagons* and the trails that they used to go down and up that way on the horse and wagon trails. And that's what he would tell us. That's what Felix would say [too]. He would almost just kind of reiterate what my [dad said]. But *not* [exactly], it was always just like hearsay.[81]

What had previously been little more than "hearsay" to Louis finally came to life as he walked to Magdalena with Felix.

LL: Like my dad would tell me, "This is where we did [trailing off] . . . and this is what we did [trailing off, again] . . . and you'll come to this mountain." And we'd come to them, [and Felix would] tell me what those mountains were. But I never really saw them growing up. I mean, I heard those stories. And he [Simon] would tell me those things, but I never [actually saw them] until I started walking. And then Felix would really kind of point out those trails. It was kind of like, "*Oh, this is what my dad was talking about!*"[82]

Through the embodied experiences of walking to Magdalena and learning about various places along the way, Louis's received oral traditional knowledge took on flesh as he himself became emplaced within the land of his ancestors that he had heard of, but had never himself experienced. For Louis, walking to Magdalena mutually and incrementally produces "real people" as well as place, as the embodied practice of walking conjoined the physicality of movement through a geographical space with his local, familial knowledge of particular places.

By attending to O'odham categories of movement as expressed in narrative discourse and as observed in practice, I meet historian and critic of anthropology James Clifford's challenge "to rethink cultures as sites of dwelling *and* travel, to take travel knowledges seriously," while insisting at the same time that "we need to know about places traveled through."[83] Movement itself, in both discourse and practice, inscribes O'odham conceptions of place and what it means to be a "real person," as well as the connections between them. Walking to Magdalena through their traditional territory to which they hold no legal title recognized by Mexico—in a procession—constitutes what de Certeau calls a "spatial practice," a pedestrian act of possession.[84] O'odham theories of "ripeness" and place making lie at the intersection between ritual studies and legal studies. O'odham conceptions of anthropology and cosmology are also mutually imbricated. Although journeys clearly make people—rather than the other way around—this analysis shows that journeys also make places. Movement then simultaneously socializes space, manufacturing place, and makes mature persons, or "real people." This resonates with both de Certeau's conception of walking as constitutive of social space and anthropologist Edith Turner's understanding of pilgrimage as "a kinetic ritual," which Sallnow builds upon in his characterization of pilgrimage as "a kinesthetic mapping of space."[85]

Although Clifford notes that the category of "travel" carries with it various gender, class, and cultural biases, this of course does not prevent O'odham themselves from using this category for their own movement between their homes and Magdalena. In addition, humans are not the only ones who "travel," since, for example, saints and staffs who are treated with respect and interacted with as persons (or O'odham) also "travel," usually (though certainly not always) "with" human O'odham.

Other categories of movement include "visiting" and "staying."[86] For example, Jonas Robles (formerly the chairman for the Gu Achi District, an elder member of the board of trustees for Tohono O'odham Community College, a substance abuse counselor with Tohono O'odham Behavioral Health, and the oldest O'odham in Felix's group of walkers) explained that he goes to Magdalena to "visit" and "stay" with Saint Francis, whom Jonas more affectionately calls Ke:li, meaning "The Old Man," or Ma:kai, meaning "Medicine Man," or "Healer."[87]

JR: One of the medicine persons that told us [Jonas's group of traditional dancers] to [go to Magdalena], 'cuz we were doing a lot of traveling and things like that, performances at different places. What he said was for the group to "go four years up to Mali:na." And that's my first time that I saw Mali:na! [Laughing] And I was way [pause] . . . *in my adult years*, you know. And I finally got to see where Mali:na was! But I had heard a lot of stories about the Saint [Francis], that they went to visit, ask for his help. And they would, *it worked*, you know. And they would get that *help*. So, we went there four years, and that's when I also started going on *my* own.[88]

Joe Joaquin, a former cultural preservation officer for the Tohono O'odham Nation, explained that the "pilgrimage" to Magdalena is about "returning" to "visit" with Saint Francis. In Joe's view, O'odham journeys to Magdalena consistently stressed the O'odham ownership of Saint Francis and Magdalena. To this end, Joe told me a story (see appendix 1) about how the O'odham tried to bring Saint Francis to their land but were unable to bring him across the border, "so they put him in a cave up there somewhere" until somebody found him there later and brought it back down to Magdalena. But, Joe emphasized, "it was really the O'odham's, *O'odham's Saint*." Saint Francis "*belonged* to the O'odham."[89]

Although many O'odham anticipate and enjoy journeys to Magdalena, taking pride in "returning" to their homeland, other O'odham are more critical of contemporary journeys to Magdalena, especially when undertaken by younger O'odham or by foot. For example, Camillus Lopez—an accomplished storyteller and language and culture teacher at Tohono O'odham Community College—who goes to Magdalena but never plans to do so on foot, stated that this group going by foot was more of "a health thing" for "exercise" than it is something "spiritual," like a pilgrimage. In defense of this position, Camillus pointed out that none of the "walkers" *walk back* to wherever they came from. "You know . . . walking to Mali:na, they say, 'Did you walk back?' [Laughing] 'Cuz it's one thing to walk that way, but another thing to walk back!"[90] Without taking a breath, Camillus switched from a biting cultural critique to historical memories of a time before O'odham could easily load into trucks in Magdalena and arrive back home only a few hours later.

CL: I mean, when we stay over there, we have to get rested. I mean, really, at least two weeks or three weeks to really get the energy to come back. And then my mother tells these stories. My mom's from Big Field. And so she would tell the story about how they're coming from Magdalena. And they're in the back of the wagon. And they would sometimes be sleeping. We'd come up and they'd get these bells, and they would ring the bells.[91]

Like the chirping of Swallows and the sound of Swallow songs (in chapter 2), the sound of bells chiming signals a return home. Even in the middle of the night, these sounds reunited families who hadn't seen one another for a month or maybe more.

CL: Because that *jiwidag*, "to return back," is a great thing, because you went over there and you came back safely. And you brought back the power from the saint. So they say the *jiwidag*. "To come back." And that's a strong thing. And they would have celebrations for that.[92]

Then, again without a breath, Camillus switched back from historical memory to cultural criticism, using the stories he grew up hearing as a corrective to those contemporary walkers, whom Camillus considers to be insufficiently "spiritual" in their motivations. Speaking of the celebrations of return, Camillus continued:

CL: They do that now, people that go. But I think that's probably what's missing is that element. Because there is some accounts of people who have died over there, or died on the way going that way, or coming back. There's accounts of people who have gotten sick and just didn't come back because they were too sick. And still now, people die over there for different reasons. So that whole element of, you know, going and coming back safely is what they celebrated. You know, when you come back you have to throw the dance on because you're calling people together so that they can partake and then also get your gift of healing, or whatever you got from Magdalena. Now, so that's the whole idea of the thing, okay.[93]

As the above narratives illustrate, the value and meaning of these categories of movement is contested. In focusing on this contestation, this interpretation follows anthropologists John Eade and Michael J. Sallnow's model of pilgrimage as "a *realm of competing discourses*."[94] The dominant ideology, then, seems to be that those who know the land—and therefore know *how* to move across the land—are more fully developed, mature, ripe persons than those who do not know the land and are therefore less capable of achieving a socially significant career. In other words, "good walkers" are more likely to bring various "blessings" from Saint Francis and Magdalena back to O'odham villages, while those who fall short of this ideal are more likely to be the third-party recipients of these second-hand "blessings." Camillus Lopez challenges the pretensions and potential inequalities that may result from this system; essentially, if journeys make mature persons—not to mention if journeys lay claim to places—then why stop half way by only walking *to* Magdalena and not walking back *from* Magdalena?

Walking, then, is not only part of everyday life; it is also a significant component of O'odham *himdag*, or ways of life. Nonetheless, as obesity and diabetes continue to afflict O'odham, in what medical anthropologist Carolyn Smith-Morris has dubbed a "landscape of (in)activity," today walking has arguably become less a part of everyday O'odham life than it was in the past.[95] Particularly in this contemporary "landscape of (in) activity," walking to Magdalena perhaps seems out of place, an ostentatious mass movement that some nonwalkers might be more inclined to see as a shameless display of pride—a character flaw, or index of immaturity. In this sense, it is no wonder that critics like Camillus might consider the group of walkers to be making the journey to Magdalena for "exercise."[96]

Linguistic anthropologist Donald Bahr noted that prideful "showing off" or "display," which he defines as "mak[ing] a scarce possession visible," renders O'odham vulnerable to the charge of "bad taste."[97] Adapting Swanson's assertion that "the moral character is a person with style," the person with no style, or "bad taste," is a person of dubious moral character.[98] For Bahr, Christianity provides O'odham a way to "show off" (with style?) when he noted that Christian "churches provide more people with ways to show off than any other kind of organization that people can belong to," and moreover that "showing off through one's church is less easily criticized than other modes of assertion," whether through "singing, honoring saints . . . leading prayers, acquiring holy images, [or, last but not least,] making a 200-mile pilgrimage to [Magdalena,] Mexico."[99] "Walkers," then, are vulnerable to the charge of ostentatious movement, particularly absent sufficient purpose and maturity. Nonetheless, if pride is a sin, many O'odham are proud to be able to use Christianity and its various powerful persons—whether God, Jesus, Mary, various saints, or others—in service to this most virtuous vice (see chapter 5 for more on O'odham pride).

Summary

Through exploring the physicality of movement in general and walking in particular—while also attending to O'odham discourses on these movements—this chapter arrives at a general, albeit a contested and historically contingent, sketch of an O'odham ideology of walking (and dancing, and perhaps movement in general) as political discourse. This political discourse constitutes what anthropologist Nancy Louise Frey has called "the polemics of movement" in her study of pilgrims on the road to Santiago de Compostela, in which the mode of transportation becomes iconic, and authentic pilgrim status is generally reserved for those who walk, and frequently withheld from those who do not.[100] More broadly, students of ideology, including religious studies scholars who have historically neglected practice in their fixation on texts, would do well to more carefully attend to movement itself, as well as discourses on movement.

A focus on both the politics and the poetics of "walking" and what it means "to be a good walker" can be useful for scholars interested in articulating O'odham (and also non-O'odham) theories of movement that go beyond abstract reifications of "pilgrimage." Walking simultaneously produces persons and places, or socially significant spaces, which in turn produce well-practiced, disciplined, "ripe" persons. When the journey to Magdalena is viewed as an embodied cosmology, or a cosmological embodiment, walking can be seen as an epistemologically, ontologically, and axiologically actualizing embodied practice. This chapter demonstrates how a particular O'odham way of walking is related to the incremental production of *siakam*, an O'odham notion of maturity pertaining to "ripening" or "ripeness," and that *siakam*, as pinnacles of O'odhamness, are inextricably linked to what it means "to be a good walker" (*himdag*). In this sense, *himdag*, as agentive tradition or culture that acts on O'odham bodies, produces *himdag* in the sense of being a good walker, which in turn produces *himdag*, or tradition. If *O'odham* refers to "people," then *siakam* means something like "real people," or those ripened, matured, modest individuals who subtly and stylishly exude O'odhamness. In short, as anthropologists Tim Ingold and Jo Lee Vergunst argue, "walking is a profoundly social activity."[101]

CHAPTER 5

Writing O'odham History

I don't know.
Sometimes it's unbelievable.
Well, I guess it's the same thing,
like between the I'itoi and the God.

Like I say, you know,
who are you gonna believe:
God or I'itoi?
And yet it's probably just one.
Maybe that's the same thing,
that the O'odham say, "Our Creator."
It's the same thing.

"So you believe in that?"
"Yeah, we believe in that."

And we can't say,
"No, I don't believe in God;
I believe in I'itoi."
We can't say that
because we know that God is God
and maybe it's the same thing.

I'itoi is probably the God.

I mean, you know,
I don't know how to put it.

But that's one thing that we can never forget,
is believing in God,
what we learn from our religions,
which is probably the same.
—Simon Lopez, Tohono O'odham elder, cowboy, traditional singer, and
ritual curer

In February 2011, during a meeting discussing the possibility of pursuing this project on O'odham pilgrimages to Magdalena at the Tohono
O'odham Nation Cultural Center & Museum, Felix Antone stated that in
order to learn anything about the walk, I must first understand that the
walk is hardly a recent development. Instead, he said, "this walk was
here in the time of I'itoi." I'itoi, as previously discussed, is the ancient
figure who is said to have successfully formed O'odham bodies and
given O'odham their *himdag*, or way of life, which, for many O'odham
today, also encompasses Christian practices. In this view, what Tohono
O'odham have made of Christianity was made for them by I'itoi. To
state it differently—and to highlight agency—Tohono O'odham did not
make Christianity their own within the last 150 years or so, as Western
scholars of all stripes have assumed (see appendix 1); I'itoi made Christianity for them at the time of the establishment of O'odham homelands.
Felix's assertion that "this walk was here in the time of I'itoi" is a stance
in deliberate opposition to Eurocentric assumptions of the history of
Christianity in the Americas.[1] In the words of linguistic anthropologist
Donald Bahr, Felix's assertion "parodies" those Western historicities, or
senses of history, that assume Christianity was brought to the Americas
by the Spanish.[2] For Felix, Christianity is not a European import brought
to O'odham lands by Father Kino and others within the last 400 years;
rather, Christianity was embedded into the land—the *jeweḍ ka:cim*, or
"staying earth"—at the founding of the O'odham cosmos (see chapter 1).
    That said, Felix's comment is more suggestive than definitive. I will

probably never be entirely certain of what he meant. I had planned to follow up on Felix's statement by eliciting elaboration with numerous questions, the following being only a sampling: When was the walk to Magdalena established in relation to other significant events in O'odham oral history? Was the walk here before the coming of Europeans? If the walk was established "in the time of I'itoi," and the walk is said to honor Saint Francis, what is the nature of the relationship between I'itoi and Saint Francis? Felix's answers to these and other questions would have had direct implications for the broader question that unites this study: What have O'odham made of Christianity? Moreover, my plan was to further elaborate upon these preliminary findings by discussing these issues in depth, not only with Felix, but also with other Tohono O'odham elders, community leaders, ordinary walkers, and nonwalkers alike, to further aid in answering this broader question.

Research with knowledgeable elders is inherently problematic; following Felix Antone's sudden death on January 31, 2012, his passing demanded reprioritization, not only for this study but also for the community. Several impromptu events—memorials, the novena, the wake, the funeral, and the burial—were held in his honor in Sells, Cold Fields, and Pozo Verde, including a short walk for Felix's "walkers" from Felix's sister Ana's house in Sells to the nearby Catholic church, and another, longer, walk from Cold Fields to his birth place and burial place in Pozo Verde. I resorted to conversations with other elders and consultants who had considered Felix to be their teacher about what Felix's teaching might mean if "this walk was here in the time of I'itoi." These O'odham related a range of senses of the past that bore direct relevance to a recent cleavage in Felix's group of walkers.

For a brief period in the decade before this study began, I was told that the number of walkers had reached four hundred. But this large group allegedly split over a dispute involving the participation of non-O'odham in the walk. By 2009 this dispute was more or less resolved. However, the group of walkers who followed Felix was reduced to about half its previous size. In short, it seems that both groups—Felix's and the primary splinter group—invoked alternate senses of the past that variously justified the inclusion or exclusion of non-O'odham—and, more specifically, non-Indians—in the walk to Magdalena. Rather than adjudicating the veracity of these senses of history, I follow Bernard Fontana, who maintains: "To the anthropologist concerned with folk histories, the truth or untruth of oral traditions is irrelevant. What is relevant is that someone else defines truth differently and sees history in a different way."[3]

History and Parody

> As we enter into the stories . . . we will find what I think is true of all stories anywhere. They are influenced by other stories. For this reason there is no good choice but to study Native American myths comparatively. If we do not compare stories, preferably between neighbors, we will not know how they were created—or so I believe, since I think that an important force on a story is the stories of neighbors. Therefore it is not true—as it is now fashionable to say—that comparison is old-fashioned and unnecessary. It is best to compare . . . . One must compare.
> —Donald Bahr, "Edenism"

Bahr defines "parody" as "the clever recasting by one person of a text of another."[4] Building on the literature of "invented tradition," Bahr suggests that parodies are not truthful accounts of what actually happened in history; they are inventions. In Bahr's words, "they are responses to *texts* and not (or not much) to past historical realities."[5] Nonetheless while scholars generally call these "myths," many O'odham regard these as "history," which—needless to say—O'odham do not claim to have "invented." And while Bahr might like to suggest that these stories are parodies of other stories and not academically sanctioned truthful accounts of what actually happened in history, he concedes that this cannot be proven. In other words, the truth of stories is essentially nonfalsifiable. For Bahr, parody is a particular mode of intertextual relation "whereby neighboring communities and peoples insist on being different from each other."[6] In turn, neighboring communities take great pleasure in being "deliberately contrary."[7] Bahr explains:

> The motivation for the parody, I claim, is community pride. . . . [W]hat neighbors say may have a greater or equal effect on texts of oratory and prose history than what actually happened in the past and, indeed,

than the stories told in the home community a hundred years prior. It is the stories . . . of neighbors, I believe, that among other factors make literatures change and adapt. The past is the past, and what makes it live and change, and what breathes life into it in the present are, among other things, the stories of neighbors.[8]

Bahr developed this notion of parody throughout the entire length of his career. Bahr's principle of parody even plays an understated but highly significant role in the penultimate paragraph of *Piman Shamanism and Staying Sickness*. At least for Juan Gregorio, Bahr's sole informant for the study, he was interested in "wandering" sicknesses—the illnesses known by Western medicine—precisely because they were so unlike "staying" sicknesses—the illnesses that he treated as a *ma:kai*, or medicine man. Bahr's commentary is extremely suggestive: "In effect, the whole of Western European germ theory provides a background of comic relief against which the undisputed qualities of *ká:cim* [*ka:cim*, or staying] sickness can better be illuminated."[9]

In *How Mockingbirds Are*, where Bahr most fully develops his principle of parody, he compares "wet" (*nawait i:'i*, or with wine drinking) and "dry" (without wine drinking) Mockingbird Speeches from Tohono O'odham and Akimel O'odham communities, respectively. On this matter, Bahr states,

> I argue that the suppression [of wine ceremonies among Akimel O'odham in the 1890s and among Tohono O'odham in the 1920s] and conversion [to Presbyterianism in Akimel O'odham communities and Catholicism in Tohono O'odham communities] were *a* cause, but another was that each community desired to be and took pleasure in being different from the other, and different not only relative to geography (desert versus river) but also, and especially, relative to character, precisely to embrace drinking or to look askance at it. The pleasure in that difference, I argue, could have preceded the suppression and differential Christian conversion.[10]

In short, Bahr hypothesizes, "I would like to think that the wish for a reworking in the direction of [Akimel O'odham] self-dignity was sufficient to produce the [dry] Pima speech even before the United States imposed its ban on their wine ceremonies."[11]

In one of his many brilliant casual asides in *How Mockingbirds Are*, Bahr suggests that character flaws are understudied in indigenous literatures. Since Bahr maintains that "the O'odham regard drinking itself as a flaw," he was struck that such behavior could be associated with attracting rain, which anthropologist Ruth Underhill argued was the main purpose of all O'odham ceremonial life. Bahr wondered "what other Original Flaws people believe lie behind their religious practices," while conceding, "I have no theory on this and mention it as a topic for future study and reflection."[12] But this cannot be true, as previously noted, because Bahr hypothesizes that "the motivation for the parody . . . is community pride."[13]

Bahr's principle of parody is an important mode of explanation, which should be of considerable interest to other scholars. I, for one, find Bahr's notion of parody to be helpful in my attempt to answer the question that unites this book: What have O'odham made of Christianity? For example, Bahr examines an admonitory speech collected by Ruth Underhill at a wine feast in the village of Santa Rosa, where the speaker says, "It was not we who established this [feast]. I'itoi gave it to us, that we all might be well and that good might come from it."[14] This statement is very similar to Felix's statement ("this walk was here in the time of I'itoi"), in that both utterances belong to the genre of preaching (*amog*), and they both (one explicitly, the other implicitly) attribute I'itoi with creating two important contemporary O'odham rituals. Significantly, to my knowledge, no known versions of *Ho'ok A:gida*, or "Witch's Telling," clearly identify I'itoi as the originator of either the wine feast or the walk to Magdalena. Regarding the statement recorded by Underhill (and, by implication, Felix's teaching as well), this is why Bahr contends, "I believe that this speaker only meant that in a general way I'itoi is responsible for everything O'odham," leaving it at that.[15] Crucially, *Ho'ok A:gida*— which scholars typically call myth, though many O'odham regard as reliable history telling things that actually happened in the past—"does not acknowledge that Christianity ever came," according to Bahr.[16]

Some O'odham, and probably most scholars, might be expected to contend that the absence of origin of Christianity in *Ho'ok A:gida*, which implies that it was always already there, is an "invented tradition."[17] Nonetheless, for many O'odham it is a pervasive and persuasive account of history. In contrast to these implicit O'odham claims to an autochthonous or indigenous Christianity, many O'odham also narrate alternate histories of the origins of Christianity, but these do not rise to the level of *Ho'ok A:gida* (see appendix 2). Whether these alternate histories are O'odham oral traditions or academically sanctioned products of literate history that rely on Spanish colonial sources, and whether these histories are happy and felicitous, or what Bahr calls "Victimist history," are secondary to the fact that O'odham relish telling such stories, not only because many O'odham regard their narratives to truthfully relay what actually happened in the past, but also because each teller is viscerally gratified in being deliberately contrary, which is presumably why O'odham tend to be loyal to their own local, family-received oral traditions.[18]

Stifling Controversy and Contrary Senses of History

In the aftermath of the controversy regarding the inclusion of non-Indians on the walk, the orthodox position that the journey to Magdalena is a Christian pilgrimage—and not an indigenous pilgrimage—was tirelessly preached by the leaders of Felix's group, perhaps especially in my presence. After all, cannot white people be Christians, too? I learned the hard way that I had to be especially tactful when inquiring about the opposing position. Discussions probed raw nerves, leading only to sore feelings; the split was too close, too personal, and too recent to rehearse for a nosy outsider with no skin in the game.

Louis Anthony Lopez, the foremost leader of Felix's group of "walkers," once stated that he sometimes asks himself, "Why do we do this?"

LL: Why are we so [pause] into doing this, when it's not our religion. It's not our tradition. It's not our *himdag*. This whole pilgrimage thing, this whole Catholicism: it's not our tradition, it's not our *himdag* as O'odham. Why have we adopted it so much that we *think* that, you know? We think, and some of our elders, you know, seem to think that this is our tradition. *And it's not*, you know! It's something that was introduced to us by the Spanish.[19]

From Louis's historical perspective, which is in harmony with the findings of academically sanctioned literate history, he knows that all of the trappings of Christianity came to O'odham from the Spanish. Therefore, from this historical perspective, nothing Catholic can be properly classified as *himdag*. However, Louis also referred to some O'odham elders (including his father, Simon Lopez—see the epigraph which begins this chapter) maintaining other positions. In response to inquiries regarding Catholicism and O'odham *himdag*, Louis offered a polemical story:

LL: I think it was at that time when these people who are not O'odham wanted to walk the journey with us. They wanted to start out [from] Cedagĭ Wahia and walk the whole way to Mali:na with us. They approached Felix and asked him if they could do that. You know, they're not O'odham, but they wanted to walk with us.[20]

With the first non-O'odham wanting to join the walk to Magdalena, Felix's group of walkers soon fragmented, divided by the issue of whether non-O'odham should be included or excluded.

LL: And at the time, a group [or rather, a part] of the group that was with us were opposed to that. And they said that they didn't want them to walk with us. And the question was "*Why*? Why don't you want them to walk with us?" And everything was, "Because they're not O'odham. Because they're not O'odham. This is *our* culture. This is our *himdag*. It's not theirs. They're not O'odham."[21]

To Louis, as well as to many other O'odham, this position was comically absurd. Louis had been taught differently, so he did the best he could to correct what he regarded as the misguided notion that Catholicism could possibly be exclusively O'odham.

LL: And that's where I came in, you know, growing up in this [laughing] as a child and being explained Catholicism. This is what was brought to us. This is not our *himdag*. This is not our tradition. But we followed this and we grew up in this way. And growing up as a child, my immediate response to that was, "But this is *not* our tradition. But this is *not* our culture. Why are you saying that this is? This is something that was introduced to us by the Spanish: the Catholicism, which is what this walk represents. You know, we're walking, we're doing this journey and this walk in honor of Saint Francis, who is a Catholic saint. It doesn't have anything to do with tradition, with culture, with being an O'odham."[22]

When I asked Bernard Siquieros—the education curator of the Tohono O'odham Nation's Cultural Center & Museum—about how he thought the pilgrimage fit within O'odham *himdag*, he began with a historical orientation similar to Louis Lopez's personal understanding of Christianity as a European import, though it was disrupted by recounting Felix's narrative of Christianity renewing basic O'odham values.

SS: How, in your view, does this pilgrimage to Magdalena fit with O'odham *himdag*?

BS: It's something that was introduced as a part of the Catholic faith. And of course, this wasn't a traditional pilgrimage. That wasn't a part of our traditional way of life prior to European contact. And when the Spanish came, they brought Christianity. And so in time a majority of our tribal members were baptized in the Catholic Church. And so we *adapted* many of these teachings from Christianity into our *himdag*, into our way of life.

And so, I asked Felix one time about why we as O'odham so readily accepted this new way of viewing things. And [Felix] went [told] this long story about how *originally* before the Spanish came . . .[23]

Bernard trailed off, remembering the story:

BS: Of course we were a spiritual people, you know. We believed in the Creator. We believed in I'itoi and the teachings of I'itoi, and the teachings of *respect*, sharing, and hard work, and family, and all these things that are a part of our basic values. And so that when these people, you people [Europeans] *came*, he says that, "There came a time when people began not to live the way that we were taught. They began to move away from those values that were a part of O'odham." And it was his feeling that it was the Creator, or Creator's way of bringing these people here, with basically those same values, those same teachings in Christianity, and that we accepted them because we are sharing people, and [we have] respect for people. But that these Christian *values*, I guess, *fit right in* with O'odham values. So we accepted that.[24]

Rather than disrupting O'odham values, according to Felix's narrative in Bernard's memory, Christianity strengthened O'odham values and helped O'odham be more O'odham. Bernard continued, adding hesitantly:

BS: It kind of *rejuvenated* our basic value system, I guess. And so we, we *adapted*. Although *we held on* to our cultural values, our cultural views, we also brought in the Christian values that really kind of *fit* with the O'odham values. So we began to recognize the fact that we were O'odham. We have our culture, but that this way of thinking *fits* pretty well with our traditional beliefs, our traditional values. And so we accepted and began to do some of those things that showed our faith in Christianity. And so, this is how we did it.[25]

As Michel de Certeau, the erudite French Jesuit scholar, stated in remarks previously quoted in the introduction, the strength of indigenous resilience "lay in procedures of 'consumption.'"[26] For Felix, as O'odham became more Christian, they became more O'odham.

Personhood, Place, and Pride

In chapter 4 I cited an unpublished manuscript in which Don Bahr noted that Christianity provided O'odham with socially sanctioned ways to show off.[27] Recall that Camillus Lopez, also in chapter 4, regarded the walk to Magdalena as "a health thing" for "exercise." Clearly, walking to Magdalena strikes some O'odham as an ostentatious display of pride—a character flaw, or index of immaturity. But if pride is a sin, many O'odham are still proud to walk to their humble Saint Francis in service of this delicious vice.

Rather than demonizing pride as a sin, let alone a cardinal sin, between

2003 and 2011 Bernard Siquieros valorized and attempted to capture, preserve, and promote the pride that he saw on the faces of the walkers whom he met on their way to Magdalena when he began to photographically document the journey in 2003 for the Tohono O'odham Nation Cultural Center & Museum.[28]

BS: And so we stopped and we got down and started greeting people and asked if I could take pictures and they all agreed. So I took pictures and shook their hands and felt really [pause]. There was a sense of, of, of *pride* that I was feeling from the people that were there. That they were happy. They were resting. They were tired, but [trailing off] . . .[29]

Bernard fell silent for a moment as he remembered the scene, transported to the moment where the feeling that kept him coming back to Magdalena to photographically document Felix's walkers for eight consecutive years first hit him:

BS: Someone had sore feet and I remember the Mexican Red Cross came. And they were tending to some of people that had severe blisters and things. [Pause] *But the group was really very positive.* There is a very positive atmosphere, a very positive aura around each of these individuals that we met. And we encouraged them [pause]. . . . And so we've tried to go back ever since. Every year since then [laughter] we've gone back to try to *show our support,* show respect for the people that chose to make the walk.[30]

In conversations with Bernard, pride pales in comparison to a lack of pride as a threat to contemporary O'odham lifeways. Rather, for Bernard, pride is a source of strength, and its lack thereof a potential weakness and threat to contemporary O'odham.

SS: What would you say is the biggest problem to be overcome by O'odham today?

Taking in a long, deep breath before another long pause, Bernard was absorbed in thought.

BS: The biggest problem? There's quite a few that are up there. [Pause] *Not having a sense of* connection with *who we are*, I guess. Not having that strong sense of pride in who we are, I guess, is something that I think needs to be worked on. As our Elders always told us, to have that sense of who you are . . . to be *grounded*, I guess. And to feel *good* about being who you are. . . . I think, that's one of the things that I see is really important in our way of life is to *be grounded*, and *live* in a very modern life but [tapping the table] *be grounded* to who we are, to who we *really* are.[31]

For Bernard, the characteristic of being "*grounded*" connects pride, place, and mature, "real people." Certainly Bernard was not the only consultant who spoke of "grounding" and the need "to be grounded." "Real people" are *grounded*, emplaced, and well traveled.

BS: I think it [walking to Magdalena] helps those people that choose to have that be a part of their life. I think it really does *strengthen them* as individuals. And that's the one thing that I sensed *the first time I met up with the group* was that these people were very strong. Not only strong *physically* to make the trip [laughter], but strong *spiritually*. Strong individuals. You're just focusing in on that commitment that you made, whatever that commitment is, but you know that you've committed to make the pilgrimage, to make that journey. And so you're a *strong individual*. And I think they go through this. They come out with that sense of pride. "I did it!" And some of them keep coming back, keep coming back. Some people go for four years and say, "I've made my commitment. And I will keep on . . ." [They] just keep coming back because it's their road of life. It *strengthens* them. Yeah, it makes them stronger.[32]

O'odham are not merely born; they are made. For example, Louis Lopez explained how he told one of his daughters that his then youngest grandchild needed to go to Magdalena in order to be a part of this journey. Louis shared that his family had been doing his grandson's "infancy rites," which included (1) the clay ceremony in which O'odham babies eat the earth, literally becoming *grounded*, (2) baptism in the Catholic

Church, and (3) the Lopez family tradition of taking their babies to Magdalena.[33] Clearly, for the Lopez family, journeys to Magdalena are intimately related to the production of disciplined, mature persons who act and carry themselves as members of a family.

Although some O'odham might proudly call themselves "Catholic," or *ka:toliga*, as if it were synonymous with "good Catholic" or even "good O'odham," other O'odham seem to shy away from this self-designation, perhaps in order to sidestep criticism from other O'odham who might see this label as immature, arrogant, or pretentious.[34] Certainly no O'odham would ever claim to be a "saint," at least not without joking. In fact, being called a "saint," or a *sa:nto*, is an expression of derision, as shown below in a conversation with Simon Lopez.[35]

ss: I'm thinking about the word *sa:nto* in O'odham. I saw in the Saxton, Saxton, and Enos dictionary, that that word *sa:nto* refers to like a saint, or those saints, *sasa:ntos*, but that it could also be used to refer to people [Catholics] who go into *sasa:nto ki:* [that is, a church, or "saints' house," or "where saints live"], that you can use that word to describe the people who are going to church. Is that right?[36]

Pointing to the saints on the home altar next to us, Simon answered affirmatively.

sL: Um hum. Yeah. Yeah, it's the same. It's the same thing. *Sa:nto* is just like Fatima here. This is a *sa:nto*. A *sa:nto*. Sacred Heart is a *sa:nto*. *Anything*, statue or picture, picture of saint is a *sa:nto*. We call it *sa:nto*. And also, the *church*. They call it *sa:nto ki:*. That's the house of the saints. Saint Francis is a *sa:nto*. And *anything* that's a saint is a *sa:nto*. Which is the same thing as the church. The *ki:* is the house of the saints. And that's why they call it *sa:nto ki:*. Or a place like Magdalena, they would say *sa:nto ki:*, because it's the plan [home] of Saint Francis.[37]

So far Simon confirmed that *sa:nto* can refer to a saint and that a *sa:nto ki:* is a saint's house. But could *santo* also be used to refer to an O'odham person who frequents a *sa:nto ki:*? Simon resumed his explanation.

SL: A lot of times these other denominations, you know, they'll call *you* or *me*, you know, as "Catholics." They'll say, "Those *sasa:nto*. Those are *sasa:nto hemajkam.*" *Sa:nto* people, saint *people*, you know. And that's what a lot of times a lot of people will say, you know, "Those are *sasa:nto*, you know, *sasa:nto hemajkam.*" That means that *we're Catholics*. And that's why they put it like that, because they know that the saints are our *sasa:nto.*[38]

Essentially, Simon answered that yes, non-Catholics do call Catholics *sasa:nto*. With this affirmation, I further inquired in order to see if the appellation is used either humorously or derogatively.

SS: Is it humorous to say, for people who maybe don't go to those churches, to call someone *sasa:nto hemajkam*? Is that like saying, "*Oh, these peoples, they think they're saints,*" or something?

SL: Sometime *before* there's a lot of . . . *jealousy or something like that* with other denominations. That's how it used to be here, here with the Presbyterians. We call them *Mi:mṣ. Mi:mṣ.* What they call the Presbyterians. And verse vice, *they* call us *sasa:nto*. And *sometimes* there's a little conflict in between, you know. I don't know if [it's] their *jealousness* or something like that. And like for instance, they'll be calling *names*. And they'll get mad and they'll say, "*Those sasa:nto* [Catholics]. *They think they're sasa:nto* [saints]!" And verse vice, we'll say, "*Oh, those mi:mṣ* [Presbyterians, or Protestants more generally], you know. *They're just mi:mṣ* [ministers], you know," and things like that.[39]

If Presbyterians, or Protestants more generally, can call Catholics *sasa:ntos*, because they think that they are saints, then Catholics can also retort that they are *mi:mṣ*, or ministers, or that Protestants think that they are ministers.

When anthropologist Deborah Neff recorded the life history of Frances Manuel, at one point Neff might have jokingly suggested that Frances was something of a "saint" and that Frances's life history might be read as something of a hagiography. In Neff's chapter entitled "I'm Not Really So Good!," though, Frances states: "I'm not all that good. If somebody reads this, they'll think, 'Well, she's so good,' but I'm *not*. . . . I don't want anybody to say about *that*. I'm just a person, just a person. I'm not that special, I don't feel special."[40] Like all O'odham, Frances Manuel is no "saint." Instead, Frances asks, "Aren't we all a little bad?," and further says that "we ourselves are devils," even implying that she was destined to become not a *sa:nto*, but a *jiawul* (or deceased devil cowboy) when she died.[41] Like a good cowgirl, Frances loved horses and even dreamed about horses. In return she knew, her grandmother told her, "they [horses, or *jiawul*] want me. . . . I can only go to this [mountain] when I die. I can't do anything else when I die. I could be a horse, I could be one of those ladies who shows horses, or a trick rider."[42]

Are devils and saints really so different? Today, *O'odham himdag*, or the O'odham way, encompasses both *sa:nto himdag* and *jiawul himdag*. Bahr might say that both ways are socially sanctioned modes for showing off. Is one disciplined, mature, sensuous, skillful, and yet modest way of walking and working and dwelling and moving through *jeweḍ ka:cim*, "the staying earth," that different from the other? When *sa:nto himdag* and *jiawul himdag* are considered to be two viable, and nonmutually exclusive paths toward maturity, one can begin to see perhaps more similarities than differences between *jejawul* and *sasa:ntos*, or O'odham "devils" and "saints." In this way O'odham are never far from *jejawul* and *sasa:ntos*, who continue to dwell within O'odham landscapes and interact in the daily lives of O'odham.

Perhaps *ban*, or Coyote, can be more usefully juxtaposed with *jejawul* and *sasa:ntos* than either can be juxtaposed with the other. After all, *jejawul* and *sasa:ntos* are powerful beings who act in social and socially sanctioned ways and therefore are models of appropriate behavior. Coyote, or *ban*, on the other hand, is a model of nonsocial behavior— deserving of a few good laughs, yes, but certainly not emulation. The early O'odham linguist Juan Dolores suggested that it is far more complimentary to be called *jiawul* than *ban*.[43] Citing linguist Madeline Mathiot's *A Dictionary of Papago Usage*, ethnobiologist Gary Nabhan noted "a rich array of words to describe not-so-praiseworthy Coyote-like attributes in humans."[44] As ethnobiologist Amadeo Rea explains, Coyote is "the archetype for several eminently human character traits; he is sometimes the braggart, the mischievous, the bumbling; he may be deceitful, a liar, lazy, or lecherous. . . . Inevitably it is Coyote's actions that drive the story to completion."[45] Like Frances Manuel, who says in her autobiography, "I'm not all that good" and "we ourselves are devils," Akimel O'odham autobiographer and storyteller Anna Moore Shaw shows her embarrassment at having taken "pages and pages" to tell her autobiography in the style of a family saga. Shaw—who converted to Presbyterianism, unlike Manuel—writes, "Perhaps the Pimas who read this book will say I am like Ban, the coyote—boastful and over-talkative about myself. No traditional Pima would ever talk long about himself for fear this charge would be thrown up to him."[46]

Anthropologist Ruth Underhill understood this ethical dimension of O'odham Coyote tales. She concluded that Coyote is

> the Papago's only substitute for the Devil. But Coyote is no devil. He is greedy, forgetful, tells fibs, and then tries to excuse himself just like a human. Of course he suffers for it, usually by getting killed. And a grandfather telling the story can make that horribly real, so that his hearers generally decide to mend their ways. Coyote does come to life again, Grandfather admits; but human sinners might not be so lucky. Efficient moral teaching, I decided.[47]

Underhill asserts that O'odham children are regarded by older O'odham as *O'odham*, or persons, in only the narrowest sense with the potential to ripen and become *O'odham* in the fullest sense of being "real people."[48] According to Underhill, a common rebuke for wayward children was "We People do not do that," usually accompanied by the threat that they will be left to live with other lesser persons or nonpersons, such as "the Apache," or *o:b*, which is also a generic term for "enemy" in O'odham.[49] Moreover, Underhill's invocation of an O'odham conception of "sin" is also quite suggestive, particularly since Joseph, Spicer, and Chesky claim that "sin" is understood by Tohono O'odham as antisocial behavior against relatives.[50] In this regard O'odham strive to be and become *O'odham*, or more like *jejawul* and *sasa:ntos* than like Coyote (*ban*), enemies (*o:b*) or other lesser persons or nonpersons.

Tohono O'odham Personhood, Place, and the History of Christianity in the Americas

When the Spaniards and Father Kino first came to the O'odham in the seventeenth century, they planned to "convert" and assimilate O'odham in four stages over a short period of approximately ten years. In the first *misión*, or mission, stage, they would establish churches. In the second stage, Spaniards expected either a *conversión*, meaning a conversion to Christianity, or a *reducción*, a reduction of their land base, or both. In the third stage, the *doctrina*, the O'odham would be given a religious education that would bring them within the fold of Catholic orthodoxy. In the final stage, the *curato*, O'odham would become taxpayers with the same rights as other "citizens." In the case of the O'odham, even centuries later, stages three and four have not yet been accomplished. O'odham in Mexico may have come closest to this fate, but in the United States, only at San Xavier (the only Tohono O'odham land to have been allotted) have the third and fourth stages even been attempted. Anthropologist Bernard Fontana suggests that only the first stage of establishing churches and the second stage of conversion have been accomplished among most Tohono O'odham in what is today the United States.[51]

In religious studies scholar Michael McNally's words, this colonial strategy of conversion and assimilation is "what *missionaries intended*," and emphatically not "what native people *made of* Christianity."[52] Since the Tohono O'odham largely Christianized themselves in the second half of the nineteenth century, building their own churches to house their *sasa:ntos*, if such a conversion did occur, it was not one that Spaniards would have imagined. Instead, like most social programs, the Spanish plan to convert and assimilate Tohono O'odham failed on its own terms because it lacked the support of local communities. When Tohono O'odham community leaders took up the project of Christianizing themselves for their own reasons and in their own ways, the results differed tremendously. As ethnographer and ethnohistorian Thomas Sheridan explains this colonial legacy, "Kino and his colleagues had their own agendas" when they rode into Tohono O'odham territory; however, "their goals fell victim to chance, circumstance, and the agendas of the Pimans themselves."[53]

Sheridan's conclusion likewise follows William King, whose study of Tohono O'odham Catholicism in Tucson, Arizona, found that Tohono O'odham have historically been reluctant "to accept change if they are not themselves [the] masters of its extent and direction."[54]

As O'odham continue to live, move, and dwell within their traditional landscapes, they are actively engaged in shaping their futures in the present as well as remaining vitally connected to the past, just as those who have gone before are said to be participating in the present moment. For example, Simon Lopez explained to me that the candle came with Christianity, and therefore that those who died before the coming of Christianity don't necessarily know what candles are. Simon related two distinct perspectives on candles at the Children's Shrine—a particularly special place near Santa Rosa that has to be remodeled every so many years—where children from long ago are said to have been sacrificed, or sent into the earth, in order to stop a great flood.

SL: When we remodel it . . . they used to tell 'em, "You don't have to burn candles over there, because those children that's there, they don't know, because they're Hohokam. And *long time before*, before Christianity comes in, *they don't know*, the kids don't know *over there*. But [pause] . . . *now* [pause] . . . *they say*, these *older* people, "*You can still do it, because they probably realize by now too*, how we realized how important the Catholicism is, like *saints* and where the saints came from, and the candle burning, and things like that. So, but now *they* still do this: *They* burn candles over there at the Children's Shrine.

In the introduction and throughout this book I have argued that O'odham have embedded, or emplaced, Christianity into their ancestral and conceptual landscapes. Though this claim might appear bold, it hardly seems so when some O'odham themselves claim that even the Hohokam, who have come and gone long before them, now appreciate the significance of Christianity in the present. In short, O'odham have embedded Christianity into the landscape because at least some O'odham claim that those who have gone before—the Hohokam—have embedded Christianity into the landscape. Significantly, these assertions not only lay claim to ancestral lands but also imply O'odham ownership of Christianity, thereby parodying Eurocentric assumptions about the history of Christianity in the Americas.

When Tohono O'odham Christianized themselves and their lands on their own terms and of their own volition, they O'odham-ized Christianity in two related senses: they made Christianity into something that was deeply meaningful and made sense to O'odham, and they established enduring relationships with powerful Christian persons. Tohono O'odham neither "converted" to nor "resisted" the Christianity of Europeans; rather, they embraced the powerful persons of Christianity (even devils!) within an O'odham cosmology. The result is neither a "syncretic" nor a "hybrid" "religion," but a unified—though certainly not monolithic—Christianity that is a "way of life" (*himdag*) that continues to be meaningful to many Tohono O'odham today. Indeed, *O'odham himdag* continues to shape contemporary O'odham as many O'odham continue to learn how "to be a good walker" (*himdag*) from Saint Francis, or as I once heard Felix put it, as he spoke to his walkers assembled around him, "We learn how to be *O'odham* from *San Flansi:sko.*" The annual pilgrimage to Mali:na renews the ancestral relationship between O'odham and Saint Francis, making journeys and places as these journeys and places make mature O'odham, providing a path for O'odham to become "real people."

When I asked Louis Lopez what Felix might have meant when he said, "We learn how to be O'odham from *San Flansi:sko,*" he explained:

LL.: I think one of the other things that as O'odham we've really adopted to [is] trying to understand what Saint Francis was about. But it's through the [oral] teachings of those that have talked about what Saint Francis is about. And if you think about what Saint Francis represents, and what he's the patron saint of, is *animals* and *nature*. And as O'odham that's what we considered ourselves. We are a people of the earth.[55]

As "a people of the earth," O'odham understand Saint Francis talking with animals and other "other-than-human persons," because their own oral traditions tell of a previous era in which O'odham and other entities spoke the same language and could communicate with one another. Even today, O'odham are connected to the earth, not only through stories that tell them that they emerged from it, but also through walking to Magdalena and eating the earth.

LL: The ceremony that we do, the clay ceremony with the babies. That clay represents our connection to the *earth*. And when you make that connection to the earth, everything on the earth is all in that way related to you. You're supposed to respect everything on the earth, you know, the animals, the trees, and everything that grows and survives off of the earth is all in that way related to you.[56]

According to Bahr, "clay eating," or "clay drinking," is a ceremony in which a medicine person gives a cup containing a gruel of white clay, owl feathers, and water to an infant or a girl at her first menstruation. Bahr regards this "swallowing/drinking of something gritty, chalky, and grey" to be an imitation or transformation—in essence, a parody—of the Christian Eucharist, which incidentally has been historically somewhat hard to come by as a result of their largely "priestless" Catholicism (see appendix 1).[57] Bahr also calls this a "Native 'baptism,'" a "girls' puberty sacrament," and a "purification." Although this study on O'odham pilgrimages to Magdalena did not include in-depth discussions of this particular O'odham ritual with O'odham consultants, Bahr contends that his O'odham informants claim both babies and pubescent girls smell badly to deceased O'odham, who remain sentient beings said to be present in the present. In turn, deceased O'odham are often said to take the form of owls, hence the use of owl feathers in this context. According to Bahr, both infants and pubescent girls smell "raw," *do'i*, a scent shared with "fresh bloody meat, menstruating women, and birth; and owls (ghosts) hate it."[58] According to ethnobiologist Amadeo Rea, "*Do'i* may also mean 'raw, unripe, unbaked,'" noting that one of his O'odham informants associated the smell with "blood and nausea."[59] Speaking of the puberty ceremony, Joseph Giff—the Akimel O'odham singer from St. John's Village who previously spoke of O'odham bodies "flowering" (see chapter 1)—said simply, "they say that they 'roast' [*cu:wa'am*] her."[60] Similarly Underhill—cited in chapter 1 speaking of O'odham "ripening"—noted that the O'odham words "*tcuuwa*, to reach puberty, and *tcuuwam*, girl at puberty, come from the same root as *tcuwa*, to bake."[61] On the basis of these statements, one might say that O'odham are not merely born as "persons"—they are born "raw," after all—but are rather "baked" or "roasted." Since O'odham personhood is gradually produced, O'odham are made, rather than born. By extension of this, one might say that O'odham are born "raw" and need to be "cooked" (though not in the sense of Claude Lévi-Strauss's work).[62]

This is true in multiple senses, it seems. For example, Simon Lopez repeatedly told me two different episodes from O'odham oral traditions that articulate how and why O'odham differ from other, putatively human persons, specifically Milga:n, or white people, and S-Cukcu, or black people. I relate both episodes here, mostly in summary form. In the first story I'itoi, Coyote, and Buzzard each try to make people, mostly without success. Each attempts to make people from clay and to "cook," or fire, them like pottery. White people are undercooked, black people are overcooked, or "burned," and O'odham are just right. There is an olfactory dimension to this as well, since most burned things stink, particularly human flesh. Simon Lopez also related another origin story—both fascinating and uncomfortable to hear—about how I'itoi killed the Eagle, which provides an alternate explanation of the origins of different peoples.[63] The Eagle had been catching O'odham for many years, eating only small parts of them and then stacking their corpses high in his cave. After killing the Eagle, I'itoi brought the decaying O'odham corpses back to life. According to Simon, "the ones that were just killed," or at the top of the heap—or even the cream of the crop, so to speak— "came back as O'odham." Midway down the heap were "the *old* ones, the *rotten* ones," who were too white and spoke an incomprehensible language. Then there were "the *real, real rotten ones* . . . just *black* . . . and *smell.*" Simon explained that both white and black people require cologne or lotion in order "to get away with *that smell that they have* . . . *because they're rotten people.*" Unlike these "rotten" people, speaking of O'odham, Simon said, "*we don't have to have any cologne or anything like that.* And we don't smell." Unlike these overpoweringly stinky, overripe bodies that rotted for too long, O'odham, of course, are just right with their unmarked odor—often jokingly referred to in everyday speech as "O'odham perfume" and "O'odham deodorant."

To briefly analyze both stories, we can easily see how typologies end up being thinly veiled hierarchies, producing gradations of personhood. In the first story, as in other constructional cosmologies, production trumps reproduction, and the model for all creative acts is craftsmanship rather than childbearing. Both persons and things are made, whether intentionally or not, but neither born nor created (from nothing, that is), and interspecific bodily differences are perhaps more a matter of degree than kind. As I'itoi produces O'odham, binding together earth and sweat, he produces nascent and vulnerable personhood. At the same time, I'itoi's production of O'odham and others produces alienation and hierarchy.

However, according to Bahr's interpretation of clay eating, O'odham do not always smell great, at least not to deceased and ancestral O'odham. Giff's comments on "roasting" O'odham and Underhill's comments on "baking" O'odham support the interpretation that O'odham need to be "made," and that there is an olfactory dimension to this as well. For example, as previously noted in this chapter, babies in the Lopez family require not one, but three, infancy rites: (1) baptism, (2) going to Magdalena, and (3) clay eating. During one of our discussions, Louis Lopez insisted that his baby grandson needed to go to Magdalena.

LL: I was telling my daughter, you know, "We need to take *the baby* and to have it be a part of this [pilgrimage]." Now that he's doing most of his infancy rites that need to be done. The clay ceremony, he needs to be baptized, and, a big part of our family tradition of carrying this on is going to Mali:na. And I told her, "I want him to be a part of that. I want him to experience that from *here*, from here on."[64]

Since the Lopez family had already done the clay ceremony and baptism ceremony for Louis's grandson, the final remaining infancy rite was to take his grandson to Magdalena in order to greet Saint Francis. In Louis Lopez's explanation of what Felix might have meant when he said, "We learn how to be O'odham from *San Flansi:sko*," Louis went on to say that the connection with the earth, which the clay ceremony substantively establishes through O'odham eating dirt, is what Saint Francis is all about. Looking straight ahead and staring off into the distance, Louis seemed to imagine far back to the very historical moment in which the O'odham were first introduced to Saint Francis, apprehending him as one of them.

LL: And that was what Saint Francis's big thing was about, that you *respect*, you know, not only people, but the animals because they're a part of you. Saint Francis was the patron saint of *animals, all animals*, you know, and that included nature itself. And so, you know, when those teachings were brought to us O'odham, I think that was our big connection to that. That's what we're supposed to be taught as O'odham, that you're a part of nature, you're a part of this earth. And so everything that is a part of this earth is all in that way related. And it was kind of like, "Well, that's who we are as O'odham anyway!"[65]

In highlighting how O'odham senses of their own history diverge from and thereby parody academic models of Tohono O'odham history and the history of Christianity in the Americas, this chapter—and this book—has shown that O'odham strength and perseverance are grounded in patterns of consumption that have made Christianity their own for many O'odham and have mutually produced O'odham places and persons that are connected not only by travel across O'odham homelands and walking to Magdalena but also by eating the earth. O'odham geophagy merges anthropology and geography, personhood and place. Having themselves emerged from the earth, eaten the earth, and moved across the earth, O'odham are profoundly people of the earth who have made Christianity their own by embedding (and ingesting) Christianity within their ancestral landscapes through songs, staffs, and stories.

Like many other Native American and indigenous peoples today, O'odham inhabit multiple ontologies, embodying different histories, and subscribe to multiple historicities. This is not to say that Native Americans and indigenous peoples are "living in two worlds" or "torn between two cultures," as in the tired and clichéd refrains from a bygone era of acculturation studies within anthropology, but rather in the sense of *occupying* multiple different worlds and living, as they move both within and between worlds, not always—or even ever—with ease, but in ways that generate and are generated by the "friction" of encounter in the "consumption" of the other, which necessarily involves the transformation of each by the other.[66]

Summary

In this book I cover much ground in exploring how O'odham produce both personhood and place. The introduction, chapter 1, and appendix 2 outline the data, methods, and theories that I employ in this study, while emphasizing the mutual imbrication of personhood and place and how some O'odham have made Christianity their own by embedding Christianity within their ancestral landscapes. Chapter 2 demonstrates how O'odham songs associated with the journey to Magdalena evoke both a sense of movement to Magdalena and back as well as senses of the past embedded in these places. Chapter 3 shows that staffs used by O'odham walkers on their way to Magdalena evoke memories of previous movements, linking walkers and their sticks, sticks and stories, people and places, the past and the present, and the living and the dead. Staffs, then, make Magdalena palpably present in the everyday lives of many O'odham who cannot help but be transported by their sticks to stories and memories made along the road to Magdalena. Chapter 4 illustrates how O'odham simultaneously produce persons and places by examining O'odham kinesthetics and kinesthetic ideologies as well as juxtapositions of "walking" and "wandering" in O'odham narrative discourse. Shifting from the polemics and politics of movement to the politics and parody of history, chapter 5 returns to the theme of O'odham embedding, or emplacing, Christianity into their ancestral and conceptual landscapes by exploring divergent O'odham senses of the past in the present, what one consultant called an O'odham need "to be grounded," and O'odham methods for connecting O'odham people to O'odham places, which include—but are not exclusively limited to—eating dirt and walking to Magdalena. The conclusion, which follows this chapter, examines Christianity, and therefore Magdalena, in unexpected places.

Conclusion

More than three years had already passed since I completed my fourth-year walking to Magdalena. During my 2015–16 winter break at Hamilton College, when I was released for a few weeks from my teaching responsibilities in the Department of Religious Studies, I took the opportunity to return to the Tohono O'odham Nation for a short season of fieldwork. As I'd often done before, early on in the trip I made a point to visit Himdag Ki:, the Tohono O'odham Nation's Cultural Center & Museum. After catching up and talking shop with both the archivist Jeannette Garcia and the curator of education, Bernard Siquieros, both separately invited me to return to Himdag Ki: on January 6, 2016, to join a large group of undergraduate and graduate students and their professors for a brief meeting at the museum, a trip to the international border at San Miguel Gate, and a "pilgrimage" (or was it a "hike"?) to I'itoi Ki:, a particular cave at the base of a steep cliff high up in the Baboquivari Mountain Range.

With the highest elevation of any geological feature in southern Arizona, the mountain can be easily seen from Himdag Ki: as well as many other parts of the Tohono O'odham Nation and surrounding areas. Himdag Ki: was designed to offer several ideal perspectives of the mountain off in the distance. The unpaved dirt road that runs beside Himdag Ki: goes to a picnic area at the base of the mountain, where a largely unmarked trailhead and a well-maintained trail leads directly to I'itoi Ki:, which is said by many—probably most—Tohono O'odham to be the residing place of I'itoi, who created both the O'odham and the Hohokam before them—said to be both similar to one another yet also different (see especially chapters 1 and 5). Many Tohono O'odham insist that this is not only the very place where I'itoi withdrew from O'odham and into the landscape but also the very place from which I'itoi led O'odham out from their subterranean home in the previous world when Hohokam reigned, in order to kill the Hohokam and drive them off (or into?) the land. As such, I'itoi Ki: is often regarded by both O'odham and non-O'odham as "the most sacred O'odham sacred place."[1] Indeed, descriptions such as these—which (1) take the category of the "sacred" to be unproblematic in describing and translating indigenous ontologies, (2) uncritically employ the discourse of "sacred space" and "sacred places," and (3) reduce the diversity of O'odham geographies to a single, official, version—fill both the academic and popular literature on Tohono O'odham.[2]

I had long been interested in visiting I'itoi Ki:, but I had never gone there myself because I didn't think that it would be appropriate to go there on my own, and I didn't want to have to ask someone to go with me. More importantly, when the Tohono O'odham Nation granted me approval to research O'odham pilgrimages to Magdalena, I sensed that for many O'odham (particularly those who subscribe to academically sanctioned literate historical chronologies), I had been given permission to study O'odham Christian traditions, but not O'odham indigenous (meaning pre-Christian) traditions. Not wanting to seem as though I was merely studying how some O'odham have made Christianity their own in order to deceitfully circumvent the tendency of most tribal governments to determine that studying indigenous religious traditions is both off-limits to outsiders and presumably of little value to tribal governments, I never brought it up. I simply never pursued it. So when I received invitations from both Bernard and Jeannette, I jumped at the opportunity.

Because I had already walked to Magdalena for four years, I took the journey to I'itoi quite seriously, making sure that (1) my name, or at least headcount, was on the official permit issued by the district; (2) I had a purpose—not just to "see what it's like"; (3) I had an offering for I'itoi; and (4) I had "a good heart." Unlike my journeys on foot to Magdalena, in which I was almost always the only Milga:n in the group, I was surrounded by Milga:n and other non-O'odham. In fact, I think there was only one O'odham on the trail with us that day, leading approximately thirty to fifty non-O'odham to I'itoi Ki:. The official caretaker of I'itoi Ki: is employed by Baboquivari District to guide groups of individuals who have secured permits from the district office from the parking and picnic area at the base of the mountain up to I'itoi Ki: and back. Before heading up, Joe Joaquin, a cultural preservation officer for the Tohono O'odham Nation, and Bernard both gave all of us instructions as to how we should comport ourselves in the picnic area, on the trail, and inside I'itoi Ki:. They asked us to honor O'odham protocols in determining for ourselves whether or not we should enter I'itoi Ki:, and even whether we should approach I'itoi Ki:. Traditionally, we were told, women were not permitted to enter. While this restriction has loosened in recent decades, we were instructed that women who are pregnant or menstruating (see chapter 5) should certainly not enter I'itoi Ki:. Furthermore, anyone who would enter I'itoi Ki: should only do so with good thoughts. Photography was unequivocally and strictly forbidden.

Undeterred by these warnings, the group of mostly twenty-somethings rushed up the mountain. Taking a slower pace, I hung back with Jeannette, which gave us time to talk. She told me about a non-O'odham archaeologist, who shall remain unnamed, who regularly offers guided tours to I'itoi Ki:. She wasn't sure whether he secured permits for these tours. She told me about a non-O'odam woman who recently accompanied the archaeologist into I'itoi's cave. I don't remember whether Jeannette said she left an offering, but once the woman had made it inside the cave, she couldn't get back out. She got stuck. Only after a long time and much effort—and maybe an offering—the woman was finally permitted to leave I'itoi's home.

Stories such as these are common. For example, in Gary Nabhan's chapter "On the Trail of I'itoi: A Pilgrimage into the Baboquivari Mountains" in *The Desert Smells Like Rain*, he relates a story told to him by a fictitious composite character whom he names "Mona":

You can't just go in there, you know, you got to leave him any little thing. When you go into the cave you just give whatever you have—a penny, a hair barrette, a cigarette.

There was a Catholic Sister who took some Papago boys up there. She went in with them, but she didn't give anything, thinking that nothing would happen because she was a Sister.

Then the boys who had each left something went back out and she turned around to go too. But it looked all dark and where she came in just kept getting smaller and smaller until she couldn't fit through. Then the boys yelled 'Give something, Sister!' and she finally left her rosary beads so it would open just enough to let her get out of there.[3]

Both "Mona's" story of a Catholic nun and the opening stanza of Ofelia Zepeda's poem "Lost Prayers" position Christianity, or more specifically Catholicism, as out of place inside of I'itoi Ki:.

Passing below the sacred peak,
here prayers signified by rosary beads are futile.
Calling on the Virgin Mary is useless.[4]

In "Mona's" story, a Catholic nun must reluctantly submit to I'itoi's protocols. Implicitly her God and her prayers had no authority there. Zepeda is more explicit. "Here," which she seems to extend to the entire mountain range, "prayers signified by rosary beads are futile" and "calling on the Virgin Mary is useless." Both the rosaries and the Hail Marys in Zepeda's poem are Jujkam ("Mexican"), rather than O'odham. Zepeda is clear: these "lost prayers," said by those undocumented Jujkam migrants who cross into the United States—both with and without success—through the Baboquivari range and O'odham territory, who do not "know the language of the land," are "futile," "useless." Both Nabhan and Zepeda seem to concur that Christianity, more specifically Catholicism, is powerless here: out of place.

When Jeannette and I finally reached I'itoi Ki:, there were still twenty-somethings streaming in and out of the narrow slit through thick rock. I waited a while longer, chatting a bit more, until everyone seemed to have left and no more sounds emanated from the cave. Jeannette decided that she would stay outside, so I went in alone. Crawling in head first, I pulled myself forward, sort of falling inside. The air was thick and hard to breathe. Dust filled the air, stirred up from all of the activity and movement in and out of the cave. As my eyes adjusted to the darkness, I realized that I was not alone. The caretaker remained inside after all of the students had left. He was making an offering of incense, either as a gift, or perhaps to purify the place after the presence of so many non-O'odham in I'itoi's home. I think he was burning *segoi*, but it might have been sage. I didn't ask. And I couldn't smell the air very well, since the air was also filled with dirt that I instinctively didn't want to breathe into my body any more than I had to. But more than that, what I saw with my eyes distracted me from what I might have otherwise smelled with my nose. The walls of the cave were lined with almost equally spaced staffs covered in ribbons, just like the staffs of O'odham walkers on their journeys to Magdalena (see chapter 3)! Searching the walls, I even discovered rosaries, more ribbons, milagros, and even a small saint. Nabhan mentioned "rosary beads" in his published account of being inside I'itoi Ki: during the late 1970s or early 1980s, but I never imagined that I would find staffs, ribbons, and saints in I'itoi Ki:! And these offerings seemed to me to have been left by O'odham, rather than non-O'odham. Were these all "lost prayers," too? Standing inside I'itoi's cave high up and inside of the mountain, I almost felt as though I were standing in the sanctuary of an O'odham chapel or even a dark gothic cathedral. How could I be standing in a place where "prayers signified by rosary beads are futile," and yet find myself surrounded with so many of the trappings of Christianity and Magdalena? I thought of Philip Deloria's provocative secret history of American Indians in modernity, *Indians in Unexpected Places*. Here I, a non-Indian, had stumbled across Christianity, and therefore Magdalena, in the most unexpected of indigenous places!

Eager to know his opinion, I asked the caretaker if he ever tries to clear I'itoi Ki: of Catholic paraphernalia. With frustration on his face and exasperation in his voice, the caretaker explained that he frequently asks O'odham to refrain from doing their rosaries (see chapter 2) while they are inside. Keeping Catholicism out of I'itoi Ki: seemed like a difficult job that had taken its toll on him. I speculated that the job of purifying indigenous

O'odham traditions of any Catholic influence was probably impossible. "Was it always this way?," I thought to myself, knowing that the answer to that question would depend on both whom I asked and the sense of history to which they subscribed (see chapter 5). I mentioned to the caretaker my astonishment that the staffs in the cave looked almost exactly like the staffs used by O'odham walkers. He didn't seem very interested. Perhaps he was already a bit annoyed by the discussion of Catholicism inside of I'itoi Ki:, where Christianity was firmly embedded or emplaced inside of a mountain of all places in what might be, at least for most Tohono O'odham, the most important place within their indigenous ancestral landscape.

May 2, 2017. Almost a year and a half later. I had been invited by Ken Madsen—a non-Indian border geographer at the Ohio State University, who returned to teach at Tohono O'odham Community College during his sabbatical leave, and who also walked to Magdalena several years before I did—and Ron Geronimo, an O'odham linguist and director of Tohono O'odham studies at Tohono O'odham Community College, to speak at the "Himdag Ki: Author Series," organized by Jeannette Garcia. I was excited to present some of the findings of my research to a predominantly O'odham audience. The event drew a moderately large audience of approximately fifty people. Most were O'odham. The official caretaker of I'itoi Ki: was also in attendance. When I came to the section of my presentation on O'odham staffs (see chapter 3), he seemed startled, almost jumping out of his seat. He asked the first question and was very eager to talk about the staffs that so clearly resembled those he had grown accustomed to seeing inside I'itoi Ki:. He may have known, as Simon Lopez had already taught me, that the sticks in I'itoi Ki: were not, in fact, pilgrims' staffs, but they did bear a striking resemblance. Indeed, they looked exactly alike, even though the understanding and uses of the staffs and ribbons—which I do not explain here—were different. Recall Louis "Tony" Lopez's (2014) statement (from chapter 3): "Truly, the ribbons itself automatically kind of reminds you of Mali:na. That's about the only place that we get the ribbons, from Mali:na. So, when you see other people wearing it, it's kind of like, 'You know, they must go to Mali:na.'" For me, seeing the staffs in I'itoi Ki: instantly evoked and invoked the presence of Magdalena. For the caretaker, I suspect that he suddenly realized that he had been fooled. Was he a victim of what Michel de Certeau had called *la perruque* (see the introduction)? In making Christianity their own, everyday O'odham *bricoleurs* (à la Lévi-Strauss) had really slipped one past the goalie.[5]

However, while the caretaker and I were both surprised, I suspect that few of my O'odham consultants would be surprised by any of this. Perhaps I should not have been surprised either. Clearly I was more right than I ever knew that O'odham have embedded, or emplaced, Christianity into their ancestral and conceptual landscape. And perhaps I had been listening too much to those O'odham—particularly in their efforts to decolonize and revitalize their own exclusively indigenous (i.e., non-Christian) traditions—who insist that there is, or even can be, a clear separation between indigenous and Catholic traditions. After all, in O'odham oral traditions, Christianity never came. Instead, Christianity was always already there. Many O'odham have so thoroughly embedded Christianity—particularly Catholicism—into their landscape and practices that they have almost become invisible for many O'odham. Indeed, as stated in the introduction, for many O'odham, Christianity is simply the way of their grandmothers and grandfathers. And this is precisely why some O'odham, particularly younger ones, have turned away from Catholicism. Given the tremendous influence of the Spanish, and later Mexicans, on O'odham and other indigenous peoples of the southwestern United States, perhaps it is not surprising that Catholicism, or better yet in Michael McNally's words, "what Native people *made of* Christianity," would become something of a new "religious establishment," making Catholicism an unmarked tradition among an indigenous people.[6] Drawing upon anthropologist Matthew Engelke's notion of "ambient faith," American studies and religious studies scholar Hillary Kaell proposes "ambient religion" to describe those religious practices and objects, like O'odham staffs in I'itoi Ki:, that are capable of "filter[ing] in and out of sensory and conscious space."[7] In her discussion of "ambient Catholicism" in Quebec, Kaell argues that wayside crosses "mark Quebec's human and physical landscape as always already Catholic," just like O'odham staffs, home altars, roadside memorials, village cemeteries, and Catholic churches in every O'odham village embed and emplace Christianity in

O'odham landscapes (and landscapes of movement), so that Christianity is always already there, almost everywhere in general, were it not for the fact that O'odham have embedded Christianity into certain (sometimes unexpected) places in particular.[8]

If I have learned anything from this study over the past decade, which I suspect many other scholars have already learned elsewhere, it is to always expect the unexpected from Native American and indigenous peoples, whose lives are simply too complex to be constrained by the expectations—what are these other than unchecked stereotypes and ideologies?—of Natives and non-Natives alike. Dynamic, living traditions, like O'odham pilgrimages to Magdalena, defy the nostalgic, primitivist, romantic, commodified, and folklorized expectations imposed upon O'odham, Native American, and indigenous traditions by both themselves and others.[9]

"This walk doesn't come with an owner's manual," I recall Verlon "Carlos" Jose saying to a large group of walkers in Pozo Verde in 2009. In my own experience of walking to Magdalena, I can affirm that this statement is true. In turn, *Walking to Magdalena* is not an owner's manual. Nor is it a travel guide. In the time that I spent with Felix before his passing, I saw that Felix was always deliberately innovating and trying new things. These innovations, however small, sometimes exasperated his O'odham assistants and kept me, as a young ethnographer, on my toes. But if pilgrimages and Christianity don't come with owner's manuals, neither does colonialism.[10] What O'odham, Native American, and indigenous peoples have *made of* all of the varied legacies of colonialism, including not only Christianity but also cowboy culture, country music, capitalism, patriotism, boarding schools, the English language, Western biomedicine, and so forth, is always changing, since these are all unfinished projects without preordained trajectories.[11] There is no room here for foregone conclusions. Too often scholars and practitioners alike, whether Native or not, think of culture change and religious acculturation as a "loss." I am hardly the first to point this out.[12] If I have accomplished nothing else in this study, I hope to have shown, at least for some O'odham, how it can also be a "gain."

Fig. 5. "Caution Walkers" sign. Photo by the author.

O'odham Religious History and the Magdalena Pilgrimage

As is the case in historical accounts of most other indigenous peoples in the southwestern United States, historians usually break up O'odham history into four eras: prehistory, Spanish, Mexican, and American. The first era precedes the colonization of the region by people of European descent. This period is usually designated as "prehistory." O'odham themselves have oral sources and material objects that they say date to these earlier times, but in spite of O'odham interest in these sources as legitimate forms of knowledge that provide direct access into their past, most academics are content to call this O'odham knowledge of their own history "myth."[1] Limited to historical sources written in European languages, most professional historians and anthropologists writing O'odham history simply skip over this era and jump into the beginning of the Spanish presence in the region.[2]

For the O'odham, the Spanish period (1687–1821) began when Father Kino began his journeys through their lands in 1687. Father Eusebio Francisco Kino, sometimes called "The Apostle to the Pimas," was a Tyrolese (in what is now Italy) Jesuit trained in Bavaria (in what is now Germany).[3] Only seven years after the Pueblo Revolt of 1680, which marked the failure of Franciscan missions among the Pueblos in what today are the states of New Mexico and Arizona, Kino introduced Christianity to the O'odham, as well as wheat and other grains, horses, cattle, livestock, goods, microbes, narratives, songs, and practices.[4] Following the lead of historian Herbert Bolton, who famously cast Kino as the "padre on horseback," the Franciscan historian Kieran R. McCarty called Kino "the cowboy missionary, a horseman par excellence."[5] From a historian's perspective, then, Kino is ultimately, if not proximally, responsible for the ongoing importance of Christianity, cowboy culture, and horsemanship, as well as the predominance of the wheat-flour tortilla over the traditional central Mexican corn tortilla among contemporary O'odham. Kino founded missions in the permanent villages among the "two villagers," whom most contemporary ethnologists call the Tohono O'odham, whether in what is today Mexico, where all of Kino's missions were founded, or in the United States, where he traveled but never founded any missions. The only exception to Kino's pattern of planting missions at the permanent winter villages of O'odham, instead of their temporary summer, or field, villages, is at Caborca, where the mission stands too close to the Río Concepcíon, which continually erodes the church's foundation. Crucially, however, Kino never established any missions north of what is today the United States–Mexico international border or, therefore, in what is now the Tohono O'odham Nation.

However, the mere fact that most O'odham today are Christians cannot be attributed to the success of Kino's missions. In fact, Kino's missions experienced many significant conflicts, both before and after his death in 1711. For example, the first O'odham revolt took place in 1695, only eight years after Father Kino's arrival. On March 29, 1695, O'odham in Tubutama rose up, killing eight at the mission, including the Jesuit priests and their Opata Indian servants, and burning all the buildings in Tubutama, Caborca, Imuris, San Ignacio, and Magdalena. Only built four years earlier in 1691, the mission church at Tubutama was likely destroyed during the revolt of 1695.[6] In retribution for their actions, forty-eight O'odham were slaughtered by the Spanish military.[7]

In 1711 Kino dedicated the church known today as the Church of Santa María Magdalena—or more simply as Magdalena de Kino—to Saint Francis Xavier, who was his patron saint and namesake, the patron saint of missionaries, and also the patron saint of his Jesuit order.[8] Dying shortly after the dedication, Padre Kino was buried at the church in Magdalena, where his bones were uncovered by archaeologists in 1966 and where they remain on public display to this day.[9]

After Kino's death his missions continued to struggle with occasional uprisings. In 1751 the second O'odham revolt took place at the village of Sáric, only a few miles north of Tubutama, the place where the first revolt began fifty-six years earlier. Luís Oacpicagigua started the revolt by killing eighteen Spaniards whom he had invited to his house. From there the revolt spread to Sonoyta and Caborca, and Jesuit priests were killed in each town. In all, Luís and his allies killed over one hundred O'odham and non-O'odham agents of the Jesuit missions, and most mission stations were temporarily abandoned. Spaniards mostly ignored the westernmost O'odham, where, for example, the mission at Sonoyta was never again rebuilt after its destruction in 1751.

Uprisings continued at missions throughout the eighteenth century. In 1776 the O'odham revolted again. The Franciscan missionary Father Pedro Font dramatically described an O'odham, Apache, and Seri attack on the mission and village of Magdalena in November 1776. In his account of the attack on the mission Font noted, among other things, that the Indians took "a lovely image of San Francisco Xavier," threw it down on the ground, and broke its arm.[10]

Following the expulsion of the Jesuits from all of New Spain by edict of the Spanish king Charles III in 1767, and the subsequent takeover by Franciscans, the date of the Magdalena fiesta in honor of Saint Francis likely changed from Saint Francis Xavier's feast day on the third day of December to Saint Francis of Assisi's feast day on the fourth day of October.[11] However, San Xavier del Bac continues to celebrate on St. Francis Xavier's feast day.

Kino visited the O'odham village of Wa:k, transformed into Spanish as Bac, in 1692. Kino began to build a church there in 1700, but it never got beyond the foundations; the present mission, which attracts thousands of tourists each year, was not completed until more than a century later. Many in San Xavier, like Mary Narcho, maintain—or at least tell the story—that their mission, and not the one at Magdalena, was supposed to have the statue of Saint Francis. As Mary Narcho, who for many years served on the Saint Francis feast committee at San Xavier, explained, the pilgrimage to Magdalena is not the result of Father Kino's intention, but Saint Francis's agency:

MN: Father Kino told the O'odham people when he started building this mission here [in San Xavier de Bac] that he was going to go to Mexico and bring them a full-sized saint of their patron saint. He would bring it to them, back to them. . . . He got as far as Magdalena, where he died. That's where he's buried. He never made it here, so that's why people make that pilgrimage to Magdalena because that's as far as Father Kino got. And that's where that statue that he was bringing laid, and I guess that's why people started going there.[12]

Moreover, in spite of Saint Francis undermining Kino's intention by lying down in Magdalena instead of San Xavier, Mary Narcho, who has also cared for Saint Francis extensively by washing his body and changing his clothes and so on, suggested that *Saint Francis himself*, who is usually lying down, later got up and *walked* from Magdalena to San Xavier:

MN: I don't know if it's true or not that this [Saint Francis at San Xavier] is the real one that they have here, because he has no legs anymore. They just made him artificial legs and he's very old and falling apart and we tied him together all over the place. But he's just really just half of a statue and we just tie him up. He's got artificial legs and feet and everything. I don't know if it's true that this is the real one, but they say that they've got a new one over there [in Magdalena].[13]

Stories such as these are common throughout the region as well as throughout Christendom in general.

In the Mexican period (1821–48) O'odham may not have ever known that Mexico had gained its independence from Spain. Although this period saw increased secularization throughout Mexico, the Franciscans were largely able to avoid attempts at secularization on the northwestern periphery of Mexico. Nonetheless the Franciscans ultimately relinquished their hold on churches in O'odham territories.

The beginning of the American period (1848 to the present), like the Mexican period before it, did not lead to any changes that were immediately noticeable in the everyday lives of most O'odham. In 1854 the

Gadsden Purchase officially split Tohono O'odham lands in half; however, most Tohono O'odham continued to live as though the boundary did not exist for many years. With the Gadsden Purchase having largely passed without notice, many O'odham were not aware of no longer being "Mexicans" and having officially become "Americans."[14] A linguistic artifact of this history is that the O'odham word *Milga:n*, which is used exclusively to refer to Anglos—and not O'odham, except in a derogatory sense, despite their status as citizens of the United States—is derived from the Spanish *Americano*, transformed into O'odham by syllable reduction, with a flap [ɾ] (spelled with <l>) replacing the trill [r]. The United States did not officially extend federal Indian policy to O'odham territory until 1857, when the first Indian agent was sent to their lands. Franciscans soon followed, when in 1859 the Catholic Church at Santa Fe sent a French priest to visit San Xavier del Bac to renew ties between O'odham and the Catholic Church in the United States.

In 1871, the same year that the Gila River was dammed and the Akimel O'odham lost the water upon which their way of life depended, the German Presbyterian missionary Charles H. Cook arrived among the Akimel O'odham on the northern reaches of O'odham territory. Anna Moore Shaw, an Akimel O'odham woman born on the Gila River Reservation in 1898 and the first American Indian woman in Arizona to graduate from high school, recounts how Presbyterianism came to her people in her autobiography and family history:

> In 1870 a kind and gentle man named Charles H. Cook arrived to live among the Pimas. This *mil-gahn* [*milga:n*] (white man) was different from anyone the River People had ever known. He told them of the Gospel message, but he was different from the Spanish missionary priests of long ago. He called himself a Presbyterian.[15]

Although it was twelve years before Cook converted any Akimel O'odham, when he finally did, "Chief" Antonio Azul was among them. After the first Akimel O'odham were baptized by Cook, according to Shaw, Presbyterianism "spread like wildfire."[16] As a result of these efforts, anthropologist Paul Ezell reports, "Pima religious culture took on a strong flavor of Presbyterian Christianity."[17] Alfretta Antone, a devout Catholic who served as the former vice president of the Pima-Maricopa Tribe for twelve years, and who addressed Pope John Paul II during the 1987 Tekakwitha Conference in Phoenix, explained contemporary Akimel O'odham in 1995 like this:

> I think, for whatever reason, this tribe has really lost a lot of its culture. I really can't say why. One time, I was talking with this woman, who is a Presbyterian, and we were talking about some of the culture. She said she didn't know any kind of cultural activities because when her parents were young, they were forbidden by the minister to have anything to do with something like that. As a result, a lot of them obeyed whatever they were told.[18]

Systematic Protestant missions to the Tohono O'odham started in 1910, when a Presbyterian missionary began to make regular trips to the reservation. Presbyterians soon established a church and school at Indian Oasis, now called Sells. By 1914 Presbyterians built a church and school at San Miguel, and by 1920 churches were built in Vamori and Topawa. In their 1949 study Alice Joseph, Rosamond Spicer, and Jane Chesky reported that the southern and eastern districts of what is today called the Tohono O'odham Nation had the most significant Presbyterian influence.[19] They also reported that "there were no Presbyterians west of Gu Achi [Santa Rosa], and no missionary work had been attempted in the western districts."[20] These Presbyterian churches are significant in part because they are largely O'odham missions to O'odham with flourishing translations of the Bible, hymns, prayers, and so forth. When I spoke to the longtime missionary-linguist Dean Saxton at the 2012 San Juan feast in Santa Rosa, he assured me that these translators were "the real O'odham theologians." O'odham Presbyterians also organize an annual camp meeting in Sells, which Simon Lopez suggested is their equivalent of the Magdalena fiesta for O'odham Catholics.

Indeed, as the growth of Presbyterianism among the O'odham has already begun to show, there were many religious influences among the Tohono O'odham beginning in the late nineteenth and early twentieth centuries. In 1891 two Mormons—or *mo:mli*, the O'odham word for Mormons—were reported to be residing at Gunsight, on the westernmost reaches of the Tohono O'odham Nation. By 1900 Mormons were reported in Topawa as well. Then, in 1906, the "Prophet Dowie," a Protestant evangelist preaching in Phoenix, sent an African American preacher and faith healer to the southeastern Tohono O'odham villages. For a while the Tohono O'odham in Topawa and neighboring villages, as well as Tuscon, were influenced. One group of families from San Miguel allegedly began to prepare themselves for the end of the world, taking their families and cattle to the Comobabi Mountains where they awaited the end, disbanding a few months later and returning to San Miguel.[21]

Catholic missionary work was renewed among the O'odham in 1908, though visits were seldom made to the westernmost districts of what became the Tohono O'odham Nation. In 1912 Father Bonaventure Oblasser began living among the Tohono O'odham, in part to limit the influence of Presbyterianism among them. These being the first American priests that the O'odham had ever seen, and perhaps even the first Franciscans, various scholars have noted that many O'odham did not recognize these Catholic priests as such.[22] When I asked Simon Lopez if his parents or grandparents talked about what these early years were like when the Franciscans started coming, he explained that his great-great-grandmother "used to *hate* these Franciscan Fathers" and that they would all hide when they saw Franciscans coming in a Model T Ford.

SL: And they would *hate* them, *seeing them*, because *they haven't known*, exactly know, what they're here for. And the only thing they know is Saint Francis, you know, what they went through with the pilgrimage to Magdalena. And so they *thought* that [is] what Saint Francis is *about*, you know, in Magdalena, where they're taught. They *think* that it's different from Franciscan fathers, and things like that.[23]

And yet while Simon added that he now thinks that the Franciscans and Saint Francis are the same, it is understandable that previous generations may have felt differently. Indeed, many American Franciscans did not recognize either the Tohono O'odham or the Magdalena fiesta as shining examples of Catholic orthodoxy.

Both before and after the Franciscans came to the Tohono O'odham, there flourished among them a largely self-directed, priest-less Catholicism often referred to in English as "Sonoran Catholicism." From the perspective of some Franciscans, the problem between Franciscans and Tohono O'odham is not that Tohono O'odham are not Christian, but rather that they are the wrong kind of Christian. Tohono O'odham were largely neglected by both Jesuits and Franciscans between the time of Padre Kino and the early twentieth century when two Franciscan fathers, Tiburtius Wand and Bonaventure Oblasser, came to convert the Tohono O'odham.[24] But before these missionaries came to the Tohono O'odham, the saint way, or *sa:nto himdag*, had already been incorporated into *O'odham himdag*, or the way of the People. Henry Dobyns, an anthropologist and ethnohistorian, also contends that the Yaquis, or Yoeme, who had already indigenized Catholicism for themselves, were principal purveyors of "folk Catholicism" to other indigenous populations of Sonora, including the Tohono O'odham.[25] David Lopez, who was a Tohono O'odham farmer, cowboy, ritual practitioner, and well-known collaborator with three generations of anthropologists from Ruth Underhill to Donald Bahr and David Kozak, corroborates the Yoeme sources of contemporary Tohono O'odham Catholicism, or *sa:nto himdag*, with his own family history:

> I want to tell you how I have a little Yaqui blood in myself. This story also tells how we, the Papago people, got *sa:nto himdag*, our saint religion. . . .
>
> Well, and they say that my late great-grandma, my grandpa's mom, is the one that brought the rosary praying to the Papago, it was what she learned how to do from the Yaqui when she lived with the Yaquis. They built a little church over there at Covered Wells and put *sasantos* [saints] in there, and they prayed and had ceremonials like San Juan because my late grandpa Lopez was named Juan. . . . So this is why I have a little Yaqui blood in me, I'm part Yaqui. And this is where our saint religion comes from.[26]

Like David Lopez's great-grandmother, who imported the material culture of Sonoran Catholicism when she came to Covered Wells from farther south in Mexico, much of the practices that encompass *sa:nto himdag* amount to bringing Magdalena—with its saints, candles, ribbons, holy water, songs, and prayers—to Tohono O'odham villages (see chapter

3). While Magdalena might have Mass, hymns and prayers in Latin, confession, baptism, marriage ceremonies, and last rites, the "Sonoran" style chapels throughout Tohono O'odham territory had none of these things, or rather, none of these to be administered by priests. Instead children were baptized by godparents, and people buried their own dead. Songs and prayers were mostly in Spanish. Though today prayers and hymns may also be in O'odham or English, some older women in Tohono O'odham villages still sing the Spanish hymns. As Henry Dobyns explains, "Older women who made the tiring pilgrimage to Magdalena for the festival of St. Francis on October 4 carefully memorized the Spanish words and music for the rosary, so they could sing and chant for their own people at home."[27] However, as religious studies scholar Pretina Stabolepszy has noted, most O'odham singing these Spanish songs do not understand the words that they are singing.[28] Adelaide Bahr's unpublished study on these Spanish hymns contributes additional evidence in support of this contention.[29] As Bahr found in her study, different villages sing different versions of these songs with different words in each. However, rather than the Spanish words being phonemically transformed into a more O'odham-friendly phonemic system, most of the words have been transformed into what O'odham imagine *sounds* Spanish, even when these sounds no longer constitute recognizably Spanish words. In short, these hymns preserve what linguist Jane Hill might call "mock Spanish."[30] But this O'odham "mock Spanish" is not meant to insult the saints, who are the primary audience for these songs; rather, the songs are made to *sound* Spanish because O'odham know that their saints—though not necessarily the O'odham themselves attending the saints' fiestas—like to hear these songs in Spanish.

Not in spite of, but rather because of, developments such as these making Tohono O'odham relatively self-sufficient Catholics who could minister to themselves so long as they could continue making journeys to Magdalena, when the Franciscan missionaries came to the Tohono O'odham in the early twentieth century, tensions erupted among both Franciscans and O'odham, with each party convinced that they were the "real Catholics."[31] Surely we should not dismiss O'odham claims regarding the authenticity of their Christianity: one need not be a Franciscan in order to be a Catholic. In the 1940s, according to Alice Joseph, a medical doctor, and anthropologists Rosamond B. Spicer and Jane Chesky, the westernmost Tohono O'odham were the most thoroughly "Sonora Catholic" and anti-Franciscan.[32] Among these peoples living in the most arid O'odham territory, there had never been a strong missionary presence.

Between the 1920s and the 1940s some Franciscans actively worked to suppress O'odham pilgrimages to Magdalena. During this period some Franciscans discouraged the annual pilgrimage to Magdalena as part of their larger attempt to remake these "Sonora Catholics" into good Roman Catholics who go to Mass, are married in the church, know some Latin songs and prayers, and have their children baptized by priests instead of godparents. According to Peter Blaine, who was the second chairman of the Papago Tribal Council,

> Father Bonaventure tried to stop us from going to Magdalena one time. He told us he didn't like the drinking that went on down there. That very same time that he told us not to go, when we got there, I'll be darned if he wasn't already there. He said Mass while he was there. It was at that time that he started a St Francis Day in December at San Xavier. That was to keep the people from going to Magdalena. It might have kept a few from going, but many still went.[33]

No O'odham with whom I spoke during the course of this project had any memory of ever having heard anything about Franciscans opposing the Magdalena pilgrimage. The very idea of Franciscans opposing O'odham journeys to Magdalena was inconceivable. Griffith relates an oral tradition among Franciscan friars at San Xavier del Bac, in which Father Tiburtius Wand converted a damaged statue of Christ into the present San Francis Xavier at Wa:k, in order to motivate O'odham to stay at home instead of taking up to one month every year to travel to Magdalena and back and, in his view, do little more than get drunk and lose money.[34] If this Franciscan tradition is true, then this Saint Francis at San Xavier del Bac is the same Saint Francis that Mary Narcho posited as the "real" Saint Francis earlier, with its legs worn off, according to the story, by walking from Magdalena to Wa:k. However, according to Griffith, the statue seen in Magdalena today is a replacement from the 1940s, after the original Saint Francis was burned in the furnaces of the Cervecería Sonora, the Sonora Brewery, on orders of the anticlerical Sonoran state government in 1934. But O'odham tell other stories than this one. For example, Joe Joaquin, a cultural preservation officer for the Tohono O'odham Nation, insists on a different story:

> JJ: During the persecution in Mexico, they [O'odham] were trying to bring the saint across. But they couldn't do it, so they put him in a cave up there somewhere. So years later, somebody found him, brought it down to where it is today [in Magdalena]. But it was really the O'odham's, *O'odham's saint*, or *belonged to the O'odham*. And since it couldn't come across, that's why they started going over *there* [to Magdalena], to pay tribute to the saint. So it's still going on today.[35]

A few Franciscans in the United States and anticlerical revolutionaries in Mexico were not the only forces that opposed O'odham journeys to Magdalena at this time. During the dourine and hoof-and-mouth disease quarantines of the 1930s, taking place at the same time as the Bureau of Indian Affair's stock-reduction program, ethnobiologist Gary Paul Nabhan noted:

> Fearing that the intermixing of livestock from both sides of the border would further endanger the American cattle industry, U.S. officials for-bade the Arizona O'odham from riding down to the ocean on their salt pilgrimage, to Magdalena on the pilgrimage for their Saint Francis, or to Stoa Doag [S-tohă Do'ag] to gather cactus fruit for summer ceremonies. Then they rounded up five hundred horses and cows, shooting, burning, and burying them near the village of Komelik. Several hundred more were massacred on the other side at Pozo Verde.[36]

Although the O'odham were granted "religious freedom" in 1933, marking the end of the persecution of O'odham summer rain ceremonies, in 1943 a severe drought struck the O'odham.[37] Some O'odham medicine men attributed the drought to the killing of horses in the dourine epidemic. For those inclined toward this interpretation, the official prohibition of the annual salt pilgrim-age and Magdalena pilgrimage, due to the dourine and hoof-and-mouth disease epidemics, brought about a general decrease in rainfall.[38]

Capital penetration and the cash economy also interfered with O'odham journeys to Magdalena. Many O'odham worked in cotton fields through much of the twentieth century.[39] Cotton growers normally enjoyed employing O'odham as cotton pickers, but every year around the end of September and the beginning of October, these O'odham cotton workers frequently abandoned the cotton fields in order to travel to Magdalena. Clearly, for many O'odham, the pilgrimage to Magdalena took priority over personal financial gain as well as national patriotism. "Faced with Papago intransigence," Dobyns writes, "most growers quickly decided to haul their Indian pilgrims to Magdalena in trucks rather than let them spend time making the trek in slow horse-drawn wagons. Thus began a shift from wagon trails to highways, from wagons to trucks, pickups and buses for pilgrimage."[40]

Indeed, contemporary O'odham continue to encounter obstacles and resistance against traveling to Magdalena. In particular, as the border zone has become increasingly militarized in the wake of 9/11, the U.S. Border Patrol, federales, and cartels regularly obstruct O'odham movement to and from Magdalena. Nonetheless many O'odham, particularly elders, insist on going to Magdalena even, from a biomedical perspective, at great risk to their health. For example, the Archie Hendricks Sr. Skilled Nursing Facility just south of Santa Rosa works to facilitate and expedite, rather than discourage, the Magdalena pilgrimage based on the concern that if the facility's staff prohibits elders from going, they may go on their own against medical advice. Instead the staff works with the elder's family in order to make the trip as safe and swift as possible.[41]

In recent years, O'odham pilgrimages to and from Magdalena have only become more difficult. Prior to Donald Trump's election as the president of the United States, one of his central campaign promises was to build a wall at the international border, and furthermore that he would force Mexico to pay for it. Then Mexican president Enrique Peña Nieto had a different idea. Verlon "Carlos" Jose, the vice-chairman of the Tohono O'odham Nation, stated that only "over my dead body" would Trump's wall be built. The statement made local, state, national, and international headlines, but Jose soon had to walk his words back, stating that he spoke those words—which he still stands by—as a private citizen, and not as a public official.

In March 2016 these national and international pressures took a decidedly local turn, when the new owners of the land just south of the San Miguel Gate in Sonora erected their own fence and posted signs in English and Spanish stating that this was "PRIVATE PROPERTY" in Mexico. The sign went on to state that neither "The Border Patrol, the Tohono O'odham Nation, nor any other agency of the United States Government has any jurisdiction over this land," and furthermore that all trespassers and their allies would be prosecuted to the fullest extent of the law. While the identity or identities of the new owner(s) remains unclear, the land in question is historically the traditional cultural property of the Tohono O'odham Nation. Some O'odham speculated that the new owners were blocking the San Miguel Gate in an attempt to pressure the Tohono O'odham Nation into buying the land and to turn a considerable profit after the nation opened a new casino in Glendale, Arizona. Other property owners had been so lucky. In 2003 the Tohono O'odham Nation paid a considerable sum to purchase a one square mile section of land near Why, Arizona, to establish a home base for Hia Ced O'odham and their descendants, whose traditional territory in the United States is now occupied by federal lands such as the Organ Pipe Cactus National Monument, the Cabeza Prieta National Wildlife Refuge, and the Barry M. Goldwater Air Force Range. Other O'odham suspected what they had known for a long time, that following Felix Antone's death, Mexican ranchers wanted to further cut off the O'odham village of Pozo Verde from the Tohono O'odham Nation in order to gain access to the site's water as a scarce resource. Regardless of motive, the new "wall" on the Mexican side has made O'odham pilgrimages to Magdalena increasingly difficult. Unable to cross the border at the San Miguel Gate, when I accompanied O'odham walkers in October 2016, we had to cross the border at Sasabe, which added several hours to our trip by automobile from Sells to Pozo Verde, before heading onto Tubutama and walking to Magdalena. In short, walking to Magdalena is anything but convenient, and increasingly so today, but this is nothing new to O'odham, who never walked to Magdalena because it was convenient.

APPENDIX 2

O'odham Speech Genres

As a framework for interpreting the songs and stories that I have recorded, I rely heavily on linguistic anthropologist Donald Bahr's analyses of O'odham speech genres in order to provide a brief narrative map outlining the scope of O'odham speech that constitutes the bulk of the primary data used in this study. By sketching a narrative map of O'odham speech genres, my intention is to indicate the special nature of the primary data for this book.[1] In particular I am fortunate that the Lopez family of Santa Rosa was willing to share their six songs that document a journey from their village to Magdalena and back. These six songs are the only songs that I analyze in this study (see chapter 2). When I asked my O'odham consultants questions about their lives and experiences, the genre in which most of them answered, most of the time, was what I call "narrative" (*ha'icu a:gidadag*). However, the O'odham with whom I spent the most time regularly and effortlessly switched to other modes as well, particularly "preaching" (*amog*) and telling me about episodes from *Ho'ok A:gida,* which I occasionally include as "narrative" or "stories."

O'odham "speech" (*ñiok*) is divided into at least five major forms: "ordinary speech" (*ñiok*), "preaching" (*amog*), "storytelling" (*a:ag*), "oration" (*ñiokculida*), and "singing" or "song" (*ñe'i*). "Storytelling" is further classified into two subgenres: "narrative" (*ha'icu a:gidadag*) and "epic legends" or "myth" (*Ho'ok A:gida*). This study excludes two genres discussed by Bahr: "speak" or "emit sounds" (*cei*), purposeless speech that accomplishes nothing, like that of Mockingbirds (*ṣu:g*), and "prayer" (*ṣoak*), which Bahr translates as "cry," "call," and "kinship cry."[2] I suspect that Bahr would not mind these exclusions, since he likes to think about O'odham critiques of the Mockingbird as "a criticism by them that extends to all of the world's ritualized speech [such as "prayer"] and canned sentiments. . . . or of what we call in English 'parroting.' "[3] Furthermore, these genres are excluded because they were neither volunteered by my O'odham consultants, nor did I ever elicit them.

In contrast to feckless and audience-less speech (*cei*), *ñiok* is ordinary speech or everyday discourse, so that *O'odham ñiok* means something like the "speech" or "language of the people." "Preaching" (*amog*) is a particular genre that "tells people directly how they should think or behave."[4] Bahr notes that this genre "thrives at fiestas, political meetings, funerals, and in all kinds of churches." In her life history Frances Manuel, a well-known Tohono O'odham basket weaver, singer, and elder, recalled with disdain in her mature old age, "Oh, I hated to be preached!," suggesting that this mode of speech is inherently condescending, as in when a grandparent directly rebukes a grandchild.[5] Viewed positively, at wakes I've regularly heard the children and grandchildren of the deceased express gratitude for "getting preached," perhaps as a public sign of having been "raised right."

Prose storytelling (*a:ag*)—or more simply "telling," according to Bahr—is "directed solely towards the people present in the room where the story is told; it is pure storytelling, for human ears alone."[6] Bahr further subdivides the category of "telling" (*a:ag*) to include (1) the long creation epic called *Ho'ok A:gida*, or "Witch's Telling," and (2) "legends" that contain "fragments of stories attributed to ancient times but lacking a defined place in the unfolding epic of creation; a stock of lore, more or less story-like, about animals, plants, etc.; and stories concerning the recent past as distinct from ancient times."[7] I refer to Bahr's "epic" as "myth," although unlike Bahr I do so without implying that it is fiction. Frances Manuel calls this "legend."[8] In contrast to this genre that contains the *Ho'ok A:gida*, or "Witch's Telling," whatever we may call the genre in English, *ha'icu a:gidadag*, literally "something told," is what I call "narrative" or "story," usually told in the first person. This is Bahr's "legend," but I call this a first-person historical narrative. Frances Manuel calls these "little stories."[9] Like all of the other O'odham speech genres, *ha'icu a:gidadag* is admittedly fuzzy. This fuzziness is particularly illustrated by the following statement made by George Webb, an Akimel O'odham, in his autobiographical family history:

> The word in the Pima language for "Something Told" is *ha'ichu'a:ga*. In the winter evenings . . . we would ask Keli:hi to tell us something. Sometimes he would tell us how to behave so that we would grow up to be good people [*amog*, or preaching], or he would tell us things that happened when his father Eaglefeathers was a boy. All these things are *ha'ichu'a:ga*. But so are legends [*Ho'ok A:gida*], and those are what we liked most to hear.[10]

"Oration" (*ñiokculida*), literally "talking for someone," according to Bahr, is a genre with a different audience than these previous genres and a greater degree of memorization.[11] Whereas "tellings" (*a:ag*) are memorized on the level of the episode, "orations" are memorized on the level of the sentence. Unlike "tellings," "orations" are not only for live human audiences; they are also "prayers" to "spirits." Observing that this genre engages multiple audiences, including living O'odham, deceased O'odham, and what might be termed "other-than-human persons," Bahr notes that the category is somewhat arbitrary. Like songs (*ñe'i*), orations are said to be the historical speech of powerful beings. In Bahr's words, "The narrators of Pima-Papago oratory—and also of songs—are ancient gods or modern spirits."[12] Accordingly, the words in both songs and orations are usually regarded as "the exact words of ancient speakers."[13]

Whereas orations are memorized on the level of the sentence, songs (*ñe'i*) are much shorter than both orations and stories and are memorized on the level of the syllable. Songs are the shortest O'odham narrative form.[14] The speech in songs is said to be the historical speech of powerful entities, but unlike orations, contemporary O'odham, even those fluent in O'odham, often cannot easily understand this speech. The songs are said to be in an obscure "song language" with extra vocables, making this sung speech more stunningly beautiful and enhanced than everyday, ordinary O'odham speech (*ñiok*).[15] Bahr argues that songs are "the preferred way for people to address spirits" and that they "resemble Japanese hai-kus, [as] terse and snap-shot-like verbal portraits" of life in the desert.[16] David Kozak calls *ñe'i* "nature poetry" because songs describe "gorgeous landscapes that contain mountains, deserts, and oceans inhabited by plants, animals, birds, insects, the sun, rain, lightning, and other natural phenomena."[17] Bahr further explains that "song texts tend to be extremely terse and ambiguous. Compared with ordinary speech there are changes in word order, vowel length, and consonant value. Syllables are added, deleted, or reduplicated 'for the sake of the song.'"[18] Ethnomusicologist John Richard Haefer translates *ñe'i*—not as a noun, but rather as a verb—as "singing" and "sings."[19]

In regard to the genres of "telling" (*a:ag*), "oration" (*ñiokculida*), and "singing" (*ñe'i*), Bahr discerns an inverse relationship between intended audience and story length.[20] Songs contain the least story, and their primary audience may be "spirits" more than living O'odham. Orations contain more story than songs and are more easily understood by audiences fluent in O'odham. "Tellings" contain the most story, but they are intended for living audiences only, not "spirits."

NOTES

INTRODUCTION

1. Mary Narcho, interview by author, July 2012, San Xavier AZ. For a description of the pilgrimage to Magdalena taken in 1947 by Mary Narcho's mother-in-law, Annie Narcho, as recorded by Muriel Thayer Painter, see Painter, "Field Notes— Magdalena," Muriel Thayer Painter Collection, MS 18.

2. Mary Narcho, interview by author, July 2012, San Xavier AZ.

3. For more on these social distinctions among O'odham, see Fontana, "Pima and Papago"; Fontana, *Of Earth*, 39–47; Hackenberg, "Pima and Papago"; Martínez, "Hiding in the Shadows"; and Madsen, "Basis for Bordering."

4. Fontana, *Of Earth*, 120; Booth, "Creation of a Nation"; Marak and Tuennerman, *At the Border*; Madsen, "Nation across Nations"; Schulze, *Are We Not Foreigners?*

5. McNally, *Ojibwe Singers*, 9.

6. McNally, *Ojibwe Singers*, 9. For an approach focused on the agency and intentions of missionaries, see Pinegar, "Church Growth."

7. V. Deloria, *God Is Red*; Treat, *Native and Christian*; Treat, *Around the Sacred Fire*; Vilaça and Wright, *Native Christians*; Martin and Nicholas, *Native Americans*; Lassiter, Ellis, and Kotay, *Jesus Road*; Hamill, *Songs of Power*; Hughes, *Biography*; Sanneh, *Whose Religion Is Christianity?*; Shorter, *We Will Dance*; Marshall, *Upward, Not Sunwise*; Vilaça, *Praying and Preying*.

8. de Certeau, *Practice of Everyday Life*, xiii.

9. Zepeda, "Sand Papago Oral History," 16.

10. Bahr, Gregorio, Lopez, and Alvarez, *Piman Shamanism*; Bahr, "Pima-Papago Christianity"; Kozak and D. Lopez, *Devil Sickness*; Kozak, "Shamanisms." Alternatively, anthropologist and ethnohistorian Daniel T. Reff argues that the Tohono O'odham devil way is pre-European in Reff, "Sympathy for the Devil."

11. Herzog, "Culture Change and Language," 69–70.

12. Griffith, "Catholic Religious Architecture"; Griffith, "Folk-Catholic Chapels."

13. Kozak and D. Lopez, *Devil Sickness*; Kozak and D. Lopez, "Translating the Boundary," 279. I should also note here that not all O'odham agree with this association. For example, Mary Narcho heartily negated this association and was offended by the idea that cowboys might have something to do with devils. She asked, "Why cowboys? Two of my boys are cowboys and one of my sons was a professional cowboy. No, I don't believe that . . . No, I don't believe that at all." Mary Narcho, interview by author, July 2012, San Xavier AZ.

14. For a discussion of reduplication and O'odham plurals, see Hill and Zepeda, "Tohono O'odham (Papago) Plurals."

15. See also Radding, *Landscapes of Power*.

16. For discussions of roadside memorials and violent death, see Kozak, "Cult of the Dead"; Kozak and C. Lopez, "Tohono O'odham Shrine Complex"; Kozak, "Dying Badly"; Kozak, "Reifying the Body."

17. Feld and Basso, *Senses of Place*; Hirsch and O'Hanlon, *Anthropology of Landscape*; Tilley, *Phenomenology of Landscape*.

18. Frey, *Pilgrim Stories*, 264–65n4.

19. Frey, *Pilgrim Stories*, 265n7.

20. Frey, *Pilgrim Stories*, 265n7.

21. Tilley, *Phenomenology of Landscape*.

22. For an example of "landscape" as merely a "backdrop" for action and movement in O'odham studies, see Bahr, *How Mockingbirds Are*, 120. For an example of "landscape" as merely a "backdrop" to movement in pilgrimage studies, see Coleman and Elsner, *Pilgrimage*, 212.

23. Snead, Erickson, and Darling, *Landscapes of Movement*.

24. Alternatively, for the movement of O'odham Feasts of Saint Francis, rather than the movement of O'odham to the Feast of Saint Francis in Magdalena, see Nabhan, "Moveable O'odham Feast." For the understudied St. Francis feast in Cu:wĭ Ge:ṣk, also known as "Rabbit Falls Down" and San Francisquito, see Schweitzer and Thomas, "Fiesta of St. Francis."

25. Nabokov, *Indian Running*; Buckley, *Standing Ground*; Shorter, *We Will Dance*; Vilaça, *Praying and Preying*.

26. Benavides, "Tyranny of the Gerund."

27. Cosgrove, *Social Formation*; Cosgrove, "Landscapes and Myths."

28. Lock, "Bowing Down," 130.

29. Clifford, *Routes*, 2.

30. Clifford, *Routes*, 2.

31. Clifford, *Routes*, 19, 22.

32. Morinis, *Sacred Journeys*, 2.

33. O'Connor, "Pilgrimage to Magdalena," 369.
34. Coleman and Eade, "Introduction," 2, 4; Morinis, *Sacred Journeys*, 3, 7; Gold, *Fruitful Journeys*.
35. Frey, *Pilgrim Stories*.
36. Coleman and Eade, "Introduction," 11.
37. Sallnow, *Pilgrims of the Andes*; Gold, *Fruitful Journeys*; Kaell, *Walking Where Jesus Walked*; Turner and Turner, *Image and Pilgrimage*.
38. O'Connor, "Pilgrimage to Magdalena," 370.
39. Dobyns, "Papago Pilgrims"; Dobyns, *Religious Festival*; Griffith, "Magdalena Revisited"; Nabhan, *Desert Smells Like Rain*, 111–19; Nabhan, "Moveable O'odham Feast"; Painter, "Field Notes—Magdalena," Muriel Thayer Painter Collection, MS 18.
40. Tooker, "Pilgrims in Church"; O'Connor, "Pilgrimage to Magdalena"; Griffith, "Magdalena Holy Picture"; Oktavec, *Answered Prayers*; Sheridan, "Female Public Drinking"; Rios and Sands, *Telling a Good One*, 148–54.
41. O'Connor, "Pilgrimage to Magdalena," 376; Griffith, *Beliefs and Holy Places*.
42. Swanson, "Through Family Eyes"; Michalowski and Dubisch, *Run for the Wall*, 20–21; see also Jill Dubisch, "Heartland of America," 113. See also Schermerhorn and McEnaney, "Through Indigenous Eyes," 48.
43. O'Connor, "Pilgrimage to Magdalena," 378.
44. Tweed, *Crossing and Dwelling*, 8–9.
45. Tweed, *Crossing and Dwelling*, 11.
46. Bahr, Giff, and Havier, "Piman Songs on Hunting," 262.
47. Tweed, *Crossing and Dwelling*, 178.
48. Tweed, *Crossing and Dwelling*, 181–82.
49. Sallnow, *Pilgrims of the Andes*; Gold, *Fruitful Journeys*; Frey, *Pilgrim Stories*; Kaell, *Walking Where Jesus Walked*.
50. O'Connor, "Pilgrimage to Magdalena," 377.
51. Clifford, *Routes*, 23.
52. de la Cadena, *Earth Beings*, 12–14.
53. Orsi, *Between Heaven and Earth*, 175.
54. Johnson, *Sacred Claims*, 160.
55. Swanson, "Through Family Eyes," 67.
56. de Certeau, *Writing of History*, xxv.
57. de Certeau, *Practice of Everyday Life*, 28.
58. de Certeau, *Practice of Everyday Life*, 25.
59. Orsi, "Everyday Miracles," 18.
60. Tedlock, *Spoken Word*; Tedlock and Mannheim, *Dialogic Emergence of Culture*; Shorter, *We Will Dance*.
61. Bakhtin, *Rabelais and His World*, 68.

62. Frisch, *Shared Authority*; Trimble, Sommer, and Quinlan, *American Indian Oral History*.

63. This study could have easily focused on Simon Lopez's interpretation of O'odham journeys to Magdalena and my interpretation of his interpretation, like Myerhoff, *Peyote Hunt*.

64. Alvarez and Hale, "Toward a Manual."

65. According to ethnobiologist Amadeo Rea, "greasewood" is a misnomer when applied to Şegoi in Rea, *Desert's Green Edge*, 153.

66. Lloyd, *Aw-Aw-Tam Indian*, 16.

67. Nabhan, *Desert Smells Like Rain*, 6.

68. To be fair, the desert makes Nabhan sneeze, too. See Nabhan, *Gathering the Desert*, 95.

69. Joseph, Spicer, and Chesky, *Desert People*, 47.

70. Underhill, *Social Organization*, 176.

71. Darling and Lewis, "Songscapes and Calendar Sticks."

72. Bahr, Paul, and Joseph, *Ants and Orioles*; Kozak and D. Lopez, "Translating the Boundary"; Darling and Lewis, "Songscapes and Calendar Sticks."

73. Darling and Lewis, "Songscapes and Calendar Sticks."

74. Swanson, "Weathered Character," 306.

75. Harrison, *Signs, Songs, and Memory*, 144–71; Lagrou, "Homesickness"; Swanson, "Singing to Estranged Lovers"; and Swanson and Reddekop, "Looking Like the Land."

76. P. Deloria, *Indians in Unexpected Places*.

1. PERSONHOOD AND PLACE

1. Astor-Aguilera, *Maya World*, 2.

2. Astor-Aguilera, *Maya World*, 3.

3. Astor-Aguilera, *Maya World*, 183–245.

4. Astor-Aguilera, *Maya World*, 204.

5. Fogelson, "Person, Self, and Identity," 93.

6. Astor-Aguilera, *Maya World*, 206–11.

7. Swanson, "Singing to Estranged Lovers," 62.

8. Oosten, "Few Critical Remarks," 32.

9. Hallowell, "Ojibwa Ontology." In the O'odham context, ethnobiologist Gary Nabhan frequently uses Hallowell's category in his own work to talk about other species. To cite one example of this, Nabhan contends that O'odham songs and stories "reflect the larger, other-than-human landscape, one intrinsic to [O'odham] literature, music, or ways of healing" in Nabhan, *Cultures of Habitat*, 11.

10. Conklin and Morgan, "Babies, Bodies,"; Lamb, "Making and Unmaking"; Schwarz, *Molded in the Image*; Schwarz, *Navajo Lifeways*; Schwarz, *"I Choose Life."*

11. Kozak, "Cult of the Dead," 156.
12. Underhill, *Papago Indian Religion*, 20; Saxton, Saxton, and Enos, *Dictionary*, 54.
13. Bahr also translates O'odham as "true humans" or "true people" in Bahr, "Oral Literatures," 211. Frank Russell also discusses "Si'atcokam," which he translates as "Examining Physicians," noting that this is the most powerful of three classes of O'odham "medicine-men" in Russell, *Pima Indians*, 256, 258–62; Elsie Clews Parsons records this title as "sai'chukam" in Parsons, "Notes on the Pima," 461.
14. Underhill, *Papago Woman*. Gretchen M. Bataille and Kathleen Mullen Sands have noted that Maria Chona's sense of place shapes her narrative in significant and intimate ways in Bataille and Sands, *American Indian Women*, 49–50. For more on Ruth Underhill's working relationship with Maria Chona, see Underhill, *Anthropologist's Arrival*, 159–72.
15. Manuel and Neff, *Desert Indian Woman*, xxxvii.
16. Giff, "Pima Blue Swallow Songs," 136–37.
17. Underhill, *Singing for Power*; Underhill, *Papago Indian Religion*; Underhill, *Social Organization*.
18. Saxton, Saxton, and Enos, *Dictionary*, 122–23.
19. McNally, *Honoring Elders*.
20. Feldhaus, *Connected Places*, 5.
21. Thomas Tweed promotes "place" as illuminating theme in American religious history, broadly conceived, in Tweed, *Our Lady*, 135–36.
22. Feldhaus, *Connected Places*, 6.
23. Feldhaus, *Connected Places*, 28. See also Feldhaus, "Walking and Thinking."
24. Verlon "Carlos" Jose, interview by author, April 2012, Sells AZ.
25. Verlon "Carlos" Jose, interview by author, April 2012, Sells AZ.
26. Nabhan, "Moveable O'odham Feast."
27. Griffith, *Beliefs and Holy Places*; Williamson, "Why the Pilgrims Come"; Schweitzer and Thomas, "Fiesta of St. Francis"; Nabhan, *Desert Smells Like Rain*; see also appendix A.
28. Feldhaus, *Connected Places*, 184.
29. Clifford, *Returns*, 82. Other scholars use the categories of "place" and "person" somewhat differently than I do, though. For two examples, see Stirrat, "Place and Person"; and Poteat, "Persons and Places."
30. Basso, *Wisdom Sits in Places*, 7.
31. Feld and Basso, *Senses of Place*, 11.
32. Feldhaus, *Connected Places*, 7.
33. For a published photograph of Michael Enis taken by Bernard Siqueiros, see Schermerhorn and McEnaney, "Through Indigenous Eyes," 34.
34. Credit must be given to Eileen Oktavec for making this point before I did in Oktavec, *Answered Prayers*, xxi.

35. Bahr, *How Mockingbirds Are*, 120.

36. Bahr, Gregorio, Lopez, and Alvarez, *Piman Shamanism*, 279.

37. For example, Kozak and D. Lopez, *Devil Sickness*.

38. Bahr, *How Mockingbirds Are*, 120.

39. For one example of compartmentalizing "Native" and "Christian" O'odham traditions, see Underhill et al., *Rainhouse and Ocean*, 5–11.

40. Foucault, "Questions on Geography," 70.

41. Soja, *Postmodern Geographies*, 15.

42. Vásquez, *More than Belief*, 267.

43. Vásquez, *More than Belief*, 268.

44. Soja, *Postmodern Geographies*, 11.

45. Appadurai, *Modernity at Large*, 33.

46. McAlister, "Madonna of 115th Street," 156.

47. Tweed, *Crossing and Dwelling*, 61–62.

48. Tweed, *Crossing and Dwelling*, 73.

49. Bahr, "O'odham Traditions," 125.

50. Bahr, "Who Were the Hohokam?"; Hayden, "Of Hohokam Origins"; Spicer, "Papago Indians"; Mason, "Papago Migration Legend"; Shaw, *Pima Indian Legends*, 27–28.

51. Lopez, "Huhugam," 118.

52. Simon Lopez, interview by author, March 2012, Santa Rosa AZ.

53. Simon Lopez, interview by author, March 2012, Santa Rosa AZ.

54. Simon Lopez, interview by author, March 2012, Santa Rosa AZ.

55. Lopez, "Huhugam," 120–21.

56. The title of this section obviously draws upon the title of Mircea Eliade's classic work; Eliade, *Cosmos and History*.

57. Bahr, "Pima-Papago Christianity," 161–64; Bahr, "Pima Heaven Songs"; Kozak and D. Lopez, *Devil Sickness*, 65–66. I must also note that Mary Narcho, who previously noted that she was offended by any association between devils and cowboys, also strenuously objected to the notion that O'odham and non-O'odham might go to different places when they die. She stated, "That's the first time I've heard that! [laughter] I totally don't believe that. That's discrimination. No, I don't believe that. I don't believe that. I've never heard that." Mary Narcho, interview by author, July 2012, San Xavier AZ.

58. Simon Lopez, interview by author, March 2012, Santa Rosa AZ.

59. For a thorough analysis of the "structure of the conjuncture," see Sahlins, *Historical Metaphors*; Sahlins, *Islands of History*.

60. For another examination of a near-death experience of Simon Lopez's grandfather, Juan D. Lopez, as memorialized in a quail song and a devil song, see Kozak and D. Lopez, "Translating the Boundary," 281–83.

61. Simon Lopez, interview by author, March 2012, Santa Rosa AZ.
62. Simon Lopez, interview by author, March 2012, Santa Rosa AZ.
63. Simon Lopez, interview by author, March 2012, Santa Rosa AZ.
64. Simon Lopez, interview by author, March 2012, Santa Rosa AZ. Kozak and
    Lopez similarly translate *sikol ṣu:dagi* as "swirling water." Kozak and Lopez,
    Devil Sickness, 134.
65. Simon Lopez, interview by author, February 2012, Santa Rosa AZ.
66. Simon Lopez, interview by author, February 2012, Santa Rosa AZ.
67. Waddell, "Place of the Cactus," 224.
68. Sallnow, *Pilgrims of the Andes*, 12.
69. Bakhtin, *Dialogic Imagination*, 84.
70. Fontana, "Pilgrimage to Magdalena," 41.
71. For more on "presence," see Orsi, *History and Presence*.

2. O'ODHAM SONGSCAPES

1. As David Kozak has claimed, the words in O'odham songs "have the ability to
   move us," in Kozak and D. Lopez, "Translating the Boundary," 275.
2. Zepeda, *Where Clouds Are Formed*, 13.
3. V. Deloria, *God Is Red*; Treat, *For This Land*; Greg Johnson, "Native Traditions";
   Bakhtin, *Dialogic Imagination*.
4. Bakhtin, *Dialogic Imagination*, 84.
5. Linguist Madeleine Mathiot claims that time and space are not differentiated
   in the O'odham language in Mathiot, "Noun Classes," 348; William Pilcher
   challenges Mathiot's findings in Pilcher, "Some Comments."
6. Basso, *Wisdom Sits in Places*, 62.
7. Darling, "O'odham Trails"; Darling and Lewis, "Songscapes and Calendar Sticks."
8. Bahr, *How Mockingbirds Are*; Bahr, Paul, and Joseph, *Ants and Orioles*; Kozak
   and D. Lopez, *Devil Sickness*; Kozak and D. Lopez, "Translating the Boundary."
9. Kozak and D. Lopez, "Translating the Boundary," 277.
10. Bahr, Paul, and Joseph, *Ants and Orioles*, 72–73.
11. Bahr, Paul, and Joseph, *Ants and Orioles*, 73.
12. Linguist David Shaul has noted verb-final positioning O'odham song syntax in
    Shaul, "Piman Song Syntax."
13. Kozak and D. Lopez, "Translating the Boundary," 278.
14. Basso, *Wisdom Sits in Places*, 45–46.
15. My interest in these songs follows the trend identified by Jane Chesky in which
    scholars generally prefer to study "older songs that are supposedly aboriginal."
    Chesky, "Indian Music," 10.
16. Kendall Jose, interview by author, April 2012, Sells AZ.
17. Kendall Jose, interview by author, April 2012, Sells AZ.

. Herzog, "Musical Styles"; Herzog, "Comparison of Pueblo."

19. Bahr, Paul, and Joseph, *Ants and Orioles*; Bahr, "Native American Dream Songs"; Bahr, "Papago Ocean Songs"; Bahr, "Pima Heaven Songs"; Bahr, "Pima Swallow Songs"; Bahr, "Four Papago Rattlesnake Songs"; Kozak and D. Lopez, *Devil Sickness*; Kozak, "Whirlwind Songs."

20. Kozak and D. Lopez, *Devil Sickness*, 128.

21. For examples of these usages, see Bahr, "Grey and Fervent Shamanism"; Bahr, Paul, and Joseph, *Ants and Orioles*, 90–91; Kozak and D. Lopez, *Devil Sickness*, 169n2. For Bahr's earliest work, where he discusses the difficulty of translating "spirit" into O'odham, see Bahr, Gregorio, Lopez, and Alvarez, *Piman Shamanism*, 12.

22. Bahr, "Pima Heaven Songs," 199.

23. Bahr, Paul, and Joseph, *Ants and Orioles*, 176; originally published as Bahr, "Native American Dream Songs."

24. Kozak and D. Lopez, *Devil Sickness*, 3, 6, 114.

25. Kendall Jose, interview by author, April 2012, Sells AZ.

26. Simon Lopez, interview by author, February 2012, Santa Rosa AZ.

27. Simon Lopez, interview by author, February 2012, Santa Rosa AZ.

28. Bahr, Paul, and Joseph, *Ants and Orioles*, 77.

29. Bahr, Paul, and Joseph, *Ants and Orioles*, 77.

30. Basso, *Wisdom Sits in Places*, 85.

31. Darling and Lewis, "Songscapes and Calendar Sticks," 131–35; songs from Bahr, Paul, and Joseph, *Ants and Orioles*, 114–43.

32. For "ethical soundscape," see Hirschkind, *Ethical Soundscape*.

33. Bahr, Paul, and Joseph, *Ants and Orioles*, 182.

34. Bahr, *How Mockingbirds Are*, 6.

35. Darling and Lewis, "Songscapes and Calendar Sticks," 138.

36. Darling and Lewis, "Songscapes and Calendar Sticks," 138.

37. Kozak and D. Lopez, *Devil Sickness*, 6.

38. Kozak and D. Lopez, *Devil Sickness*, 8–9.

39. Ortiz, "Some Concerns"; Morrison, *Solidarity of Kin*; Shorter, *We Will Dance*, 197–209.

40. Shorter, "Spirituality."

41. Bahr, *How Mockingbirds Are*, 6.

42. Simon Lopez, interview by author, March 2012, Santa Rosa AZ.

43. Simon Lopez, interview by author, March 2012, Santa Rosa AZ.

44. Bahr and Haefer, "Song in Piman Curing," 119. For an example of the limitations of analyzing miscellaneous songs in isolation from one another, see Stricklen, "Eight Papago Songs."

45. Bahr, "Format and Method."

46. Simon Lopez, interview by author, February 2012, Santa Rosa AZ.
47. Louis Anthony Lopez, interview by author March, 2012, Sells AZ.
48. Lévi-Strauss, *Raw and the Cooked*.
49. Simon Lopez, interview by author, March 2012, Santa Rosa AZ.
50. Louis Anthony Lopez, interview by author, March 2012, Sells AZ.
51. Kozak, "Swallow Dizziness," 7.
52. Bahr, "Pima Swallow Songs"; Kozak, "Swallow Dizziness," 7.
53. Louis Anthony Lopez, interview by author, March 2012, Sells AZ.
54. Simon Lopez, interview by author, March 2012, Santa Rosa AZ.
55. Underhill, et al., *Rainhouse and Ocean*, 125.
56. Schermerhorn, "O'odham Songscapes," 248–49; Schermerhorn, "Walking to Magdalena," 103–4.
57. Winters, *'O'odham Place Names*, 525. See also Bolton, *Rim of Christendom*, 306–7, 434, 451, 466, 474, 478, 493, 496, 526, 539, 552, 589.
58. Winters, *'O'odham Place Names*, 526.
59. Geronimo, "Establishing Connections to Place," 222.
60. If Louis Lopez and I have been mistaken in translating "siwok" as "siwol," at least we have been in good company in misapprehending this place-name. Curiously, Kozak and Lopez translate "Si:woda dodoag" as "Dazzling Mountain(s)." They offer no explanation for this translation, which subsequently inspired the title of a large anthology of southwestern oral literatures edited by Kozak. Kozak and Lopez, *Devil Sickness*, 132; Kozak, *Inside Dazzling Mountains*, 10.
61. Griffith, *Beliefs and Holy Places*, 161, 162.
62. Winters, *'O'odham Place Names*, 515–16, 531.
63. Louis Anthony Lopez, interview by author, March 2012, Sells AZ.
64. Simon Lopez, interview by author, March 2012, Santa Rosa AZ.
65. Louis Anthony Lopez, interview by author, March 2012, Sells AZ.
66. Simon Lopez, interview by author, February 2012, Santa Rosa AZ.
67. Louis Anthony Lopez, interview by author, March 2012, Sells AZ.
68. Louis Anthony Lopez, interview by author, March 2012, Quijotoa AZ.
69. For an excellent example focusing on such connections in another indigenous community, see Feld, *Sound and Sentiment*.
70. Nabhan, *Desert Smells Like Rain*, 96.
71. Simon Lopez, interview by author, March 2012, Santa Rosa AZ.
72. Simon Lopez, interview by author, March 2012, Santa Rosa AZ.
73. Simon Lopez, interview by author, March 2012, Santa Rosa AZ.
74. Bahr, "Pima Swallow Songs," 184.
75. Bahr, "Pima Swallow Songs," 184.
76. Simon Lopez, interview by author, March 2012, Santa Rosa AZ; Simon Lopez's statement also resonates with Ofelia Zepeda's interpretive inclinations regarding

movements and changes in the desert, which according to Zepeda, "almost always include people," in Zepeda, "Autobiography," 414.

77. Soja, *Postmodern Geographies*, 15.

78. V. Deloria, *God Is Red*, 62.

79. Louis Anthony Lopez, interview by author, March 2012, Sells AZ.

3. WALKERS AND THEIR STAFFS

1. I intentionally use both "staff" and "walking stick" to preserve ambiguity in order to suggest that there are "multiple ways of being a thing," as does anthropologist Fernando Santos-Granero in Santos-Granero, *Occult Life of Things*, 105–27. Furthermore, during the course of my research different consultants used different terms. I can't prove it, but I suspect that walking sticks date back farther historically and that Felix's staffs are a more historically recent innovation. Finally, I use the generic category of "sticks" because it allows me to compare walking sticks with calendar sticks, scraping sticks, and flutes made of reeds that are somewhat "stick-like."

2. Although the plural of "staff" is often represented as "staves," I consciously used "staffs" as the plural to reflect the practice in the community. Furthermore, the *Oxford English Dictionary* finds both versions in common use.

3. For photography and further discussion of staffs as part of moveable altars, see Schermerhorn and McEnaney, "Through Indigenous Eyes," 42–45.

4. Darling and Lewis, "Songscapes and Calendar Sticks."

5. Other "sticks" with which these staffs might be compared, and to which O'odham also compare them, include the following: the staffs or canes of office held by a *kowinal*, or "governor," first given to O'odham—and other indigenous peoples of the Americas—by the Spanish, as well as by the Mexican and American governments; and United States Marine Corps–issued rifles. Both of these "sticks" (a rifle is merely a "boomstick") are relevant to O'odham understandings of contemporary staffs, or walking sticks, not only because Felix Antone was the governor of O'odham in Mexico, but also because—in spite of not being born within the United States or possessing U.S. citizenship—he served in the United States Marine Corps. While few O'odham are governors, most are certainly aware of this hereditary office. Furthermore, while most O'odham are not marines, many O'odham walkers and support are marines, and probably just about every O'odham is related to a marine. During my first year walking to Magdalena, I recall one O'odham man in particular half-jokingly reciting the "Rifleman's Creed"—popularized in Stanley Kubrick's 1987 *Full Metal Jacket*—switching out the word "rifle" for "staff." I do not compare staffs to either canes of office or rifles simply because they do not seem to relate to O'odham theories and representations of space and time.

6. According to ethnobiologist Amadeo Rea, most O'odham do not use flutes in the present. Historically young O'odham men used flutes to seduce or woo women. When an O'odham boy became interested in a girl and wanted her to be attracted to him, he would play "love songs" on a flute nearby the desired young woman while she worked or slept. The intent was to arouse the woman and move her to the young man playing the flute. For more on O'odham flutes, see Rea, *Desert's Green Edge*, 102. Chona, the subject of Ruth Underhill's classic *Papago Woman*, had this to say about flutes:

> I used to think about boys when I was . . . thirteen. Sometimes I thought I heard flutes at night. I do not know if it was really boys playing them or if I only dreamed it. But the music drove me wild. The flute is what our boys play when they want a woman to come to them and I wanted to go. . . . They told me that there were women who went alone to those dances, the wild women, who did not work and who went about painted every day. Corn ears they painted on their breasts, and birds and butterflies, each breast different for the men to see. . . . I began to dream of those wild women. . . . They make men and women crazy, sometimes so that they run out and die. . . . And I kept hearing flutes: flutes in the morning and evening. (Underhill, *Papago Woman*, 55–57)

7. Saxton and Saxton, *O'othham Hoho'ok A'agitha*, 221.
8. Saxton and Saxton, *O'othham Hoho'ok A'agitha*, 24–25.
9. Saxton and Saxton, *O'othham Hoho'ok A'agitha*, 221–22. For more on Reed Mountain, see Winters, *'O'odham Place Names*, 453.
10. Saxton and Saxton, *O'othham Hoho'ok A'agitha*, 222.
11. Saxton and Saxton, *O'othham Hoho'ok A'agitha*, 223.
12. Saxton and Saxton, *O'othham Hoho'ok A'agitha*, 225.
13. Note that the terms used in discussing the women who became the Pleiades are frequently value-laden. These women are often referred to with even more value-laden terms in the ethnographic literature, such as "wild women," "whores," and "prostitute women." According to linguistic anthropologist Don Bahr, "The whores' goals are to hear singers, not to acquire mates," in Bahr, Paul, and Joseph, *Ants and Orioles*, 29. Strictly speaking, they are neither sex-crazed nor engaging in sexual activity in exchange for payment, but rather they are involuntarily moved by song. However, they cannot stop dancing. In this state, they abandon their families, which is perhaps the worst thing that women can do in this particular patriarchal society. So, O'odham are prone to use moralizing language in speaking about these women.
14. Underhill, *Social Organization*, 183.
15. Nabokov, *Forest of Time*, 150.
16. Santos-Granero, *Occult Life of Things*, 8.

17. Fontana, "Pilgrimage to Magdalena," 60.

18. For more on saguaros, see Rea, *Desert's Green Edge*, 253–60.

19. Bahr, *How Mockingbirds Are*, 12.

20. Swanson, "Weathered Character," 299.

21. Swanson, "Weathered Character," 299.

22. Darling and Lewis, "Songscapes and Calendar Sticks," 137.

23. Haefer, "Musical Thought," 50.

24. Grossmann, "Pima Indians of Arizona," 407.

25. Russell, "Pima Annals," 76.

26. Russell, "Pima Annals," 76.

27. Underhill, "Papago Calendar Record," 13–14.

28. Kilcrease, "Ninety-Five Years," 297; Papago Tribe of Arizona, Appendix A, A1.

29. For an authoritative refutation of Western literate biases of what generally constitutes both "writing" and "history" that marginalize indigenous historicities, or senses of history, see Shorter, *We Will Dance*, 197–209.

30. Simon Lopez, interview by author, February 2012, Santa Rosa AZ.

31. For a discussion of greasewood, see Rea, *Desert's Green Edge*, 152–53.

32. Haefer, "Musical Thought," 296–97.

33. Russell, *Pima Indians*, 167.

34. Darling and Lewis, "Songscapes and Calendar Sticks," 136.

35. Darling and Lewis, "Songscapes and Calendar Sticks," 136–37.

36. Swanson, "Weathered Character."

37. Simon Lopez, interview by author, February 2012, Santa Rosa AZ.

38. Herzog, "Music in the Thinking," 12.

39. For a discussion of mesquite, see Rea, *Desert's Green Edge*, 183–92.

40. Russell, *Pima Indians*.

41. Simon Lopez, interview by author, February 2012, Santa Rosa AZ.

42. Simon Lopez, interview by author, February 2012, Santa Rosa AZ.

43. Rea, *Desert's Green Edge*, 157.

44. Saxton, Saxton, and Enos, *Dictionary*, 45.

45. Bahr, "Ages of O'odham Architecture," 499.

46. Saxton, Saxton, and Enos, *Dictionary*, 25.

47. Kozak and D. Lopez, *Devil Sickness*, 135.

48. Louis Anthony Lopez, interview by author, March 2014, Santa Rosa AZ.

49. Verlon "Carlos" Jose, interview by author, August 2012, Sells AZ.

50. Verlon "Carlos" Jose, interview by author, August 2012, Sells AZ.

51. Pels, "Modern Fear of Matter," 265.

52. Bahr, "Ages of O'odham Architecture," 499–500.

53. Verlon "Carlos" Jose, interview by author, August 2012, Sells AZ.

54. Kendall Jose, interview by author, July 2012, Sells AZ. For a published photograph of Kendall Jose taken by Bernard Siquieros, see Schermerhorn, "Walkers and Their Staffs," 488; and Schermerhorn and McEnaney, "Through Indigenous Eyes," 34.

55. Mary Narcho, interview by author, July 2012, San Xavier AZ. For other published photographs of Mary Narcho taken by Bernard Siquieros and Mary Narcho, see Schermerhorn and McEnaney, "Through Indigenous Eyes," 27, 41; see also Castillo and Cowan, *Not Our Fault*, 47, 91.

56. Mary Narcho, interview by author, July 2012, San Xavier AZ.

57. Mary Narcho, interview by author, July 2012, San Xavier AZ.

58. Mary Narcho, interview by author, July 2012, San Xavier AZ.

59. Verlon "Carlos" Jose, interview by author, August 2012, Sells AZ.

60. Verlon "Carlos" Jose, interview by author, August 2012, Sells AZ.

61. Verlon "Carlos" Jose, interview by author, August 2012, Sells AZ.

62. Verlon "Carlos" Jose, interview by author, August 2012, Sells AZ.

63. Verlon "Carlos" Jose, interview by author, August 2012, Sells AZ.

64. Louis Anthony Lopez, interview by author, March 2014, Santa Rosa AZ.

65. Mary Narcho, interview by author, July 2012, San Xavier AZ.

66. Mary Narcho's equally spaced knots might also be compared to knotted cords carried by Pueblo Runners during and after the Pueblo Revolt of 1680. For an account of knotted cords in this revolt, see Schermerhorn, "Christianity, Kachinas, Crosses." For scholarship on Andean khipus, see Salomon, *Cord Keepers*; Quilter and Urton, *Narrative Threads*; Urton, *Signs of the Inka Khipu*; Urton, *Inka History in Knots*.

67. Mary Ann Ramirez, interview by author, July 2012, Tucson AZ.

68. Mary Ann Ramirez, interview by author, July 2012, Tucson AZ.

69. Mary Narcho, interview by author, July 2012, San Xavier AZ.

70. Kendall Jose, interview by author, April 2012, Sells AZ.

71. Kendall Jose, interview by author, July 2012, Sells AZ.

72. Royetta Thomas, interview by author, April 2012, Sells AZ.

73. Royetta Thomas, interview by author, April 2012, Sells AZ.

74. Bahr, Gregorio, Lopez, and Alvarez, *Piman Shamanism*.

75. Simon Lopez, interview by author, February 2012, Santa Rosa AZ.

76. Simon Lopez, interview by author, February 2012, Santa Rosa AZ.

77. Swanson, "Weathered Character."

78. Verlon "Carlos" Jose, interview by author, August 2012, Sells AZ.

79. Verlon "Carlos" Jose, interview by author, August 2012, Sells AZ.

80. Nabokov, *Forest of Time*, 150; Santos-Granero, *Occult Life of Things*, 8.

81. Darling and Lewis, "Songscapes and Calendar Sticks."

1. Although this list is far from being exhaustive, a few noteworthy examples follow: Bahr, "Pima-Papago Christianity"; Begay et al., "San Xavier"; De Grazia, "Papago Pilgrimage"; Dobyns, "Papago Pilgrims"; Dobyns, "Religious Festival"; Dobyns, "*Do-It-Yourself* Religion"; Dolores, "Autobiography," 14–15; Dolores and Mathiot, "Reminiscences of Juan Dolores," 307; Fontana, "Pilgrimage to Magdalena"; Fontana, "Pilgrimage to San Xavier"; Gaillard, "Papago of Arizona," 296; Galinier, "From Montezuma to San Francisco"; Gill, *Native American Religions*, 74–78; Griffith, "Magdalena Revisited"; King, "Folk Catholicism"; Kozak and D. Lopez, *Devil Sickness*; Manuel and Neff, *Desert Indian Woman*; Nabhan, *Desert Smells Like Rain*; O'Connor, "Pilgrimage to Magdalena"; Oktavec, *Answered Prayers*; Painter, "Field Notes—Magdalena," Muriel Thayer Painter Collection, MS 18; Shaul, "Piast and Pilgrimage," unpublished manuscript; Stewart, "Southern Papago Salt Pilgrimages"; Taylor, "Centre and Edge"; Underhill, *Papago Indian Religion*; Underhill, "Intercultural Relations," 649; Zepeda, *Ocean Power*, 41–45.
2. For previously published examples of these usages, see Siquieros, "Magdalena Pilgrimage," 3; F. Lewis and Bahr, "Whither T-himdag."
3. In particular see Morinis, *Sacred Journeys*; as well as Coleman and Eade, *Reframing Pilgrimage*. See also Feldhaus, *Connected Places*, 28; and Feldhaus, "Walking and Thinking," 452.
4. Bahr, Gregorio, Lopez, and Alvarez, *Piman Shamanism*; Kozak and D. Lopez, *Devil Sickness*.
5. Saxton and Saxton, *O'othham Hoho'ok A'agitha*, 24–25.
6. I borrow the notion of "disciplined sensuality" from Swanson, "Singing to Estranged Lovers."
7. I borrow these analytic categories from Sturman, "Movement Analysis."
8. Sallnow, *Pilgrims of the Andes*, 201.
9. Shorter, *We Will Dance*, 18; see also Marshall, *Upward, Not Sunwise*, 204n4.
10. Mauss, *Sociology and Psychology*, 97; Foucault, "Technologies"; Bourdieu, *Outline of a Theory*, 72–95.
11. Mauss, *Sociology and Psychology*, 100.
12. Mauss, *Sociology and Psychology*, 100.
13. Mauss, *Sociology and Psychology*, 102.
14. Mauss, *Sociology and Psychology*, 100; emphasis added.
15. Bourdieu, *Logic of Practice*, 53.
16. Mauss, *Sociology and Psychology*, 108.
17. Mauss, *Sociology and Psychology*, 105; Bourdieu, *Outline of a Theory*, 19, 166.
18. Bourdieu, *Outline of a Theory*, 19; Derrida, "Structure, Sign, and Play."
19. Bourdieu, *Outline of a Theory*, 166.
20. Vásquez, *More than Belief*, 241–42.

21. Bourdieu, *Outline of a Theory*, 214n1.
22. Bourdieu, *Outline of a Theory*, 87.
23. Bourdieu, *Outline of a Theory*, 19, 166–67.
24. Bourdieu, *Outline of a Theory*, 167; de Certeau, *Practice of Everyday Life*, 56.
25. de Certeau, *Practice of Everyday Life*, 93.
26. Tweed, *Crossing and Dwelling*, 13.
27. Tweed, *Crossing and Dwelling*, 18.
28. Bourdieu, "Genesis and Structure," 5.
29. The journey to Magdalena is generally consistent with Underhill's conception of Tohono O'odham economics in that "heavy labor, everywhere, was done by the young, under the direction of the old," in Underhill, *Social Organization*, 91.
30. See chapter 1 for an explanation of why I use the categories of place and cosmology more or less interchangeably.
31. Narayanan, "Embodied Cosmologies."
32. Geertz, "Deep Play."
33. Vásquez, *More than Belief*, 252.
34. Zepeda, *Where Clouds Are Formed*, 24–26.
35. Zepeda, *Where Clouds Are Formed*, 24.
36. Like Zepeda, Bernard Fontana also describes O'odham walking as "shuffling," when he observed some O'odham walkers who "shuffle along, painfully determined to make it all the way to their destination," in Fontana, "Pilgrimage to San Xavier," 47.
37. Baylor, *Yes Is Better*.
38. For Byrd Baylor's juxtaposition of the movements of O'odham and Mexican women, see Baylor, *Yes Is Better*, 7–8. For Baylor's juxtaposition of the movements of O'odham and Anglo women, see Baylor, *Yes Is Better*, 95.
39. Baylor, *Yes Is Better*, 7–8.
40. Zepeda, *Where Clouds Are Formed*, 25. One possible explanation for this distinctive way of walking was given by one O'odham woman to Zepeda, who relates that O'odham dancers should dance with "the dirt under their feet so that when the dancers got going, the dust would rise into the air and mix with everything else and result in rain, the ultimate goal." Zepeda, "Autobiography," 411.
41. Sturman, "Movement Analysis," 56.
42. Sturman, "Movement Analysis," 53.
43. Sturman, "Movement Analysis," 53; emphasis added.
44. Sturman, "Movement Analysis," 54.
45. For "hidden transcripts," see Scott, *Domination and the Arts*.
46. For another example of "painful" dancing as undesirable in a different Native Christian context in the Southwest, see Marshall, *Upward, Not Sunwise*, 141.
47. Titus, "Waila as Transnational Practice," 158.

48. Griffith, "Waila," 196.

49. Titus, "Waila as Transnational Practice," 159.

50. Titus, "Waila as Transnational Practice," 159.

51. Titus, "Waila as Transnational Practice," 159.

52. Titus, "Waila as Transnational Practice," 159.

53. Marie Gunst claimed that for O'odham, "every movement of the body expresses something." in Gunst, "Ceremonials of the Papago."

54. Kozak and D. Lopez, *Devil Sickness*, 92.

55. Bahr, Giff, and Havier, "Piman Songs on Hunting," 263.

56. Kozak and D. Lopez, *Devil Sickness*, 111.

57. Underhill, *Singing for Power*, 2.

58. Sturman, "Movement Analysis," 59.

59. For example, see Siquieros, "Magdalena Pilgrimage," 3; and F. Lewis and Bahr, "Whither T-himdag."

60. Saxton, Saxton, and Enos, *Dictionary*, 22.

61. Swanson, "Weathered Character," 306; see also Swanson, "Singing to Estranged Lovers." For the division of ethics and aesthetics, see Kant, *Critique of Pure Reason*; Kant, *Critique of Judgment*.

62. Narayanan, "Embodied Cosmologies."

63. Vásquez, *More than Belief*, 242.

64. Harrison, *Signs, Songs, and Memory*, 144–71; Swanson, "Singing to Estranged Lovers"; Swanson and Reddekop, "Looking Like the Land"; and Lagrou, "Home-sickness"; similarly, Don Bahr juxtaposes *ki:*, that is, "living" or "dwelling," with *oimeḍ*, or "wandering," or perhaps even better as "fooling around," in Bahr, "Santa Rosa, Arizona," unpublished manuscript, 19; Bahr also discusses "distracted travel" in Bahr, "Four Papago Rattlesnake Songs," 122; see also Kozak and D. Lopez, "Echoes of Mythical Creation."

65. Underhill, *Social Organization*, 184.

66. La Fontaine, "Person and Individual," 139.

67. In this regard the findings of this study are consistent with what an unnamed Tohono O'odham woman from San Xavier told George Williamson in 1950. Williamson, "Why the Pilgrims Come," 6.

68. Simon Lopez, interview by author, July 2011, Santa Rosa AZ.

69. Simon Lopez, interview by author, July 2011, Santa Rosa AZ.

70. Simon Lopez, interview by author, July 2011, Santa Rosa AZ.

71. Simon Lopez, interview by author, July 2011, Santa Rosa AZ.

72. Simon Lopez, interview by author, July 2011, Santa Rosa AZ.

73. Simon Lopez, interview by author, July 2011, Santa Rosa AZ.

74. Simon Lopez, interview by author, July 2011, Santa Rosa AZ.

75. Simon Lopez, interview by author, July 2011, Santa Rosa AZ; Simon's use of the English third-person singular pronoun "him" to refer back to his daughter is not an "error." As linguistic anthropologist William Leap has noted, "Indian English varieties do not always maintain the standard English gender distinctions indicated by the third person singular personal pronouns (he, she, it). As a result, gender and number features associated with a speaker's choice of subject or object pronoun do not always correspond with the gender and number features of its antecedent." Leap further suggests that this may be a substrate lexical influence from American Indian languages. Leap, *American Indian English*, 58–60. Other scholars have found this feature in O'odham English as well; see Manuel and Neff, *Desert Indian Woman*, xvi; and Waddell, "Mesquite and Mountains," 83n4. According to Don Bahr, the O'odham language "does not have gender-specific personal pronouns," in Bahr, Smith, Allison, and Hayden, *Short Swift Time*, 313n2.
76. Simon Lopez, interview by author, July 2011, Santa Rosa AZ.
77. Simon Lopez, interview by author, July 2011, Santa Rosa AZ.
78. Simon Lopez, interview by author, July 2011, Santa Rosa AZ.
79. Bahr, *Pima and Papago*, 5.
80. Simon Lopez, interview by author, July 2011, Santa Rosa AZ. The importance of never looking back during a journey is also discussed in Stewart, "Southern Papago Salt Pilgrimages," 90.
81. Louis Anthony Lopez, interview by author, March 2012, Quijotoa AZ.
82. Louis Anthony Lopez, interview by author, March 2012, Quijotoa AZ.
83. Clifford, *Routes*, 31, 36.
84. de Certeau, *Practice of Everyday Life*, 91–130.
85. Turner and Turner, *Image and Pilgrimage*, xiii; Sallnow, *Pilgrims of the Andes*, 184.
86. Cultural anthropologist Kirstin Erickson also found these categories of movement among her Yoeme, or Yaqui, collaborators in Erickson, *Yaqui Homeland and Homeplace*, 52–53. Folklorist James Griffith also reported that Mayo dancers in Magdalena stated their primary reason for attending the Magdalena fiesta in 1965 was to "visit with the Saint" in Griffith, "Magdalena Revisited," 84.
87. Jonas Robles, interview by author, April 2012, Santa Rosa AZ.
88. Jonas Robles, interview by author, April 2012, Santa Rosa AZ.
89. Joe Joaquin, interview by author, April 2012, Sells AZ.
90. Camillus Lopez and Deacon Alfred Gonzales, interview by author, April 2012, Santa Rosa AZ.
91. Camillus Lopez and Deacon Alfred Gonzales, interview by author, April 2012, Santa Rosa AZ.
92. Camillus Lopez and Deacon Alfred Gonzales, interview by author, April 2012, Santa Rosa AZ.

93. Camillus Lopez and Deacon Alfred Gonzales, interview by author, April 2012, Santa Rosa AZ.
94. Eade and Sallnow, *Contesting the Sacred*, 5. See also Chidester and Linenthal, *American Sacred Space*, 15–20; Johnson, *Sacred Claims*.
95. Smith-Morris, *Diabetes among the Pima*, 15.
96. Smith-Morris, *Diabetes among the Pima*, 15.
97. Bahr, "Santa Rosa, Arizona," 41–42.
98. Swanson, "Weathered Character," 306.
99. Bahr, "Santa Rosa, Arizona," 46.
100. Frey, *Pilgrim Stories*, 17–19.
101. Ingold and Vergunst, *Ways of Walking*, 1.

5. WRITING O'ODHAM HISTORY

1. Bahr, *How Mockingbirds Are*, 5, 154n8. Some O'odham stories of the origin of Christianity might also be in conversation with Yoeme, or Yaqui, Talking Tree stories. For example, see twelve versions of the Talking Tree story and an accompanying analysis in Shorter, *We Will Dance*, 111–46.
2. Several Western traditions, including Mormonism, have also assumed that some form of Christianity was in the Americas prior to the arrival of Europeans in the fifteenth and sixteenth centuries.
3. Fontana, "American Indian Oral History," 370.
4. Bahr, *How Mockingbirds Are*, 118.
5. Bahr, *How Mockingbirds Are*, 154n8.
6. Bahr, *How Mockingbirds Are*, 122.
7. Bahr, "Easter, Keruk, and Wi:gita," 191.
8. Bahr, *How Mockingbirds Are*, 119.
9. Bahr, Gregorio, Lopez, and Alvartez, *Piman Shamanism*, 280.
10. Bahr, *How Mockingbirds Are*, 12–13.
11. Bahr, *How Mockingbirds Are*, 18–19.
12. Bahr, *How Mockingbirds Are*, 54.
13. Bahr, *How Mockingbirds Are*, 119.
14. Underhill, *Papago Indian Religion*, 58; also in Bahr, *How Mockingbirds Are*, 60.
15. Bahr, *How Mockingbirds Are*, 157n3.
16. Bahr and Fenger, "Indians and Missions," 309. The core of Bahr and Fenger's article is based on their study of the photography of Father Augustine Schwarz, O.F.M., which is housed in the Labriola Center's archives at the Arizona State University Library in Tempe, Arizona.
17. Hobsbawm and Ranger, *Invention of Tradition*.
18. For "Victimist history," see Bahr and Fenger, "Indians and Missions," 316–17.
19. Louis Anthony Lopez, interview by author, March 2012, Quijotoa AZ.

20. Louis Anthony Lopez, interview by author, March 2012, Quijotoa AZ.
21. Louis Anthony Lopez, interview by author, March 2012, Quijotoa AZ.
22. Louis Anthony Lopez, interview by author, March 2012, Quijotoa AZ.
23. Bernard Siquieros, interview by author, April 2012, Topawa AZ.
24. Bernard Siquieros, interview by author, April 2012, Topawa AZ.
25. Bernard Siquieros, interview by author, April 2012, Topawa AZ.
26. de Certeau, *Practice of Everyday Life*, xiii.
27. Bahr, "Santa Rosa, Arizona."
28. For more on Bernard Siquieros's photography of O'odham pilgrimages to Magdalena, see Schermerhorn and McEnaney, "Through Indigenous Eyes."
29. Bernard Siquieros, interview by author, April 2012, Topawa AZ.
30. Bernard Siquieros, interview by author, April 2012, Topawa AZ.
31. Bernard Siquieros, interview by author, April 2012, Topawa AZ.
32. Bernard Siquieros, interview by author, April 2012, Topawa AZ.
33. Louis Anthony Lopez, interview by author, March 2012, Sells AZ.
34. For a similar example, see Hughes, *Biography*, 176–78.
35. Pretina Kathleen Stabolepszy also notes that those O'odham who go to Catholic chapels are called "santos" by those who do not in Stabolepszy, "Laughing Softly," 59.
36. Simon Lopez, interview by author, February 2012, Santa Rosa AZ.
37. Simon Lopez, interview by author, February 2012, Santa Rosa AZ.
38. Simon Lopez, interview by author, February 2012, Santa Rosa AZ.
39. Simon Lopez, interview by author, February 2012, Santa Rosa AZ.
40. Manuel and Neff, *Desert Indian Woman*, 165.
41. Manuel and Neff, *Desert Indian Woman*, 11, 88–89.
42. Manuel and Neff, *Desert Indian Woman*, 11.
43. Dolores, "Papago Nicknames," 45.
44. Nabhan, *Desert Smells Like Rain*, 79.
45. Rea, *Folk Mammology*, 195.
46. Shaw, *Pima Past*, 169–70.
47. Underhill, *Papago Woman*, 90.
48. Underhill, *Papago Woman*, 89–90. Anthropologist David Kozak's findings also support this determination in Kozak, "Cult of the Dead," 167–68; and Kozak, "Dying Badly," 214.
49. Underhill, *Papago Woman*, 90.
50. Joseph, Spicer, and Chesky, *Desert People*, 92n15.
51. Fontana, *Of Earth*, 55–57, 77–79.
52. McNally, *Ojibwe Singers*, 9.
53. Sheridan, "Kino's Unforeseen Legacy," 155–67.
54. King, "Folk Catholicism," 114.

55. Louis Anthony Lopez, interview by author, March 2012, Quijotoa AZ.

56. Louis Anthony Lopez, interview by author, March 2012, Quijotoa AZ.

57. Don Bahr also says that this is "one sacrament," with "two occasions," which he claims "play on or respond to the Christian rights of baptism and, surprisingly, communion," in Bahr, "La Longue Conversion," 15.

58. Bahr, "La Longue Conversion," 15.

59. Rea, *Desert's Green Edge*, 131.

60. Giff, "Pima Blue Swallow Songs," 132.

61. Underhill, *Social Organization*, 165.

62. Lévi-Strauss, *Raw and the Cooked*.

63. Simon Lopez, interview by author, February 2012, Santa Rosa AZ; also Simon Lopez, interview by author, October 2016, Santa Rosa AZ.

64. Louis Anthony Lopez, interview by author, March 2012, Sells AZ.

65. Louis Anthony Lopez, interview by author, March 2012, Quijotoa AZ.

66. Tsing, *Friction*; de Certeau, *Practice of Everyday Life*.

CONCLUSION

1. For example, in an explanatory note at the end of one of her poems, Ofelia Zepeda calls Baboquivari, or Waw Giwulig, "the most sacred mountain for the Tohono O'odham" in Zepeda, *Where Clouds Are Formed*, 59.

2. For excellent scholarly interventions against these trends, see Wenger, *Religious Freedom*; and Wenger, *We Have a Religion*.

3. Nabhan, *Desert Smells Like Rain*, 16.

4. Zepeda, *Where Clouds Are Formed*, 15.

5. According to Claude Lévi-Strauss, "The 'bricoleur' has no precise equivalent in English. He is a man who undertakes odd jobs and is a Jack of all trades or a kind of professional do-it-yourself man." Lévi-Strauss, *Savage Mind*, 17.

6. See Sullivan and Beaman, *Varieties of Religious Establishment*; for discussion of "unmarked Christianity" in another context, see Fessenden, *Culture and Redemption*, 3–5; and Albanese, *America*, 402.

7. Kaell, "Seeing the Invisible," 136, 139.

8. Kaell, "Seeing the Invisible," 162.

9. Schermerhorn, "Global Indigeneity," 199.

10. Sanneh, *Whose Religion Is Christianity?*; Schwarz, *Fighting Colonialism*; Clifford, *Returns*.

11. Iverson, *When Indians Became Cowboys*; Iverson, *Riders of the West*; Samuels, *Putting a Song*; Marshall, *Upward, Not Sunwise*, 101–28; Jacobsen, *Sound of Navajo Country*; Miller, *Reservation "Capitalism"*; Rosier, *Serving Their Country*; Child, *Boarding School Seasons*; Leap, *American Indian English*; Moss, "English"; Bahr, Gregorio, Lopez, and Alvarez., *Piman Shamanism*; Alvord and Van Pelt, *Scalpel*.

12. For example, see Smoak, *Ghost Dances and Identity*, 199.

1. In their work to conceive of these so-called oral traditions, or "myths," as "history," and in so doing denaturalize what normally gets to count as "history," I am influenced by and build upon the work of the following scholars: Ortiz, "Some Concerns"; Morrison, *Solidarity of Kin*; Shorter, *We Will Dance.*

2. Spicer, *Cycles of Conquest*; Dobyns, *Papago People*; Fontana, *Of Earth*; W. Erickson, *Sharing the Desert.*

3. Lorini, "Pageant of Father Kino," 412–14.

4. For seventeenth-century New Mexico and the revolt of 1680, see Schermerhorn, "Christianity, Kachinas, Crosses." For Kino's impact on the O'odham, see Sheridan, "Kino's Unforeseen Legacy."

5. Bolton, *Padre on Horseback*; McCarty, "Jesuits and Franciscans," 36.

6. Schuetz-Miller and Fontana, "Mission Churches," 67; Bayne, "Willy-Nilly Baptisms."

7. As a side note, the Tohono O'odham organizers of the walk to Magdalena are all aware of this revolt; yet despite having hard feelings about the revolt and its gruesome aftermath, Tubutama is the town where we begin actually walking to Magdalena, about sixty kilometers away.

8. For more on the life of Eusebio Francisco Kino, see Bolton, *Rim of Christendom.*

9. Joseph, Spicer, and Chesky, *Desert People*, 85–86; Griffith, *Beliefs and Holy Places*, 36; Fontana, *Of Earth*, 103.

10. Font, "Letters." While contemporary ethnographers may observe affectionate interaction between O'odham and Saint Francis in Magdalena today, it is worth noting that in the past, if not the present, O'odham have clearly had other ways of relating with Saint Francis as well.

11. Griffith, *Beliefs and Holy Places*, 38.

12. Mary Narcho, interview by author, July 2012, San Xavier AZ.

13. Mary Narcho, interview by author, July 2012, San Xavier AZ.

14. Andrae Marak and Laura Tuennerman illustrate how during this time O'odham were viewed by both United States and Mexican governments as "proto-citizens," who had not yet earned the rights and responsibilities of full citizenship, in Marak and Tuennerman, *At the Border.*

15. Shaw, *Pima Past*, 91.

16. Shaw, *Pima Past*, 92.

17. Ezell, "History of the Pima," 158.

18. Antone and Pack, "Life History," 346.

19. Joseph, Spicer, and Chesky, *Desert People*, 25.

20. Joseph, Spicer, and Chesky, *Desert People*, 92.

21. Spicer, *Cycles of Conquest*, 139–40; Waddell, "Mesquite and Mountains."

22. Joseph, Spicer, and Chesky, *Desert People*; Fontana, *Of Earth*; Griffith, *Beliefs and Holy Places*; for an account of Father Bonaventura Oblasser's life that smacks of hagiography, see Rohder, *Padre*.

23. Simon Lopez, interview by author, February 2012, Santa Rosa AZ.

24. Griffith, *Beliefs and Holy Places*, 70; Bonaventure Oblasser's papers are housed in the Special Collections Library at the University of Arizona in Tucson, Arizona.

25. Dobyns, "Do-It-Yourself Religion," 63–64; for discussions of Yoeme Christianity see Shorter, *We Will Dance*; Painter, *With Good Heart*.

26. Kozak and D. Lopez, *Devil Sickness*, 77–78. David Lopez's narrative is also corroborated by Father Bonaventure Oblasser, O.F.M.:

> FR. VENTURA: The first chapel, the only chapel built before we came was when these two fellows came back from, from, a, from, a, Magdalena.
>
> FONTANA: Mmm.
>
> FR. VENTURA: See, they had gone, gone to Magdalena. . . . And then they came back and they started that, a little chapel at, little chapel at Santa Rosa, one man, about as big as this room.

Oblasser, Oral History Interview by Bernard Fontana, n.d., Bonaventure Oblasser Papers, MS 300, box 8, folder 9, 77.

27. Dobyns, *Papago People*, 38.

28. Stabolepszy, "Laughing Softly," 38–39, 61.

29. A. Bahr, "Spanish Songs," unpublished manuscript.

30. Hill, *Everyday Language*, 119–57.

31. Griffith, *Beliefs and Holy Places*, 87.

32. Joseph, Spicer, and Chesky, *Desert People*, 89.

33. Blaine, *Papagos and Politics*, 20. Peter Blaine Sr.'s papers are housed in the Arizona Historical Society Library and Archives, Oral History Collection, in Tucson, Arizona.

34. Griffith, *Beliefs and Holy Places*, 47.

35. Joe Joaquin, interview by author, April 2012, Sells AZ.

36. Nabhan, *Desert Legends*, 21.

37. For the path toward Native American "religious freedom," see Wenger, "We Are Guaranteed Freedom"; Wenger, *We Have a Religion*; and Wenger, "Indian Dances."

38. For more on the transformations taking place in this period, see D. Lewis, *Neither Wolf nor Dog*, 149–67.

39. Dobyns, "Papagos in the Cotton Fields."

40. Dobyns, *Papago People*, 67; see also Meeks, "Tohono O'odham," 484.

41. Kukar et al., "Spiritual Norms."

1. One might also ask why some speech genres are translated as verbs, or actions that produce speech, and why others are nouns, or products of speech. My understanding of the O'odham language is too limited to answer this question with much certainty, but I can say that the O'odham language, like many indigenous languages, has far fewer words than English and, more importantly, that many of these words can be translated into English both as nouns and as verbs. See chapter 4 on *himdag*, for example. Finally, I should note that these grammatical categories are Western, rather than indigenous, categories.

2. Bahr, *How Mockingbirds Are*, 110–11, 151n3.

3. Bahr, *How Mockingbirds Are*, 18.

4. Bahr, *Pima and Papago*, 5.

5. Manuel and Neff, *Desert Indian Woman*, xxi.

6. Bahr, *Pima and Papago*, 6.

7. Bahr, *Pima and Papago*, 7–8.

8. Manuel and Neff, *Desert Indian Woman*, 142.

9. Frances Manuel explained to Deborah Neff, "I think it is going to be better when the person tells the things that happen, remembers what happened in their life. I'm sure everybody has these stories. I think that's what should be told! Legends have already been told!" Manuel and Neff, *Desert Indian Woman*, 141–42.

10. Webb, *Pima Remembers*, 91.

11. Bahr, *How Mockingbirds Are*, 6–7.

12. Bahr, "Oral Literatures," 222.

13. Bahr, "Oral Literatures," 227; see also Bahr, *O'odham Creation*, xxxi.

14. Bahr and Haefer, "Song in Piman Curing," 103.

15. Bahr, "Oral Literatures," 226.

16. Bahr, *Pima and Papago*, 6.

17. Kozak, "Whirlwind Songs," 340.

18. Bahr, Giff, and Havier, "Piman Songs on Hunting," 246.

19. Haefer, "Musical Thought," 164.

20. Bahr, *Pima and Papago*, 7.

BIBLIOGRAPHY

ARCHIVES AND MANUSCRIPTS

Bahr, Adelaide. "The Spanish Songs of Papago Indians." 1980. Unpublished manuscript in possession of the author.

Bahr, Donald M. "Santa Rosa, Arizona." 1964. Unpublished manuscript in possession of the author.

Blaine, Peter, Sr. Peter Blaine, Sr. Collection. AV 0362-01 and AV 0384v. Arizona Historical Society Library and Archives, Tucson.

Dolores, Juan. "Autobiography." N.d. Bancroft Library, University of California, Berkeley.

Oblasser, Bonaventure. Oral History Interview by Bernard Fontana, n.d. Bonaventure Oblasser Papers, MS 300, box 8, folder 9. University of Arizona, Special Collections Library.

Painter, Muriel Thayer. "Field Notes—Magdalena." Muriel Thayer Painter Collection, MS 18. Arizona State Museum Library and Archives, Tucson.

Rios, Theodore, and Kathleen Mullen Sands. Theodore Rios–Kathleen Mullen Sands Collection. Tohono O'odham Nation Cultural Center and Museum, Himdag Ki: Hukĭhu, Hemu, Im B I-Ha'ap, Library and Archives, Topawa AZ.

Schwarz, Augustine. Father Augustine Schwarz Collection. MSS 153. Arizona State University Archives, Tempe.

Shaul, David L. "Piast and Pilgrimage: Cultural and Linguistic Accommodation in a Piman Worldview." N.d. Unpublished manuscript in possession of the author.

Underhill, Ruth Murray. Papers. Denver Museum of Nature and Science.

PUBLISHED WORKS

Albanese, Catherine. *America: Religions and Religion*. 2nd ed. Belmont CA: Wadsworth, 1992.

Alvarez, Albert, and Kenneth Hale. "Toward a Manual of Papago Grammar: Some Phonological Terms." *International Journal of American Linguistics* 36, no. 2 (April 1970): 83–97.

Alvord, Lori Arviso, and Elizabeth Cohen Van Pelt. *The Scalpel and the Silver Bear: The First Navajo Woman Surgeon Combines Western Medicine and Traditional Healing*. New York: Bantam Books, 1999.

Antone, Alfretta, and Sam Peck. "The Life History of a Pima-Maricopa Woman and Her Speech to Pope John Paul II." In *Inside Dazzling Mountains: Southwest Native Verbal Arts*, edited by David L. Kozak, 339–55. Lincoln: University of Nebraska Press, 2012.

Appadurai, Arjun. *Modernity at Large: Cultural Dimensions of Globalization*. Minneapolis: University of Minnesota Press, 1996.

———, ed. *The Social Life of Things: Commodities in Cultural Perspective*. Cambridge: Cambridge University Press, 1988.

Astor-Aguilera, Miguel Angel. *The Maya World of Communicating Objects: Quadripartite Crosses, Trees, and Stones*. Albuquerque: University of New Mexico Press, 2010.

Astor-Aguilera, Miguel, and Robert Jarvenpa. "Comparing Indigenous Pilgrimages: Devotion, Identity, and Resistance in Mesoamerica and North America." *Anthropos* 103, no. 2 (2008): 483–506.

Bahr, Donald M. "Ages of O'odham Architecture." *Journal of the Southwest* 47, no. 3 (Autumn 2005): 497–521.

———. "Easter, Keruk, and Wi:gita." In *Performing the Renewal of Community: Indigenous Easter Rituals in North Mexico and Southwest United States*, edited by Rosamond B. Spicer and N. Ross Crumrine, 185–217. Lanham MD: University Press of America, 1997.

———. "Edenism: On the Star Husband-less Southwest." In *Inside Dazzling Mountains: Southwest Native Verbal Arts*, edited by David L. Kozak, 557–97. Lincoln: University of Nebraska Press, 2012.

———. "A Format and Method for Translating Songs." *Journal of American Folklore* 96, no. 380 (1983): 170–82.

———. "Four Papago Rattlesnake Songs." In *Speaking, Singing and Teaching: A Multidisciplinary Approach to Language Variation—Proceedings of the Eighth Annual Southwestern Areal Language and Linguistics Workshop*, edited by Florence Barkin and Elizabeth Brandt, 118–26. Anthropological Research Papers no. 20. Tempe: Arizona State University, 1980.

———. "A Grey and Fervent Shamanism." *Journal de la Société des Américanistes* 77 (1991): 7–26.

———. *How Mockingbirds Are: O'odham Ritual Orations.* Albany: State University of New York Press, 2011.

———. "La Longue Conversion des Pimas-Papagos." *Recherches Amérindiennes au Québec* 21, no. 4 (1991): 5–20.

———. "La Modernisation du Chamanisme Pima-Papago." *Recherches Amérindiennes au Québec* 18, nos. 2–3 (1988): 69–81.

———. "Native American Dream Songs, Myth, Memory, and Improvisation." *Journal de la Société des Americanistes* 80 (1994): 73–94.

———, ed. *O'odham Creation and Related Events: As Told to Ruth Benedict in 1927 in Prose, Oratory, and Song by the Pimas William Blackwater, Thomas Vanyiko, Clara Ahiel, William Stevens, Oliver Wellington, and Kisto.* Tucson: University of Arizona Press, 2001.

———. "O'odham Traditions about the Hohokam." In Fish and Fish, *Hohokam Millennium*, 123–29.

———. "The Oral Literatures of Small Nations." In *Ethnographic Essays in Cultural Anthropology: A Problem-Based Approach*, edited by R. Bruce Morrison and C. Roderick Wilson, 211–34. Belmont CA: Wadsworth/Thomson, 2002.

———. "Papago Ocean Songs and the Wi:gita." *Journal of the Southwest* 33, no. 4 (Winter 1991): 539–56.

———. *Pima and Papago Ritual Oratory: A Study of Three Texts.* San Francisco: Indian Historian Press, 1975.

———. "Pima Heaven Songs." In *Recovering the Word: Essays on Native American Literature*, edited by Brian Swann and Arnold Krupat, 198–246. Berkeley: University of California Press, 1987.

———. "Pima-Papago Christianity." *Journal of the Southwest* 30, no. 2 (Summer 1988): 133–67.

———. "Pima Swallow Songs." *Cultural Anthropology* 1, no. 2 (May 1986): 171–87.

———. "Who Were the Hohokam? The Evidence from Pima-Papago Myths." *Ethnohistory* 18, no. 3 (Summer 1971): 245–66.

Bahr, Donald M., and Susan Fenger. "Indians and Missions: Homage to and Debate with Rupert Costo and Jeanette Henry." *Journal of the Southwest* 31, no. 3 (Autumn 1989): 300–321.

Bahr, Donald M., Joseph Giff, and Manuel Havier. "Piman Songs on Hunting." *Ethnomusicology* 23, no. 2 (May 1979): 245–96.

Bahr, Donald M., Juan Gregorio, David I. Lopez, and Albert Alvarez. *Piman Shamanism and Staying Sickness (Ká:cim Múmkidag).* 1973. Tucson: University of Arizona Press, 1981.

Bahr, Donald M., and J. Richard Haefer. "Song in Piman Curing." *Ethnomusicology* 22, no. 1 (January 1978): 89–122.

Bahr, Donald M., Lloyd Paul, and Vincent Joseph. *Ants and Orioles: Showing the Art of Pima Poetry.* Salt Lake City: University of Utah Press, 1997.

Bahr, Donald M., Juan Smith, William Smith Allison, and Julian Hayden. *The Short Swift Time of Gods on Earth: The Hohokam Chronicles.* Berkeley: University of California Press, 1994.

Bakhtin, Mikhail M. *The Dialogic Imagination: Four Essays.* Edited by Michael Holquist. Translated by Caryl Emerson and Michael Holquist. Austin: University of Texas Press, 1981.

———. *Rabelais and His World.* Translated by Hélène Iswolsky. Bloomington: Indiana University Press, 1984.

Basso, Keith H. *Western Apache Language and Culture: Essays in Linguistic Anthropology.* Tucson: University of Arizona Press, 1990.

———. *Wisdom Sits in Places: Landscape and Language among the Western Apache.* Albuquerque: University of New Mexico Press, 1996.

Bataille, Gretchen M., and Kathleen Mullen Sands. *American Indian Women: Telling Their Lives.* Lincoln: University of Nebraska Press, 1984.

Baylor, Bird. *Yes Is Better Than No.* 1977. New York: Avon Books, 1980.

Bayne, Brandon. "Willy-Nilly Baptisms and *Chichimeca* Freedoms: Missionary Disputes, Indigenous Desires and the 1695 O'odham Revolt." *Journal of Early Modern History* 21, nos. 1–2 (2017): 9–37.

Begay, Alice, Jamie Encinas, Shamie Encinas, Michael Enis, Daniel Franco, Alexandria Lopez, and Dawn Lopez. "San Xavier: Learning History . . . Making History." Tucson: San Xavier District and the Tucson/Pima Arts Council, 2000.

Benavides, Gustavo. "The Tyranny of the Gerund in the Study of Religion." In *Temi E Problemi Della Storia Delle Religioni Nell'europa Contemporanea,* edited by Giulia Sfameni Gasparro, 53–66. Cosenza: Edizioni Lionello Giordano.

Blaine, Peter, Sr. *Papagos and Politics.* Tucson: Arizona Historical Society, 1981.

Bolton, Herbert Eugene. *The Padre on Horseback.* 1932. Chicago: Loyola University Press, 1963.

———. *Rim of Christendom: A Biography of Eusebio Francisco Kino, Pacific Coast Pioneer.* 1936. Tucson: University of Arizona Press, 1984.

Booth, Peter M. "Creation of a Nation: The Development of the Tohono O'odham Political Culture, 1900–1937." PhD diss., Purdue University, 2000.

Bourdieu, Pierre. "Genesis and Structure of the Religious Field." *Comparative Social Research* 13 (1991): 1–44.

———. *The Logic of Practice.* Stanford: Stanford University Press, 1990.

———. *Outline of a Theory of Practice.* 1972. Translated by Richard Nice. Cambridge: Cambridge University Press, 1977.

Buckley, Thomas. *Standing Ground: Yurok Indian Spirituality, 1850–1990.* Berkeley: University of California Press, 2002.

Casey, Edward S. "How to Get from Space to Place in a Fairly Short Stretch of Time: Phenomenological Prolegomena." In *Senses of Place*, edited by Steven Feld and Keith H. Basso, 13–52. Santa Fe: School of American Research Press, 1996.

Castillo, Guadalupe, and Margo Cowan, eds. *It Is Not Our Fault: The Case for Amending Present Nationality Law to Make All Members of the Tohono O'odham Nation United States Citizens, Now and Forever*. Sells AZ: Tohono O'odham Nation, Executive Branch, 2001.

Chana, Leonard F., Susan Lobo, and Barbara Chana. *The Sweet Smell of Home: The Life and Art of Leonard F. Chana*. Tucson: University of Arizona Press, 2009.

Chesky, Jane. "Indian Music of the Southwest." *Kiva* 7, no. 3 (December 1941): 9–12.

———. "The Nature and Function of Papago Music." Master's thesis, University of Arizona, 1943.

Chidester, David, and Edward T. Linenthal, eds. *American Sacred Space*. Bloomington: Indiana University Press, 1995.

Child, Brenda J. *Boarding School Seasons: American Indian Families, 1900–1940*. Lincoln: University of Nebraska Press, 1998.

Clifford, James. *Returns: Becoming Indigenous in the Twenty-First Century*. Cambridge MA: Harvard University Press, 2013.

———. *Routes: Travel and Translation in the Late Twentieth Century*. Cambridge MA: Harvard University Press, 1997.

Coleman, Simon, and John Eade. "Introduction: Reframing Pilgrimage." In *Reframing Pilgrimage: Cultures in Motion*, edited by Simon Coleman and John Eade, 1–25. London: Routledge, 2004.

Coleman, Simon, and John Eade, eds. *Reframing Pilgrimage: Cultures in Motion*. London: Routledge, 2004.

Coleman, Simon, and John Elsner. *Pilgrimage: Past and Present in the World Religions*. Cambridge MA: Harvard University Press, 1995.

———. "Pilgrim Voices: Authoring Christian Pilgrimage." In *Pilgrim Voices: Narrative and Authorship in Christian Pilgrimage*, edited by Simon Coleman and John Elsner, 1–16. New York: Berghahn Books, 2002.

Conklin, Beth A., and Lynn M. Morgan. "Babies, Bodies, and the Production of Personhood in North America and a Native Amazonian Society." *Ethos* 24, no. 4 (December 1996): 657–94.

Cosgrove, Denis. "Landscapes and Myths, Gods and Humans." In *Landscape: Politics and Perspectives*, edited by Barbara Bender, 281–305. Oxford: Berg, 1993.

———. *Social Formation and Symbolic Landscape*. London: Croom Helm, 1984.

Counts, David R., and Dorothy A. Counts. "Conclusions: Coping with the Final Tragedy." In *Coping with the Final Tragedy: Cultural Variation in Dying and Grieving*, edited by David R. Counts and Dorothy A. Counts, 277–91. Amityville NY: Baywood, 1991.

Daniel, E. Valentine. *Fluid Signs: Being a Person the Tamil Way*. Berkeley: University of California Press, 1984.

Darling, J. Andrew. "S-cuk Kavick: Thoughts on Migratory Process and the Archaeology of O'odham Migration." In *Rethinking Anthropological Perspectives on Migration*, edited by Graciela S. Cabana and Jeffery J. Clark, 68–83. Gainesville: University Press of Florida, 2011.

———. "O'odham Trails and the Archaeology of Space." In *Landscapes of Movement: Trails, Paths, and Roads in Anthropological Perspective*, edited by James E. Snead, Clark L. Erickson, and J. Andrew Darling, 61–83. Pittsburgh: University of Pennsylvania Museum of Archaeology and Anthropology, 2009.

Darling, J. Andrew, and B. Sunday Eiselt. "Trails Research in the Gila Bend Area." In *Trails, Rock Features and Homesteading in the Gila Bend Area: A Report on the State Route 85, Gila Bend to Buckeye Archaeological Project*, edited by J. C. Czarzasty, K. Peterson, G. E. Rice, and J. A. Darling, 199–227. Anthropological Research Papers no. 4. Arizona State University Anthropological Field Studies no. 43. Sacaton AZ: Gila River Indian Community, 2009.

Darling, J. Andrew, and Barnaby V. Lewis. "Songscapes and Calendar Sticks," In *Living in the Ancient Southwest*, edited by David Grant Noble, 149–58. Santa Fe: School for Advanced Research Press, 2014. Originally published in Fish and Fish, *Hohokam Millennium*.

de Certeau, Michel. *The Practice of Everyday Life*. 1980. Translated by Steven Rendall. Berkeley: University of California Press, 1984.

———. *The Writing of History*. 1975. Translated by Tom Conley. New York: Columbia University Press, 1988.

De Grazia, Ted. "Papago Pilgrimage." *Arizona Highways* 35, no. 10 (October 1959): 10–13.

de la Cadena, Marisol. *Earth Beings: Ecologies of Practice across Andean Worlds*. Durham NC: Duke University Press, 2015.

Deloria, Philip J. *Indians in Unexpected Places*. Lawrence: University of Kansas Press, 2004.

Deloria, Vine, Jr. *God Is Red: A Native View of Religion*. 1972. Golden CO: Fulcrum, 1992.

Densmore, Frances. *Papago Music*. 1929. New York: De Capo Press, 1972.

Derrida, Jacques. "Structure, Sign, and Play in the Discourse of the Human Sciences." In *Writing and Difference*, translated by Alan Bass, 351–70. 1978. Chicago: University of Chicago Press, 2005.

Dobyns, Henry F. "*Do-It-Yourself* Religion: The Diffusion of Folk Catholicism on Mexico's Northern Frontier, 1821–46." In *Pilgrimage in Latin America*, edited by N. Ross Crumrine and Alan Morinis, 53–67. New York: Greenwood Press, 1991.

———. *The Papago People*. Phoenix: Indian Tribal Series, 1972.

———. "Papago Pilgrims on the Town." *Kiva* 16, nos. 1–2 (September–October 1950): 27–32.

———. *Papagos in the Cotton Fields*. Tucson, 1951.

———. "The Religious Festival." PhD diss., Cornell University, 1960.

Dolores, Juan. "Papago Nicknames," In *Essays in Anthropology in Honor of Alfred Kroeber*, edited by J. Alden Mason, 45–47. Berkeley: University of California Press, 1936.

Dolores, Juan, and Madeleine Mathiot. "The Reminiscences of Juan Dolores, an Early O'odham Linguist." *Anthropological Linguistics* 33, no. 3 (1991): 232–315.

Dubisch, Jill. "'Heartland of America': Memory, Motion and the (Re)construction of History on a Motorcycle Pilgrimage." In *Reframing Pilgrimage: Cultures in Motion*, edited by Simon Coleman and John Eade, 105–32. London: Routledge, 2004.

———. *In a Different Place: Pilgrimage, Gender, and Politics at a Greek Island Shrine*. Princeton NJ: Princeton University Press, 1995.

Eade, John, and Michael J. Sallnow. Introduction to *Contesting the Sacred: The Anthropology of Christian Pilgrimage*, edited by John Eade and Michael J. Sallnow, 1–29. London: Routledge, 1991.

Eliade, Mircea. *Cosmos and History: The Myth of the Eternal Return*. Translated by Willard R. Trask. 1949. New York: Harper and Row, 1959.

———. *The Sacred and the Profane: The Nature of Religion*. Translated by Willard R. Trask. 1959. New York: Harcourt Brace, 1987.

Engelke, Matthew. "Angels in Swindon: Public Religion and Ambient Faith in England." *American Ethnologist* 39, no. 1 (February 2012): 155–70.

Erickson, Kirstin C. *Yaqui Homeland and Homeplace: The Everyday Production of Ethnic Identity*. Tucson: University of Arizona Press, 2008.

Erickson, Winston P. *Sharing the Desert: The Tohono O'odham in History*. Tucson: University of Arizona Press, 1994.

Evers, Larry, ed. *The South Corner of Time: Hopi, Navajo, Papago, Yaqui Tribal Literature*. 1980. Tucson: University of Arizona Press, 1983.

Ezell, Paul H. "History of the Pima." In Ortiz, *Handbook of North American Indians*, 10: 149–60.

Feld, Steven. *Sound and Sentiment: Birds, Weeping, Poetics, and Song in Kaluli Expression*. 1982. Durham NC: Duke University Press, 2012.

Feld, Steven, and Keith H. Basso, eds. *Senses of Place*. Santa Fe: School of American Research Press, 1996.

Feldhaus, Anne. *Connected Places: Region, Pilgrimage, and Geographical Imagination in India*. New York: Palgrave MacMillan, 2003.

———. "Walking and Thinking." In *Mārga: Ways of Liberation, Empowerment, and Social Change in Maharashtra*, edited by E. Naito, I. Shima, and H. Kotani, 441–53. New Delhi: Manohar, 2008.

Fessenden, Tracy. *Culture and Redemption: Religion, the Secular, and American Literature*. Princeton NJ: Princeton University Press, 2007.

Fish, Suzanne K., and Paul R. Fish, eds. *The Hohokam Millennium*. Santa Fe: School for Advanced Research Press, 2007.

Fitzgerald, Colleen M. "Language Change and Motion Verbs in Tohono O'odham." Paper presented at the 23rd Annual Meeting of the Linguistic Association of the Southwest, New Orleans, September 10, 2004: 1–6. Accessed August 2017, http://www.uta.edu/faculty/cmfitz/2004lassohandout.pdf.

Fogelson, Raymond D. "Person, Self, and Identity: Some Anthropological Retrospects, Circumspects, and Prospects." In *Psychosocial Theories of the Self*, edited by Benjamin Lee, 67–109. New York: Plenum Press, 1982.

Font, Pedro. "Letters of Friar Pedro Font, 1776–1777." Translated by Dan S. Matson. *Ethnohistory* 22, no. 3 (Summer 1975): 263–93.

Fontana, Bernard L. "American Indian Oral History: An Anthropologist's Note." *History and Theory* 8, no. 3 (1969): 366–70.

———. "History of the Papago." In Ortiz, *Handbook of North American Indians*, 10: 137–48.

———. *Of Earth and Little Rain: The Papago Indians*. Tucson: University of Arizona Press, 1989.

———. "Pilgrimage to Magdalena." *American West* 18, no. 5 (1981): 40–45, 60.

———. "Pilgrimage to San Xavier." *Arizona Highways* 62, no. 11 (November 1986): 44–48, inside back cover.

———. "Pima and Papago: Introduction." In Ortiz, *Handbook of North American Indians*, 10: 125–36.

Foucault, Michel. "Questions on Geography." In *Power/Knowledge: Selected Interviews and Other Writings: 1972–1977*, edited by Colin Gordon, 63–77. New York: Pantheon Books, 1980.

———. "Technologies of the Self." In *Technologies of the Self: A Seminar with Michel Foucault*, edited by Luther H. Martin, Huck Gutman, and Patrick H. Hutton, 16–49. Amherst: University of Massachusetts Press, 1988.

Frey, Nancy Louise. *Pilgrim Stories: On and off the Road to Santiago*. Berkeley: University of California Press, 1998.

Frisch, Michael. *A Shared Authority: Essays on the Craft and Meaning of Oral and Public History*. Albany: State University of New York Press, 1990.

Gaillard, David D. "The Papago of Arizona and Sonora." *American Anthropologist* 7, no. 3 (July 1894): 293–96.

Galinier, Jacques. "From Montezuma to San Francisco: The Wi:gita Ritual in Papago (Tohono O'odham) Religion." Translated by Adelaide Bahr and Donald Bahr. *Journal of the Southwest* 33, no. 4 (Winter 1991): 486–538.

Geertz, Clifford. "Deep Play: Notes on the Balinese Cockfight." In *The Interpretation of Cultures*, 412–53. New York: Basic Books, 1973.

Geronimo, Ronald. "Establishing Connections to Place: Identifying O'odham Place Names in Early Spanish Documents." *Journal of the Southwest* 56, no. 2 (Summer 2014): 219–32.

Giff, Joseph. "Pima Blue Swallow Songs of Gratitude." Translated by Donald M. Bahr. In *Speaking, Singing and Teaching: A Multidisciplinary Approach to Language Variation—Proceedings of the Eighth Annual Southwestern Areal Language and Linguistics Workshop*, edited by Florence Barkin and Elizabeth Brandt, 127–39. Anthropological Research Paper no. 20. Tempe: Arizona State University, 1980.

Gill, Sam D. *Native American Religions: An Introduction.* Belmont CA: Wadsworth/Thomson Learning, 2005.

Gold, Ann Grodzins. *Fruitful Journeys: The Ways of Rajasthani Pilgrims.* 1988. Prospect Heights IL: Waveland Press, 2000.

Griffith, James S. *Beliefs and Holy Places: A Spiritual Geography of the Pimeria Alta.* Tucson: University of Arizona Press, 1992.

———. "The Catholic Religious Architecture of the Papago Reservation, Arizona." PhD diss., University of Arizona, 1973.

———. "The Folk-Catholic Chapels of the Papagueria." *Pioneer America* 7, no. 2 (July 1975): 21–36.

———. *Folk Saints of the Borderlands: Victims, Bandits, and Healers.* Tucson: Rio Nuevo, 2003.

———. "The Magdalena Holy Picture: Religious Folk Art in Two Cultures." *New York Folklore Quarterly* 8, nos. 3–4 (Winter 1982): 71–82.

———. "Magdalena Revisited: The Growth of a Fiesta." *Kiva* 33, no. 2 (December 1967): 82–86.

———. *Saints of the Southwest.* Tucson: Rio Nuevo, 2000.

———. "Waila: The Social Dance Music of the Tohono O'odham." In *Musics of Multicultural America: A Study of Twelve Musical Communities*, edited by Kip Lornell and Anne K. Rasmussen, 187–207. London: Schirmer Books, 1997.

Grossmann, Frederick E. "The Pima Indians of Arizona." In *Annual Report of the Board of Regents of the Smithsonian Institution for 1871*, 407–19. Washington DC: Government Printing Office, 1873.

Gunst, Marie Louise. "Ceremonials of the Papago and Pima Indians, with Special Emphasis on the Relation of the Dance to Their Religion." Master's thesis, University of Arizona, 1930.

Hackenberg, Robert A. "Pima and Papago Ecological Adaptations." In Ortiz, *Handbook of North American Indians*, 10: 161–77.

Haefer, John Richard. "Musical Thought in Papago Culture." PhD diss., University of Illinois, 1981.

———. *Papago Music and Dance.* Tsaile AZ: Navajo Community College Press, 1977.

Hale, Kenneth. "A Papago Grammar." PhD diss., Indiana University, 1959.

Hall, Sharlot M. "The Story of a Pima Record Rod." *Out West: A Magazine of the Old Pacific and the New* 26 (1907): 413–23.

Hallowell, A. Irving. "Ojibwa Ontology, Behavior, and World View." In *Culture in History: Essays in Honor of Paul Radin*, edited by Stanley Diamond, 18–52. New York: Columbia University Press, 1960. Reprinted in Dennis Tedlock and Barbara Tedlock, eds. *Teachings from the American Earth: Indian Religion and Philosophy*, 139–78. New York: Liveright Press, 1975.

Hamill, Chad S. *Songs of Power and Prayer in the Columbia Plateau: The Jesuit, the Medicine Man, and the Indian Hymn Singer*. Corvallis: Oregon State University Press, 2012.

Harrison, Regina. *Signs, Songs, and Memory in the Andes: Translating Quechua Language and Culture*. Austin: University of Texas Press, 1989.

Hayden, Julian D. "Of Hohokam Origins and Other Matters." *American Antiquity* 35, no. 1 (January 1970): 87–93.

Herzog, George. "A Comparison of Pueblo and Pima Musical Styles." *Journal of American Folk-Lore* 49, no. 194 (October–December 1936): 283–417.

———. "Culture Change and Language: Shifts in the Pima Vocabulary." *Language, Culture, and Personality: Essays in Memory of Edward Sapir*, edited by Leslie Spier, A. Irving Hallowell, and Stanley S. Newman, 66–74. Menasha WI: Sapir Memorial Fund, 1941.

———. "Musical Styles in North America." *Proceedings: Twenty-Third International Congress of Americanists*, New York, September 17-22, 1928, 455–58.

———. "Music in the Thinking of the American Indian." *Peabody Bulletin* 34, no. 1 (1938): 8–12.

Hill, Jane H. *The Everyday Language of White Racism*. Malden MA: Wiley-Blackwell, 2008.

Hill, Jane H., and Ofelia Zepeda. "Tohono O'odham (Papago) Plurals." *Anthropological Linguistics* 40, no. 1 (Spring 1998): 1–42.

Hirsch, Eric, and Michael O'Hanlon, eds. *The Anthropology of Landscape: Perspectives on Space and Place*. Oxford: Clarendon Press, 1995.

Hirschkind, Charles. *The Ethical Soundscape: Cassette Sermons and Islamic Counterpublics*. New York: Columbia University Press, 2006.

Hobsbawm, Eric, and Terence Ranger, eds. *The Invention of Tradition*. Cambridge: Cambridge University Press, 1983.

Hughes, Jennifer Scheper. *Biography of a Mexican Crucifix: Lived Religion and Local Faith from the Conquest to the Present*. Oxford: Oxford University Press, 2010.

Ingold, Tim, and Jo Lee Vergunst. Introduction to *Ways of Walking: Ethnography and Practice on Foot*, edited by Tim Ingold and Jo Lee Vergunst, 1–19. Burlington VT: Ashgate, 2008.

Iverson, Peter. *Riders of the West: Portraits from Indian Rodeo*. Seattle: University of Washington Press, 1999.

———. *When Indians Became Cowboys: Native Peoples and Cattle Ranching in the American West*. Norman: University of Oklahoma Press, 1994.

Jacobsen, Kristina M. *The Sound of Navajo Country: Music, Language, and Diné Belonging*. Chapel Hill: University of North Carolina Press, 2017.

Johnson, Greg. "Native Traditions of North America." *Brill Dictionary of Religion*, edited by Kocku von Stuckrad, 1341–50. Leiden: E. J. Brill, 2006.

———. *Sacred Claims: Repatriation and Living Tradition*. Charlottesville: University of Virginia Press, 2007.

Joseph, Alice, Rosamond B. Spicer, and Jane Chesky. *The Desert People: A Study of the Papago People*. 1949. Chicago: University of Chicago Press, 1974.

Kaell, Hillary. "Seeing the Invisible: Ambient Catholicism on the Side of the Road." *Journal of the American Academy of Religion* 85, no. 1 (March 2017): 136–67.

———. *Walking Where Jesus Walked: American Christians and Holy Land Pilgrimage*. New York: New York University Press, 2014.

Kant, Immanuel. *Critique of Judgment*. Translated by James Creed Meredith. 1790. Oxford: Clarendon, 1988.

———. *Critique of Pure Reason*. Translated by Marcus Weigelt and Max Muller. 1781. New York: Penguin Classics, 2008.

Kilcrease, A. T. "Ninety-Five Years of History of the Papago Indians." *Southwestern Monuments Monthly Report, Supplement for April*, 297–310. Coolidge AZ: U.S. Department of Interior, National Park Service, 1939.

King, William S. "The Folk Catholicism of the Tucson Papagos." Master's thesis, University of Arizona, 1954.

Kozak, David. "The Cult of the Dead: Neocolonialism, Violent Mortality, and Religious Change." Master's thesis, Arizona State University, 1990.

———. "Dying Badly: Violent Death and Religious Change among the Tohono O'odham." *Omega* 23, no. 3 (November 1991): 207–16.

———, ed. *Inside Dazzling Mountains: Southwest Native Verbal Arts*. Lincoln: University of Nebraska Press, 2012.

———. "Reifying the Body through the Medicalization of Violent Death." *Human Organization* 53, no. 1 (Spring 1994): 48–54.

———. "Shamanisms: Past and Present." *Religion and Culture: An Anthropological Focus*. Edited by Raymond Scupin, 106–21. Upper Saddle River NJ: Prentice Hall, 1999.

———. "Swallow Dizziness, the Laughter of Carnival, and Kateri." *Wicazo Sa Review* 8, no. 2 (Autumn 1992): 1–10.

———. "Whirlwind Songs." In *Contemporary Translations of the Native Literatures of North America*, edited by Brian Swann, 340–49. Lincoln: University of Nebraska Press, 2004.

Kozak, David, and Camillus Lopez. "The Tohono O'odham Shrine Complex: Memorializing the Locations of Violent Death." *New York Folklore* 17, nos. 1–2 (Winter–Spring 1991): 1–20.

Kozak, David L., and David I. Lopez. *Devil Sickness and Devil Songs: Tohono O'odham Poetics*. Washington DC: Smithsonian Institution Press, 1999.

——. "Echoes of Mythical Creation: Snakes, Sex, Voice." *Wicazo Sa Review* 10, no. 1 (Spring 1994): 52–58.

——. "Translating the Boundary between Life and Death in O'odham Devil Songs." In *Born in the Blood: On Native American Translation*, edited by Brian Swann, 275–85. Lincoln: University of Nebraska Press, 2011.

Kukar, Scott, Delitha Livingston, Laurel Mallett, and Veronica Nieto. "Spiritual Norms and Other Cultural Considerations for Tohono O'odham Elders (information received from person communication)." Robin Bonifas, School of Social Work, College of Public Programs, Arizona State University, n.d. Accessed August 2017, http://clas.uiowa.edu/socialwork/files/socialwork/NursingHomeResource /documents/SpiritualNormsforTohono_personalinterview_NativeAmericans _Supp2.pdf.

La Fontaine, J. S. "Person and Individual: Some Anthropological Reflections." In *The Category of the Person: Anthropology, Philosophy, History*, edited by Michael Carrithers, Steven Collins, and Steven Lukes, 123–40. Cambridge: Cambridge University Press, 1985.

Lagrou, Elsje Maria. "Homesickness and the Cashinahua Self: A Reflection on the Embodied Condition of Relatedness." In *The Anthropology of Love and Anger: The Aesthetics of Conviviality in Native Amazonia*, edited by Joanna Overing and Alan Passes, 152–69. London: Routledge, 2000.

Lamb, Sarah. "The Making and Unmaking of Persons: Notes on Aging and Gender in North India." *Ethos* 25, no. 3 (September 1997): 279–302.

Lassiter, Luke Eric, Clyde Ellis, and Ralph Kotay. *The Jesus Road: Kiowas, Christianity, and Indian Hymns*. Lincoln: University of Nebraska Press, 2002.

Leap, William L. *American Indian English*. Salt Lake City: University of Utah Press, 1993.

Lévi-Strauss, Claude. *The Raw and the Cooked*. 1964. New York: Harper and Row, 1969.

——. *The Savage Mind*. Chicago: University of Chicago Press, 1966.

Lewis, David Rich. *Neither Wolf nor Dog: American Indians, Environment, and Agrarian Change*. Oxford: Oxford University Press, 1984.

Lewis, Frank, and Donald Bahr. "Whither T-himdag." *Wicazo Sa Review* 8, no. 1 (Spring 1992): 70–90.

Lloyd, John William. *Aw-Aw-Tam Indian Nights: The Myths and Legends of the Pimas*. 1911. [London]: Forgotten Books, 2008.

Lock, Charles. "Bowing Down to Wood and Stone: One Way to Be a Pilgrim." In *Pilgrim Voices: Narrative and Authorship in Christian Pilgrimage*, edited by Simon Coleman and John Elsner, 110–32. New York: Berghahn Books, 2002.

Lopez, Daniel. "Huhugam." In Fish and Fish, *Hohokam Millennium*, 117–21.

Lorini, Alessandra. "The Pageant of Father Kino: From History to Public Memory and the Making of Usable Pasts." *Southern California Quarterly* 99, no. 4 (Winter 2017): 395–424.

Madsen, Kenneth. "A Basis for Bordering: Land, Migration, and Inter–Tohono O'odham Distinction along the US-Mexico Line." In *Placing the Border in Everyday Life*, edited by Reece Jones and Corey Johnson, 93–116. Burlington VT: Ashgate, 2014.

———. "A Nation across Nations: The Tohono O'odham and the U.S.-Mexico Border." PhD diss., Arizona State University, 2005.

Manuel, Frances, and Deborah Neff. *Desert Indian Woman: Stories and Dreams*. Tucson: University of Arizona Press, 2001.

Marak, Andrae M., and Laura Tuennerman. *At the Border of Empires: The Tohono O'odham, Gender, and Assimilation, 1880–1934*. Tucson: University of Arizona Press, 2013.

Marshall, Kimberly J. *Upward, Not Sunwise: Resonant Rupture in Navajo Neo-Pentecostalism*. Lincoln: University of Nebraska Press, 2016.

Martínez, David. "Hiding in the Shadows of History: Revitalizing Hia Ced O'odham Peoplehood." *Journal of the Southwest* 55, no. 2 (Summer 2013): 131–73.

Martin, Joel W., and Mark A. Nicholas, eds. *Native Americans, Christianity, and the Reshaping of the American Religious Landscape*. Chapel Hill: University of North Carolina Press, 2010.

Mason, J. Alden. "The Papago Migration Legend." *Journal of American Folk-Lore* 34, no. 133 (July–September 1921): 254–68.

Mathiot, Madeleine. *An Approach to the Cognitive Study of Language*. The Hague: Mouton, 1968.

———. *A Dictionary of Papago Usage*. 2 vols. Bloomington: Indiana University Press, 1973.

———. "Noun Classes and Folk Taxonomy in Papago." *American Anthropologist* 64, no. 2 (April 1962): 340–50.

Mauss, Marcel. *Sociology and Psychology: Essays*. Translated by Ben Brewster. 1950. London: Routledge and Keegan Paul, 1979.

McAlister, Elizabeth. "The Madonna of 115th Street Revisited: Vodou and Haitian Catholicism in the Age of Transnationalism." In *Gatherings in Diaspora: Religious Communities and the New Immigration*, edited by Stephen Warner and Judith Wittner, 123–60. Philadelphia: Temple University Press, 1998.

McCarthy, James. *A Papago Traveler: The Memories of James McCarthy*. Tucson: University of Arizona Press, 1985.

McCarty, Kieran R. "Jesuits and Franciscans." In *The Pimería Alta: Missions and More*, edited by James E. Officer, Mardith Scheutz-Miller, and Bernard L. Fontana, 35–46. Tucson: Southwestern Mission Research Center, 1996.

McNally, Michael. *Honoring Elders: Aging, Authority, and Ojibwe Religion*. New York: Columbia University Press, 2009.

————. *Ojibwe Singers: Hymns, Grief, and a Native Culture in Motion*. 2000. Saint Paul MN: Minnesota Historical Society Press, 2009.

Meeks, Eric V. *Border Citizens: The Making of Indians, Mexicans, and Anglos in Arizona*. Austin: University of Texas Press, 2007.

————. "The Tohono O'odham, Wage Labor, and Resistant Adaptation, 1900–1930." *Western Historical Quarterly* 34, no. 4 (Winter 2003): 468–89.

Merrell, James H. *The Indians' New World: Catawbas and Their Neighbors from European Contact through the Era of Removal*. New York: Norton, 1989.

Michalowski, Raymond J., and Jill Dubisch. *Run for the Wall: Remembering Vietnam on a Motorcycle Pilgrimage*. New Brunswick NJ: Rutgers University Press, 2001.

Miller, Robert J. *Reservation "Capitalism": Economic Development in Indian Country*. Lincoln: University of Nebraska Press, 2012.

Morinis, E. Alan, ed. *Pilgrimage in the Hindu Tradition: A Case Study of West Bengal*. Delhi: Oxford University Press, 1984.

————. *Sacred Journeys: The Anthropology of Pilgrimage*. Westport CT: Greenwood Press, 1992.

Morrison, Kenneth M. *The Solidarity of Kin: Ethnohistory, Religious Studies, and the Algonkian-French Religious Encounter*. Albany: State University of New York Press, 2002.

Moss, Meredith. "English with a Navajo Accent: Language and Ideology in Heritage Language Advocacy." PhD diss., Arizona State University, 2015.

Myerhoff, Barbara G. *Peyote Hunt: The Sacred Journey of the Huichol Indians*. Ithaca: Cornell University Press, 1974.

Nabhan, Gary Paul. *Cultures of Habitat: On Nature, Culture, and Story*. Washington DC: Counterpoint, 1997.

————. *Desert Legends: Re-Storying the Sonoran Borderlands*. New York: Henry Holt, 1994.

————. *The Desert Smells Like Rain: A Naturalist in Papago Indian Country*. San Francisco: North Point Press, 1982.

————. *Gathering the Desert*. Tucson: University of Arizona Press, 1985.

————. "The Moveable O'odham Feast of San Francisco." *Native Peoples* 4, no. 2 (Winter 1991): 28–34.

Nabokov, Peter. *A Forest of Time: American Indian Ways of History*. Cambridge: Cambridge University Press, 2002.

————. *Indian Running: Native American History and Tradition*. Santa Fe: Ancient City Press, 1981.

Narayanan, Vasudha. "Embodied Cosmologies: Sights of Piety, Sights of Power." *Journal of the American Academy of Religion* 71, no. 3 (September 2003): 495–520.

Oblasser, Bonaventure. "Present Day Religion of the Papagos." *Provincial Annals* 3, no. 3 (1941): 35–37.

O'Connor, Mary I. "The Pilgrimage to Magdalena." In *Anthropology of Religion: A Handbook*, edited by Steven D. Glazier, 369–89. Westport CT: Praeger, 1999.

Officer, James E., Mardith Scheutz-Miller, and Bernard L. Fontana, eds. *The Pimería Alta: Missions and More*. Tucson: Southwestern Mission Research Center, 1996.

Oktavec, Eileen. *Answered Prayers: Miracles and Milagros along the Border*. Tucson: University of Arizona Press, 1995.

Oosten, Jasper J. "A Few Critical Remarks on the Concept of Person." In *Concepts of Person in Religion and Thought*, edited by Hans G. Kippenberg, Yme B. Kuiper, and Andy F. Sanders, 25–33. Berlin: Mouton de Gruyter, 1990.

Orsi, Robert A. *Between Heaven and Earth: The Religious Worlds People Make and the Scholars Who Study Them*. Princeton NJ: Princeton University Press, 2005.

——. "Everyday Miracles: The Study of Lived Religion," In *Lived Religion in America: Toward a History of Practice*, edited by David Hall, 3–21. Princeton NJ: Princeton University Press, 1997.

——. *History and Presence*. Cambridge MA: Belknap Press of Harvard University Press, 2016.

Ortiz, Alfonso, ed. *Handbook of North American Indians*. Vol. 10: *Southwest*. Washington DC: Smithsonian Institution, 1983.

——. "Some Concerns Central to the Writing of 'Indian' History." *Indian Historian* 10, no. 1 (Winter 1977): 17–22.

Painter, Muriel Thayer. *With Good Heart: Yaqui Beliefs and Ceremonies in Pascua Village*. Tucson: University of Arizona Press, 1986.

Papago Tribe of Arizona. "Appendix A: A Chronology of Papago and Pima History Taken from Calendar Sticks." In *Facts about the Papago Indian Reservation and the Papago People*, A1–A11. 1939. Sells AZ: Bureau of Indian Affairs, Papago Agency, and the U.S. Public Health Service, 1972.

Parsons, Elsie Clews. "Notes on the Pima, 1926." *American Anthropologist* 30, no. 3 (July–September 1928): 445–64.

Pels, Peter. "The Modern Fear of Matter: Reflections on the Protestantism of Victorian Science." *Material Religion: The Journal of Objects, Art and Belief* 4, no. 3 (September 2008): 264–83.

Pilcher, William W. "Some Comments on the Folk Taxonomy of the Papago." *American Anthropologist* 69, no. 2 (April 1967): 204–8.

Pinegar, James Wendell. "Church Growth among the Papago Indians of Southern Arizona." Master's thesis, Abilene Christian College, 1971.

Poteat, W. H. "Persons and Places: Paradigms in Communication." In *Art and Religion as Communication*, edited by James Waddell and F. W. Dillistone, 185–89. Atlanta: John Knox Press, 1974.

Quilter, Jeffrey, and Gary Urton, eds. *Narrative Threads: Accounting and Recounting in Andean Khipu*. Austin: University of Texas Press, 2002.

Radding, Cynthia. *Landscapes of Power and Identity: Comparative Histories in the Sonoran Desert and the Forests of Amazonia from Colony to Republic*. Durham NC: Duke University Press, 2005.

Rea, Amadeo M. *At the Desert's Green Edge: An Ethnobotony of the Gila River Pima*. Tucson: University of Arizona Press, 1997.

————. *Folk Mammalogy of the Northern Pimans*. Tucson: University of Arizona Press, 1998.

————. *Wings in the Desert: A Folk Ornithology of the Northern Pimans*. Tucson: University of Arizona Press, 2007.

Reff, Daniel T. "Sympathy for the Devil: Devil Sickness and Lore among the Tohono O'odham." *Journal of the Southwest* 50, no. 4 (Winter 2008): 355–76.

Rios, Theodore, and Kathleen M. Sands. *Telling a Good One: The Process of a Native American Collaborative Biography*. Lincoln: University of Nebraska Press, 2000.

Rohder, Regis, O.F.M. *Padre to the Papagos: Father Bonaventura Oblasser*. Tucson AZ: Oblasser Library, San Xavier Mission, 1982.

Rosier, Paul C. *Serving Their Country: American Indian Politics and Patriotism in the Twentieth Century*. Cambridge MA: Harvard University Press, 2012.

Russell, Frank. "Pima Annals." *American Anthropologist* 5, no. 1 (January 1903): 76–80.

————. *The Pima Indians*. 1908. Tucson: University of Arizona Press, 1980.

Sahlins, Marshall. *Historical Metaphors and Mythical Realities: Structure in the Early History of the Sandwich Islands Kingdom*. Ann Arbor: University of Michigan Press, 1981.

————. *Islands of History*. Chicago: University of Chicago Press, 1985.

Sallnow, Michael J. "Pilgrimage and Cultural Fracture in the Andes." In *Contesting the Sacred: The Anthropology of Christian Pilgrimage*, edited by John Eade and Michael J. Sallnow, 137–53. London: Routledge, 1991.

————. *Pilgrims of the Andes: Regional Cults in Cusco*. Washington DC: Smithsonian Institution Press, 1987.

Salomon, Frank L. *The Cord Keepers: Khipus and Cultural Life in a Peruvian Village*. Durham NC: Duke University Press, 2004.

Samuels, David W. *Putting a Song on Top of It: Expression and Identity on the San Carlos Apache Reservation*. Tucson: University of Arizona Press, 2004.

Sanneh, Lamin. *Whose Religion Is Christianity? The Gospel beyond the West*. Grand Rapids MI: Eerdmans, 2003.

Santos-Granero, Fernando, ed. *The Occult Life of Things: Native Amazonian Theories of Materiality and Personhood*. 2009. Tucson: University of Arizona Press, 2013.

Saxton, Dean and Lucille Saxton. *O'othham Hoho'ok A'agitha: Legends and Lore of the Papago and Pima Indians*. Tucson: University of Arizona Press, 1973.

Saxton, Dean, Lucille Saxton, and Susie Enos. *Tohono O'odham/Pima to English, English to Tohono O'odham/Pima Dictionary*, edited by R. L. Cherry. 2nd ed. 1983. Tucson: University of Arizona Press, 1998.

Schermerhorn, Seth. "Christianity, Kachinas, Crosses, and Kivas: Religion, Resistance, and Revolt in Seventeenth Century New Mexico." *Next: The Graduate Student Journal for the Academic Study of Religion* 1 (2007).

———. "Global Indigeneity and Local Christianity: Performing O'odham Identity in the Present." In *Handbook of Indigenous Religion(s)*, edited by Greg Johnson and Siv Ellen Kraft, 192–203. Leiden: Brill, 2017.

———. "O'odham Songscapes: Journeys to Magdalena Remembered in Song." *Journal of the Southwest* 58, no. 2 (Summer 2016): 237–60.

———. "Walkers and Their Staffs: O'odham Walking Sticks by Way of Calendar Sticks and Scraping Sticks." *Material Religion: The Journal of Objects, Art and Belief* 12, no. 4 (December 2016): 476–500.

———. "Walking to Magdalena: Place and Person in Tohono O'odham Songs, Sticks, and Stories." PhD diss., Arizona State University, 2013.

Schermerhorn, Seth, and Lillia McEnaney. "Through Indigenous Eyes: A Comparison of Two Tohono O'odham Photographic Collections Documenting Pilgrimages to Magdalena." *Religious Studies and Theology* 36, no. 1 (2017): 21–54.

Schuetz-Miller, Mardith, and Bernard L. Fontana. "Mission Churches of Northern Sonora." In *The Pimería Alta: Missions and More*, edited by James E. Officer, Mardith Scheutz-Miller, and Bernard L. Fontana, 61–95. Tucson: Southwestern Mission Research Center, 1996.

Schulze, Jeffrey M. *Are We Not Foreigners Here? Indigenous Nationalism in the U.S.-Mexico Borderlands*. Chapel Hill: University of North Carolina Press, 2018.

Schwarz, Maureen Trudelle. *Fighting Colonialism with Hegemonic Culture: Native American Appropriation of Indian Stereotypes*. Albany: State University of New York Press, 2013.

———. *"I Choose Life": Contemporary Medical and Religious Practices in the Navajo World*. Norman: University of Oklahoma Press, 2008.

———. *Molded in the Image of Changing Woman: Navajo Views on the Human Body and Personhood*. Tucson: University of Arizona Press, 1997.

———. *Navajo Lifeways: Contemporary Issues, Ancient Knowledge*. Norman: University of Oklahoma Press, 2001.

Schweitzer, John, and Robert K. Thomas. "Fiesta of St. Francis at San Francisquito, Sonora." *Kiva* 18, nos. 1–2 (September–October 1952): 1–8.

Scott, James C. *Domination and the Arts of Resistance: Hidden Transcripts*. New Haven CT: Yale University Press, 1990.

Shaul, David L. "Piman Song Syntax: Its Historical Significance." *Proceedings of the Seventh Annual Meeting of the Berkeley Linguistics Society*, February 14–16, 1981: 275–83.

Shaw, Anna Moore. *Pima Indian Legends*. 1968. Tucson: University of Arizona Press, 1972.

——. *A Pima Past*. 1974. Tucson: University of Arizona Press, 1994.

Sheridan, Thomas. "Female Public Drinking Patterns among the 1971 Magdalena Pilgrims." *Student Anthropologist* 4, no. 2 (1972): 47–52.

——."Kino's Unforeseen Legacy: The Material Consequences of Missionization among the Northern Piman Indians of Arizona and Sonora." *Smoke Signal*, no. 49–50 (1988): 155–67.

Shorter, David Delgado. "Spirituality." In *The Oxford Handbook of American Indian History*, edited by Frederick E. Hoxie, 433–52. Oxford: Oxford University Press, 2016.

——. *We Will Dance Our Truth: Yaqui History in Yoeme Performances*. Lincoln: University of Nebraska Press, 2009.

Siquieros, Bernard. "The Magdalena Pilgrimage: In My Own Words." *We:sii T-we:m: All of Us Together*. Tohono O'odham Nation Executive Newsletter 2 (2009): 3.

Slater, Candace. *Trail of Miracles: Stories from a Pilgrimage in Northeast Brazil*. Berkeley: University of California Press, 1986.

Smith, Mrs. White Mountain. "Time Marches On in Pimeria." *Desert Magazine* 5, no. 6 (April 1942): 22–24.

Smith-Morris, Carolyn. *Diabetes among the Pima: Stories of Survival*. Tucson: University of Arizona Press, 2006.

Smoak, Gregory E. *Ghost Dances and Identity: Prophetic Religion and American Indian Ethnogenesis in the Nineteenth Century*. Berkeley: University of California Press, 2006.

Snead, James E., Clark L. Erickson, and J. Andrew Darling, eds. *Landscapes of Movement: Trails, Paths, and Roads in Anthropological Perspective*. Pittsburgh: University of Pennsylvania Museum of Archaeology and Anthropology, 2009.

Soja, Edward W. *Postmodern Geographies: The Reassertion of Space in Critical Social Theory*. London: Verso, 1989.

Southworth, C. H. "A Pima Calendar Stick." *Arizona Historical Review* 4, no. 2 (1931): 44–51.

Spicer, Edward H. *Cycles of Conquest: The Impact of Spain, Mexico, and the United States on the Indians of the Southwest, 1533-1960*. 1962. Tucson: University of Arizona Press: 1970.

——. "The Papago Indians." *Kiva* 6, no. 6 (March 1941): 21–24.

Spicer, Rosamond B., and N. Ross Crumrine, eds. *Performing the Renewal of Community: Indigenous Easter Rituals in North Mexico and Southwest United States*. Lanham MD: University Press of America, 1997.

Stabolepszy, Pretina Kathleen. "Laughing Softly: O'odham Song Ritual as Orientation to the World." Master's thesis, University of Colorado, 1988.

Stewart, Kenneth M. "Southern Papago Salt Pilgrimages." *The Masterkey for Indian Lore and History* 39, no. 3 (1965): 84–91.

Stirrat, Roderick L. "Place and Person in Sinhala Catholic Pilgrimage." In *Contesting the Sacred: The Anthropology of Christian Pilgrimage*, edited by John Eade and Michael J. Sallnow, 122–36. London: Routledge, 1991.

Stricklen, E. G. "Notes on Eight Papago Songs." *University of California Publications in American Archaeology and Ethnology* 20 (1923): 363–65. Berkeley: University of California Press. Reprint, New York: Krauss, 1965.

Sturman, Janet. "Movement Analysis as a Tool for Understanding Identity: Retentions, Borrowings, and Transformations in Native American *Waila*." *World of Music* 39, no. 3 (1997): 51–70.

Sullivan, Winnifred Fallers, and Lori G. Beaman, eds. *Varieties of Religious Establishment*. London: Routledge, 2013.

Swanson, Tod. "Singing to Estranged Lovers: Runa Relations to Plants in the Ecuadorian Amazon." *Journal for the Study of Religion, Nature and Culture* 3, no. 1 (2009): 36–65.

———. "Through Family Eyes: Towards a More Adequate Perspective for Viewing Native American Religious Life." *American Indian Quarterly* 21, no. 1 (Winter 1997): 57–71.

———. "Weathered Character: Envy and Response to the Seasons in North and South American Indian Morality." *Journal of Religious Ethics* 20, no. 2 (1992): 279–308.

Swanson, Tod D., and Jarrad Reddekop. "Looking Like the Land: Beauty and Aesthetics in Amazonian Quichua Philosophy and Practice." *Journal of the American Academy of Religion* 85, no. 3 (September 2017): 682–708.

Taylor, Lawrence J. "Centre and Edge: Pilgrimage and the Moral Geography of the US/Mexico Border." *Mobilities* 2, no. 3 (November 2007): 383–93.

Tedlock, Dennis. *The Spoken Word and the Work of Interpretation*. Philadelphia: University of Pennsylvania Press, 1983.

Tedlock, Dennis, and Bruce Mannheim, eds. *The Dialogic Emergence of Culture*. Urbana: University of Illinois Press, 1995.

Tilley, Christopher. *A Phenomenology of Landscape: Places, Paths and Monuments*. Oxford: Berg, 1994.

Titus, Joan. "*Waila* as Transnational Practice." In *Transnational Encounters: Music and Performance at the U.S.-Mexico Border*, edited by Alejandro L. Madrid, 149–67. Oxford: Oxford University Press, 2011.

Tooker, Elisabeth. "The Pilgrims in Church." *Kiva* 16, nos. 1–2 (October–November 1950): 9–13.

Treat, James. *Around the Sacred Fire: Native Religious Activism in the Red Power Era—A Narrative Map of the Indian Ecumenical Conference.* New York: Palgrave Macmillan, 2003.

————, ed. *For This Land: Writings on Religion in America.* London: Routledge, 1999.

————, ed. *Native and Christian: Indigenous Voices on Religious Identity in the United States and Canada.* New York: Routledge, 1996.

Trimble, Charles E., Barbara W. Sommer, and Mary Kay Quinlan. *The American Indian Oral History Manual: Making Many Voices Heard.* Walnut Creek CA: Left Coast Press, 2008.

Tsing, Anna L. *Friction: An Ethnography of Global Connection.* Princeton NJ: Princeton University Press, 2005.

Turner, Victor, and Edith L. B. Turner. *Image and Pilgrimage in Christian Culture: Anthropological Perspectives.* New York: Columbia University Press, 1978.

Tweed, Thomas A. *Crossing and Dwelling: A Theory of Religion.* Cambridge MA: Harvard University Press, 2006.

————. *Our Lady of the Exile: Diasporic Religion at a Cuban Catholic Shrine in Miami.* Oxford: Oxford University Press, 1997.

Underhill, Ruth M. "Acculturation at the Papago Village of Santa Rosa." In *Papago Indians 1: American Indian Ethnohistory, Indians of the Southwest,* edited by David A. Horr, 309–448. New York: Garland, 1974.

————. *An Anthropologist's Arrival: A Memoir.* Edited by Chip Colwell-Chanthaphonh and Stephen E. Nash. Tucson: University of Arizona Press, 2014.

————. "Intercultural Relations in the Greater Southwest." *American Anthropologist* 56, no. 4 (August 1954): 645–56.

————. "A Papago Calendar Record." *University of New Mexico Bulletin,* no. 322, Anthropological series 2, no. 5 (1938): 1–66.

————. *Papago Indian Religion.* 1946. New York: AMS Press, 1969.

————. *Papago Woman.* 1936. Prospect Heights IL: Waveland Press, 1979. Originally published as *Autobiography of a Papago Woman.*

————. *Singing for Power: The Song Magic of the Papago Indians of Southern Arizona.* 1938. Tucson: University of Arizona Press, 1993.

————. *Social Organization of the Papago Indians.* 1939. New York: AMS Press, 1969.

Underhill, Ruth M., Donald M. Bahr, Baptisto Lopez, Jose Pancho, and David Lopez. *Rainhouse and Ocean: Speeches for the Papago Year.* 1979. Tucson: University of Arizona Press, 1997.

Urton, Gary. *Inka History in Knots: Reading Khipus as Primary Sources.* Austin: University of Texas Press, 2017.

————. *Signs of the Inka Khipu: Binary Coding in the Andean Knotted-String Records.* Austin: University of Texas Press, 2003.

Vásquez, Manuel. *More than Belief: A Materialist Theory of Religion.* Oxford: Oxford University Press, 2011.

Vilaça, Aparecida. *Praying and Preying: Christianity in Indigenous Amazonia.* Oakland: University of California Press, 2016.

Vilaça, Aparecida, and Robin M. Wright, eds. *Native Christians: Modes and Effects of Christianity among Indigenous Peoples of the Americas.* London: Ashgate Books, 2009.

Waddell, Jack O. "Mesquite and Mountains with Money and Messiah: A Papago Indian Case of Cultural Revitalization." *Journal of the Steward Anthropological Society* 2, no. 1 (Fall 1970): 51–88.

———. "The Place of the Cactus Wine Ritual in the Papago Indian Eco-system." In *The Realm of the Extra-Human: Ideas and Actions,* edited by Agehananda Bharati, 213–28. The Hague: Mouton, 1976.

Webb, George. *A Pima Remembers.* Tucson: University of Arizona Press, 1959.

Wenger, Tisa. "Indian Dances and the Politics of Religious Freedom, 1870–1930." *Journal of the American Academy of Religion* 79, no. 4 (December 2011): 850–78.

———. *Religious Freedom: The Contested History of an American Ideal.* Chapel Hill: University of North Carolina Press, 2017.

———. "'We Are Guaranteed Freedom': Pueblo Indians and the Category of Religion in the 1920s." *History of Religions* 45, no. 2 (November 2005): 89–113.

———. *We Have a Religion: The 1920s Pueblo Indian Dance Controversy and American Religious Freedom.* Chapel Hill: University of North Carolina Press, 2009.

Williamson, George H. "Why the Pilgrims Come." *Kiva* 16, nos. 1–2 (October–November 1950): 2–8.

Winters, Harry J., Jr. *'O'odham Place Names: Meanings, Origins, and Histories Arizona and Sonora.* Tucson: Nighthorse, 2012.

Zepeda, Ofelia. "Autobiography." In *Here First: Autobiographical Essays by Native American Writers,* edited by Arnold Krupat and Brian Swann, 405–20. New York: Modern Library, 2000.

———. *Ocean Power: Poems from the Desert.* Tucson: University of Arizona Press, 1995.

———. "The Sand Papago Oral History Project." Division of Archeology, Western Archeological and Conservation Center, National Park Service. Tucson: 1985.

———. *A Tohono O'odham Grammar.* 1983. Tucson: University of Arizona Press, 2016. Originally published as *A Papago Grammar.*

———. *When It Rains: Papago and Pima Poetry.* Tucson: University of Arizona Press, 1982.

———. *Where Clouds Are Formed.* Tucson: The University of Arizona Press, 2008.

INDEX

Page numbers in italic indicate illustrations.

Bahr, Donald (*continued*)
   on personhood, 29, 35–36, 179n13;
   on sickness, 93, 94; and songs, 24,
   47, 50, 53, 54, 56, 57, 61, 70; on
   speech genres, 171–74; on sticks,
   78, 80, 82, 84; at Tohono O'odham
   Nation, 18; on "walking," 12; on
   women as Pleiades, 185n13
Bakhtin, Mikhail, 43, 46–47
ban. *See* coyote
baptism, 134, 142, 144, 194n57
Barry M. Goldwater Air Force Range, 169
Basso, Keith, 34, 47, 53
Bataille, Gretchen M., 179n14
Baylor, Byrd, 100, 103, 105, 106
bells, 119–20
Benavides, Gustavo, 7
Big Fields, 53
birds, 48, 50–51, 55, 67–68, 76. *See
   also* animals; Eagle; Mocking-
   birds; Orioles; owls; Swallows;
   whip-poor-wills
black people, 143
Blaine, Peter, 166
Blue Swallow songs, 30
Bolton, Herbert, 158
Bourdieu, Pierre, 100, 102–4
Brown, Eddie F., 16
Bureau of Indian Affairs, 167
Burnt Seeds. *See* Santa Rosa
Buzzard, 143

Cabeza Prieta National Wildlife Refuge, 169
Caborca, 62, 158, 159
calendar sticks, 75, 78–81, 96. *See also*
   sticks
candles, 140
Casey, Edward, 31
Catholic Church at Santa Fe, 161

Catholicism: at I'itoi Ki:, 150–52; influ-
   ence on O'odham, 72, 127, 129–31,
   134–35, 139, 140, 142, 153–54, 163–
   66; saints in, 135–36, 193n35; and
   staffs, 24, 75. *See also* Christianity;
   religion
Cebolla, 60, 62, 63
Cedagĭ Wahia, 20, 34, 41, 84, 130
Cervecería Sonora, 167
Charles III, King, 159
Chesky, Jane, 22, 138, 162, 166
children, 134–35, 138, 142, 144
Children's Shrine, 140
Chona, Maria, 29–30, 179n14, 185n6
Christianity: and candles, 140; con-
   versions to, 139, 161–62; at I'itoi
   Ki:, 150–52; material culture of, 75;
   natives' claiming of, 4–8, 23, 25,
   124, 128–29, 131–32, 139–42, 145,
   153–54, 192n1, 194n57; of O'odham,
   2–3, 43, 148, 157–58, 164–66; and
   O'odham landscapes, 71–72, 140;
   and personhood, 28, 36; "showing
   off" through, 121, 132; and walk to
   Magdalena, 129–31. *See also* Cathol-
   icism; religion
chromaticism, 59, 60
chronotopes, 43, 46–47
Church of Santa María Magdalena, 35, 158
Cibuta, 63. *See also* Si:woda
Civil War, 79
clay ceremony, 134, 142, 144, 194n57
Clifford, James, 8, 12, 13, 118
Cold Fields, 34, 125
Coleman, Simon, 9
Collins, Richard, 11
colonialism, 154
Colorado River, 4
communion, 142, 194n57
Comobabi Mountains, 163

Conklin, Beth A., 28

Cook, Charles H., 161

cosmologies: and afterlife, 40; and history of Christianity, 124, 141; and personhood, 35–36, 118; place in, 31, 38–39, 104, 118; studies of indigenous, 27; and ways of walking, 110–11, 122

cotton, 168

Covered Wells, 58, 164

cowboys, 41–42, 50, 109, 137, 176n13. *See also* devils

coyote, 28, 30, 137–38, 143. *See also* animals

creosote. *See* greasewood

cumbia, 108

Cu:wĭ Geṣk. *See* San Francisquito

dancing: maturation through, 107–9; and return from Magdalena, 120; as undisciplined movement, 76, 77, 99, 108–9, 185n13; in waila performances, 100, 106–8; and walking, 100, 189n40

Darling, J. Andrew, 24, 47, 53, 54, 75, 80, 96

death, 40–43, 91, 120, 143. *See also* sickness

de Certeau, Michel, 4–5, 14, 38, 100, 103, 117–18, 132, 153

de la Cadena, Marisol, 13–14

Deloria, Philip, 26, 151

Deloria, Vine, Jr., 46, 71

Derrida, Jacques, 102

Desert Diamond Casinos, 16

The Desert Smells Like Rain (Nabhan), 21, 149

devils: as cowboys, 176n13; in Papago culture, 138; qualities of, 98, 137, 138; songs associated with, 49–50, 54–55, 83; and undisciplined movement, 109; way of, 6, 23. *See also* cowboys

Devil Sickness and Devil Songs (Kozak and Lopez), 109

A Dictionary of Papago Usage (Mathiot), 137

Diné (Navajo), 28

Dobyns, Henry, 164, 165, 168

Dolores, Juan, 76, 98, 137

dourine epidemic, 167

drinking, 127–28

Dubisch, Jill, 11

Eade, John, 9, 120

Eagle, 143. *See also* animals

earth, 32, 39, 105, 124, 134, 137, 141–45. *See also* landscapes

East, 40–41

Eliade, Mircea, 35, 36–37, 38

Encinas, Francisco "Harry," 45

Engelke, Matthew, 153

English language, 165

Enis, Michael, 34–35

Enos, Susie, 29, 30, 82, 83

Erickson, Kirstin, 191n86

ethics: of coyote, 137–38; and movement, 100, 110, 111; and O'odham religious tradition, 131–32; and songs, 53–54; and walk to Magdalena, 114–16, 121; and wine ceremonies, 128; of women, 185n13. *See also* sin

ethnography. *See* anthropology

Ezell, Paul, 161

Feld, Steven, 34

Feldhaus, Anne, 31, 33, 34

Florence Village, 3

"flowering" bodies, 30, 142

Jose, Jojo, 49
Jose, Kendall, 48–51, 84–85, 92–93
Jose, Verlon "Carlos," 21, 32, 49, 83–84, 87–89, 95, 154, 168–69
Jose family, 53, 71
Joseph, Alice, 22, 162, 166

Kaell, Hillary, 10, 13, 153
Kaij Mek. *See* Santa Rosa
Kant, Immanuel, 110
Kilcrease, A. T., 79
kinesthetics, 106–10, 118. *See also* dancing; walking: styles and pace of
King, William, 140
Kino, Eusebio Francisco, 11, 62, 72, 124, 139, 157–60, 164
Kohatk, 45, 51
Komelik, 167
Kozak, David: on immodesty, 109; on personhood, 29, 35; and place-names, 183n60; research of, 24, 164; on songs, 47, 48, 50, 54, 60, 83, 174
Ku'ukcul (Ko'okol, or Chili Mountain), 41

La Fontaine, Jean Sybil, 111
Lagrou, Elsje Maria, 25
Lamb, Sarah, 28
"Landscape" (Zepeda), 104–5
landscapes: Christianity tied to, 5–8, 23, 25–26, 140–41, 153–54; description of Magdalena area, 116–17; movement through, 37, 43, 47–48, 120, 145; and O'odham dead, 41; O'odham relations with, 98, 140; as places, 31; sacredness of, 25–26, 148, 152, 194n1; and songs, 24, 53–54, 59. *See also* earth; places
Leap, William, 191n75
Lévi-Strauss, Claude, 59, 143

Lewis, Barnaby V., 24, 47, 53, 54, 75, 80, 96
light, 58–61
Lock, Charles, 7
Lopez, Camillus, 119–21
Lopez, Danny, 38, 39
Lopez, David I., 24, 50, 54, 83, 93, 109, 164, 183n60, 196n26
Lopez, Dora, 63
Lopez, Florence, 18
Lopez, Juan, 40, 41, 81
Lopez, Louis "Tony": on being O'odham, 141, 144–45; leadership of, 116–17; and place-names, 63, 183n60; relationship with author, 17, 20; on ribbons, 89; on songs, 48, 57–60, 62, 65–68, 72; on sticks, 83, 152; on walking, 97, 98, 129–31, 134–35
Lopez, Simon, 52; on candles, 140; on Catholic priests, 163; on "good walkers," 111–16; on offerings to Saint Teresa, 66–67; on O'odham afterlife, 40–43; on O'odham origins, 38–39, 143; on O'odham religious history, 124, 130; prayers for, 112–14; on Presbyterian camp meetings, 162; relationship with author, 17–20; on saints, 135–36; and songs, 51–70; on sticks, 73, 79–82, 84, 94, 152; on Swallows, 68–69; use of pronouns, 191n75
Lopez family: infancy rites in, 144; songs of, 53, 56–57, 71, 171; at wake, 45–46; walks to Magdalena, 134–35
"Lost Prayers" (Zepeda), 150

Madsen, Ken, 152
Magdalena: Christian tradition in, 5, 98, 158, 164, 165; experience of walking to, 20–23, 134–35, 144, 154;

Magdalena (*continued*)
history of walk to, 74, 75, 89–91,
124–25, 128; length of walk to, 22;
modes of travel to and from, 116–20;
O'odham dead at, 42–43; personhood tied to, 34; as place, 33–34;
power of, in objects, 78, 96; reasons
for walking to, 2, 32–33, 75, 112–14,
118–21, 129–30, 132–33, 159–60, 167;
reference to, at wake, 45–46; revolt
in, 159; routes to, 62, 63, 67; Saint
Francis in, 35–38, 166–67; studies
of walk to, 9–20; suppression of
pilgrimages to, 166–69; as territory,
32. *See also* Magdalena fiesta
Magdalena de Kino. *See* Church of
Santa María Magdalena
Magdalena fiesta: date of, 159; Fran-
ciscans' attitudes toward, 163, 166;
reasons for attending, 191n86; stud-
ies of, 10–12. *See also* Magdalena
Magdalena River, 65
Mahabharata, 111
Maharashtra, 31, 33
Mali:na. *See* Magdalena
Manuel, Frances, 30, 79, 136–38, 172,
197n9
materiality, 75, 77–78, 84, 92, 96
Mathiot, Madeline, 137
Mauss, Marcel, 100–102
Mayo dancers, 191n86
McAlister, Elizabeth, 37
McCarty, Kieran R., 158
McDowell Mountain, 76
McNally, Michael, 4–8, 139, 153
mesquite, 81
Mexicans, 105–6, 150, 153, 184n5
Mexico: anticlericalism in, 167; border
with U.S., 168–69; Catholicism
in, 164; missions in, 139, 158–59;

O'odham in, 3–5, 117, 160–61,
195n14; pilgrimage studies in, 11;
place-names in, 63. *See also* Sonora,
Mexico
Michalowski, Raymond J., 11
Milga:n. *See* white people
Mission San Xavier del Bac, 22, 33
Mockingbirds, 50, 51, 71. *See also* birds
Mockingbird Speeches, 127
Mo'okam Do'ag. *See* Seven Headed
Mountain
Morgan, Lynn M., 28
Morinis, E. Alan, 8–10, 98
Mormons, 162–63, 192n2
Mullen Sands, Kathleen, 179n14
music. *See* flutes; songs
myth. See *Ho'ok A:gida*; stories

Nabhan, Gary Paul, 21–22, 68, 137, 149,
151, 167, 178n9
Nabokov, Peter, 77
Narayanan, Vasudha, 104, 110–11
Narcho, Mary: on cowboys as devils,
176n13; grieving for husband, 1–2; on
O'odham afterlife, 180n57; on Saint
Francis statue, 159–60, 166; walking
stick of, *85*, 85–86, 89–90, 92,
187n66; on walk to Magdalena, 16
Navajo, 28
Ñe:big Do'ag (Sucking Monster Moun-
tain), 59–61
Neff, Deborah, 136–37, 197n9
New Mexico, 157
Nieto, Enrique Peña, 168
Nolik, 48, 53

Oacpicagigua, Luís, 159
Oblasser, Father Bonaventure, 163, 164,
166, 196n26
O'Connor, Mary I., 9–11

Ojibwe Indians, 4

Onion Mountain. *See* Siwol Do'ag (Onion Mountain)

O'odham: adaptability of, 154; aesthetics of, 108–11; afterlife of, 40–44, 180n57; attitudes toward Christianity, 139–46, 153–54, 157–58, 164; attitudes toward walk to Magdalena, 23, 25, 167–68; author's relationships with, 11–12; church built by, 64; citizenship of, 161, 195n14; classifications of, 3, 6; creator of, 148; culture of, 157–58, 162; differences among, 128; dispute about walkers, 125–26, 129, 130; historical record of, 75, 78–81, 128–32, 157, 195n1; kinship relations of, 98, 99, 104, 111, 112, 115, 120, 134–35; meaning of word, 29; modesty and pride of, 109–10, 121, 127–28, 132–33, 137; personhood of, 23, 27–30, 34–44, 75, 78, 104, 107, 109, 111, 117–18, 122, 134, 138, 141–46; scent of, 142, 143, 144; sociability of, 69–70; and water symbol, 66. *See also* Akimel O'odham; Hia Ced O'odham; Tohono O'odham

O'odham language: author's transcription of, 20; hymns in, 165; nicknames in, 21, 22; songs in, 47–48, 55–57, 61, 62; speech genres of, 171–74, 197n1; term for Anglos in, 161

o'ohon, 80

Opata Indians, 158

orations, 173, 174

Organ Pipe Cactus National Monument, 169

Orioles, 24, 50, 53. *See also* birds

Orsi, Robert, 14

owls, 142. *See also* birds

Papago Indians. *See* Sonoran Papagos; Tohono O'odham

Papago Tribal Council, 166

Papago Tribe of Arizona. *See* Tohono O'odham Nation

Papago Woman (Underhill), 29–30, 185n6

parodies, 126–29, 142

Pels, Peter, 84

Phoenix AZ, 3, 162, 163

pilgrimages, 7–15, 97–98, 100, 118, 122, 188n1

Pima Indians. *See* Akimel O'odham

Pima language, 3

Pima-Maricopa Tribe, 162

Piman Shamanism and Staying Sickness (Bahr), 35, 127

Pitiquito, Sonora, 64

place-names, 59–65

places: making of, 30–34, 122, 145; movement to and from, 46, 75, 80–81, 103, 104; and personhood, 27–28, 34–44, 116–18, 141; and songs, 47, 51–54, 71; and sticks, 96. *See also* landscapes

Pleiades, 76, 98–99, 111, 185n13

Pozo Verde, 41, 125, 154, 167, 169

prayers, 173. *See also* rosaries

preaching, 115, 128, 171, 172

Presbyterians, 127, 136, 138, 161–63

pride. *See* O'odham: modesty and pride of

pronouns, first person, 48, 58, 68–71

"Prophet Dowie," 163

Protestant optic, 7

Protestants, 136

puberty ceremony, 76, 98–99, 142

Pueblo Revolt, 157, 187n66

Puerto Peñasco, 3

43, 46, 97–101, 121, 122; and songs, 58, 67; sticks for, 73–74; styles and pace of, 12–15, 22–23, 25, 99–106, 110–14, 120, 189n36, 189n40

walking sticks. *See* sticks

Wand, Tiburtius, 164, 166

wandering, 12–15, 95, 99, 111, 116, 127

water, 66, 92, 95

water, holy, 87

Webb, George, 173

whip-poor-wills, 76. *See also* birds

white people, 105–6, 143, 149, 161

Why az, 169

wine ceremonies, 127–28

Winters, Harry J., Jr., 62, 63

"Witches Telling." *See Ho'ok A:gida*

women, 76, 98–99, 105–6, 149

Wu:ṣkam Hemajkam, 38–39

Yaquis, 76–77, 164, 191n86, 192n1

Yoeme. *See* Yaquis

Zepeda, Ofelia, 46, 100, 103–6, 150, 189n40, 194n1

Everywhen: Australia and the
Language of Deep History
Ann McGrath, Laura Rademaker,
and Jakelin Troy

All My Relatives: Exploring Lakota
Ontology, Belief, and Ritual
David C. Posthumus

Standing Up to Colonial Power:
The Lives of Henry Roe and
Elizabeth Bender Cloud
Renya K. Ramirez

Walking to Magdalena: Personhood
and Place in Tohono O'odham
Songs, Sticks, and Stories
Seth Schermerhorn

To order or obtain more information on these or other University of Nebraska
Press titles, visit nebraskapress.unl.edu.

Printed in the USA
CPSIA information can be obtained
at www.ICGtesting.com
CBHW031908220724
11974CB00001B/30